Physical Justice

A Guide to Preventative & Medical Breakthroughs

Dwaine R. Klein
&
Douglas J. Geving

Order this book online at www.trafford.com
or email orders@trafford.com

Most Trafford titles are also available at major online book retailers.

Print information available on the last page.

ISBN: 978-1-4120-2769-4 (sc)

Trafford rev. 08/21/2019

 www.trafford.com

North America & international
toll-free: 1 888 232 4444 (USA & Canada)
fax: 812 355 4082

2

MY CREDIANTIALS

My story began with a desire to become a medical missionary. I received a B.A. from Northwest College. From there I went to Eastern Washington University, where I received a B.S. degree. Then I continued my education until I had received a M.S. degree also from Eastern Washington University.

My plans changed drastically when my wife had an automobile accident and was severely hurt. My eight-month-old son was also severely injured and he was paralyzed on his right side. We almost lost him. He is now 44 years of age and is healthy but has little use of his right arm. I used my degree for a short time to teach science at Spokane Falls College. My interests gradually changed from traditional medicine, to alternative treatments. They seem to have substantially fewer side effects and have led many people from sickness to health. I now receive calls from many parts of the United States from people who have failed to find healing from traditional medicine. One man had seen 27 doctors, he and his wife had all but given up saying, "enough is enough." He could not work and expressed to me that he did not have the desire to try anymore. I spent two hours with him over the phone. He seemed to believe me and decided it may be worth one more try. Within several weeks of the phone call, he was almost completely free of pain, back on the job and full of hope. You see I was his 28th try. That mans desperation and hope for renewed health and his desire never to give up showed me the reason not to give up. I truly thank God for the wisdom to touch a few lives and to see people happy and well again. Please note I have never accepted one dollar in my efforts to help people. I do not sell remedies and am not sponsored by endorsements. My only reward is your health and happiness. I do not own stock in any chemical or vitamin companies, so my advice is prejudiced by nothing.

Always remember medicine is a practice. The practice of medicine is a common term and is the absolute truth - it is a practice. I wish medicine were a pure science where 2 + 2 always equaled four. Unfortunately, it is not that way. Some people call me several times before I am able to hit on the cause and possible cure for their problem. I have studied alternative medicine for over 40 years and this book is an attempt not to let those 40 years of research and study go to waste. What you are about to read in this book might seem unbelievable, some of it is just plain old wisdom from Grandma's first aid notes (Grandma always knew best). My hopes are that you find something that will be of some help to you. I hope that this information will change your life as much as it has changed mine.

MY STORY

This book is not intended to put down allopathic medicine. Neither, is it intended to replace. There is a great need for traditional medicine, but I believe there is an even greater need for alternative medicine. You should have a choice and the knowledge to make that choice. I do not presume to make diagnoses; I only try to change the chemistry of your body in a natural way, so it can respond favorably against the disease you may confront. Please know this, it is always, always, easier to prevent the disease rather than try to cure it. This book contains more ideas on preventative medicine than cures for disease.

If only your sixteen-year-old could have the knowledge presented here, life might be much easier for him. Too often, I am presented with a problem that has been neglected and has lasted so long that the cure looks almost impossible. Please know that almost nothing is impossible and it is never too late unless you are six feet under. Never forget the power of prayer, as I have learned through the years, faith and a higher power sometimes has a greater healing effect than any medical efforts traditional or alternative.

I have done a great deal of research concerning the immune system, and how it responds to various herbs and other natural treatments. I am definitely not a health food nut and enjoy my food. You should not let alternative medicine be the controlling factor in your life. Instead, use it as a tool to help you make informed health choices.

This book is based on chemistry and how certain foods and chemicals cause your body to respond in certain ways. American physicians learn precious little about prevention or nutrition in medical school. However, in their defense, this can be easily understood. How many of us would pay two to three hundred dollars an hour to consult with someone about the disease we do not have yet. You see, we have created this situation ourselves. Then by the time, we have developed a serious condition it is too late for the doctor to cure the illness. The real key to health is prevention, not cure. Many of the things presented in this book will change your life drastically not today, but ten years from now. You see, preventative medicine always works better before you need it.

I will try to avoid any wow fads that is, I will try to direct you to what truly works. The chemistry used will be in layman's terms as much as possible. To the best of my abilities, I will avoid chemistry as much as possible. Nevertheless, there will be times you may need to know the scientific process of healing as it relates to alternative treatments.

In this book, you will learn about a revolutionary burn treatment. Incidentally, this may be the only place that you will learn about this product. You will also learn about the most prescribed hormone replacement, that almost guarantees cancer later in life. You will learn how to re-grow hair without chemicals that may change your body's chemistry, and have serious side effects.

Now back to my story. The reason that I am motivated to write this book stems from a desire, a desire that I had at the age of 62. It was my intention to compete in the Ironman Triathlon competition in Hawaii. I was hoping to make a good showing in my age class, maybe win. I was running 50 miles a week, swimming 300 laps in the pool and was just beginning to prepare for the cycling phase, all of this while I was working 10 to 12 hours a day, 7 days a week. I was eager to go; I had trained myself to the point that I felt stronger than I ever had, even in my youth. Everything showed a green light, and then came the twinge. It erupted into pain, it was my heart. I was rushed to the hospital where they did an emergency bypass operation. After the surgery was over, and I was sent home. My doctors had me on so much medication that the use of it might kill me just as surely as the heart attack. Physically I was going down hill fast and felt as if it was all over, or soon would be. Then a friend of mine brought up the idea of hormone replacement. I began to study. It seemed to be a promising option so I contacted a doctor that I had a great deal of confidence in. I asked him what he thought and if I should try it. He told me "Dwaine you have little or nothing to lose, and you probably won't make it the way that things are going now."

I decided to go to the foremost hormone replacement clinic in the world. It is located in Palm Springs Florida. This technology is very revolutionary and until 1980 was only for the rich and famous. At its inception, treatments were around $25,000 a month so you can understand why the clinic was started in

Palm Springs, possibly the richest per capita city in the country. When I arrived in Palm Springs, I could barely negotiate my way through the airport. I had to call a cab just to take me two blocks from the airport to the clinic. Just three months later, I was beginning to notice a great deal of change taking place and by 6 months, I was running and swimming again. Amazing well perhaps, but I will cover the details of this subject in a later chapter.

BURNS AND HOW TO DEAL WITH THEM

The product that you will be introduced to was first revealed on the CBS show 60 Minutes. The report was titled Dock Willard's Wonder Water. Dr. John Wesley Willard invented a new form of water and called it catalytic water. You can find it at your health food store as Willard's Water. Doctor Willard accidentally burned himself in his laboratory and to ease his pain he immersed his hand in a jar of his catalytic water. Much to his surprise the pain disappeared immediately and the burn healed much faster than normal, leaving no scar. The speed with which the pain was relieved is unbelievable. A friend of mine just had to know if Willard Water worked, so he intentionally burned himself with a match until he had a third degree burn. He waited until the pain was evident and then sprayed the burn with the catalytic water. The pain was gone almost immediately. In addition, when it had healed, there was no scarring. Not to mention the fact that it had healed in half of the time. Still not convinced, he burned himself again. Again, with the same results. Then he decided to test it on me, as I was rather skeptical myself. I could not believe it when he burned me with a match! However, the water was remarkable, the pain subsided almost immediately, it healed in half of the time and there was no scar. Acting like a kid with a new toy, he began testing it on all of his friends (note: don't try this as your circle of friends will get very small in a big hurry) but, everyone that tried it also wound up with the same results.

If you have sunburn get a spray bottle and mist the Willard's Water on as often as needed. You can also soak a cloth in the water and lay it over the burn. Always mix the solution exactly as the instructions describe. Mixing it stronger will actually lessen the effects. If the pain returns, continue to mist on the solution, believe me it works. Always keep a spray bottle handy but don't get as carried away as my friend did. Try to convince your friends with conversation, you will keep more friends that way.

There are other qualities about Willard's Water that I will be discussing throughout this book, but believe me if the general public only knew of the amazing properties of this substance, everyone would have some. One more example to try to convince you was an incident where a woman dropped a pan of boiling water and it splashed on her hand and arm.

Immediately she grabbed a spray bottle full of Willard's Water and sprayed the burned area. In just a short time of misting, the pain was gone; there was no redness, no wrinkling and no blistering.

The mechanism of this amazing product is that it seems to put a film around the exposed nerves caused by the burns. Thus, restoring it to almost full operation – hence no pain. This also allows the smooth muscle to pump the fluid away from the area. Now just a little bit of chemistry, as it relates to Willard's Water. It is a very strong anti-oxidant and that makes it a reducing agent. A reducing agent gives up electrons. Oxidizing agents attract electrons and the most powerful of these oxidizers are called free radicals. In living organism's free radicals, react to damaged cell membranes and nuclei. It causes changes in genetic material and these changes cause aging, cancer, infections and a whole range of other diseases. The water is a magnetic condenser, gathering free electrons and making them available to various chemical reactions. It is also a source of free protons, or hydrogen ions that are vital to many chemical reactions, of life processes. I promised to keep the chemistry as short as possible but, the above explanation may be of some value to you, in your ability to evaluate the tremendous healing properties of Willard's Water. It may also help you to understand its abilities to prevent infection as the burn heals.

CONSTIPATION AND HEMOROIDS

These two problems often go together so, I will classify them together. The reason for this is that it is usually difficult to cure one without the other. There is no sophisticated chemistry here, just common sense. Let's cure the constipation first. First, let me state unequivocally that the measure of your colon's health is probably the easiest thing in the world to diagnose. If your feces floats, your colon is probably very healthy. If it sinks, you probably aren't getting enough fiber and are heading for trouble down the line. This is a great diagnostic tool, but it is so simple that it is usually overlooked. Some of you may need to take a gentle laxative such as senna or cascara, better yet a combination of the two. Never, never take mineral oil or milk of magnesia, as these products both change the body's chemistry in a deleterious manner. The best approach to healthy regularity is fiber, fiber and to top it off more fiber. One of the best natural fibers is flax seed. Flax seed is one of the highest fiber seeds available. It is also very inexpensive, but it pays back gigantic dividends in many ways. Besides the fiber content, it has Omega 3 and Omega 6 oils, which will lower the LDL (bad cholesterol) and raise the HDL (good cholesterol). Here is how to use flax seed. Buy one pound of flax seed (I buy it 50 pounds at a time). Then purchase an inexpensive coffee grinder, the kind with a two-sided blade. Grind about 2 cups at a time, as you will want to use it while it is fresh. Flax seed in its un-ground form will virtually never spoil, but when ground it can turn rancid in a very short time. When the seed is, fresh it has a wonderful nut like flavor and tastes good in water, juices or as a topping on your breakfast. I keep the ground seed refrigerated. You don't need to refrigerate the un-ground seed, as it never spoils. I recommend two heaping tablespoons in the morning and two heaping tablespoons at night, along with a tablespoon of psyllium seed such as Metamucil. However, psyllium seed is psyllium seed so go ahead and get the most inexpensive brand possible. You can almost convince yourself that this concoction actually tastes good but I've never been that good a liar. I also recommend acidophilus, which is the bacterium in yogurt. If you have taken an anti-biotic in the last month, this is very important. The anti-biotic destroys most of the beneficial bacteria in the intestine and needs to be replaced. You will now begin to see your feces float. Guess what, you are on the road to a healthy colon. You will probably double your bowel movements but that is O.K. just think of how much reading you will get done.

Now that we've conquered the constipation problem and it's under control let's start working on those hemorrhoids. Here I'll admit that in some cases surgery might have to be preformed, as many suggestions won't cure the worst cases. However, once you have had the surgery I can keep the problem from coming back. If you use these suggestions early in life, you will never need to use the word hemorrhoids. Before I had the knowledge that I have now, I had to have a hemorrhoid surgery myself, and the doctor told me that it was a sure thing and that he would never need to do the surgery again. I told him the reason that he would never do it twice to me was that he couldn't run fast enough to catch me again. Thankfully today's treatments are better then when I had my surgery but if you can catch it in time surgery will never be an option that you need to deal with. Preparation H has some benefit and has no bad side effects but in order to keep free of hemorrhoids you need to follow these rules. Number one, never use toilet paper. It is very abrasive and it does very little to control odor. Always wash after every bowel movement. After a thorough washing use, some kind of lubricant a light un-scented mineral oil is fine. Now for the real key to success get yourself an enema bottle and wash yourself on the inside too. Wash at least once a day twice if you can. Doing this will help prevent those painful internal fissures and your hemorrhoids will become a thing of the past. If you are pregnant and are confronted with hemorrhoids, just remember that the problem you are having at this time is caused by pressure from the baby and will in most cases resolve itself after the baby is born.

Diarrhea

Diarrhea has such a simple solution, that I can cover it in just a few sentences. You can go to the drug store and buy Kayopectate. Alternatively, you can go to your physician and get a prescription and spend all of the money that you want. However, I have found a very simple remedy that costs almost nothing. Just take a glass of milk and boil it for ten minutes, let it cool, drink it and voila your problem is solved. Is this an old wife's tale, I don't know. All that I know is that it works. Try it and let me know about your results. You have almost nothing to lose and a lot to gain. There was one instance where I consumed two whole bottles of Kayopectate in one sitting, with absolutely no results. Then I tried the boiled milk and my problem was solved in just a few short hours. I have used this remedy several times over the years and have suggested it to friends, and there has always been a successful result to this problem.

YEAST INFECTION

Let's talk about one of the most common problems facing women and occasionally men. The first thing that you need to know is that under normal conditions your body has a very low PH (acid condition) in your urinary tract. The reason for this is that having a low PH cleans the urinary tract and stops the speed of yeast and other harmful bacteria. If a woman douches regularly, the PH is raised to a neutral level or alkaline state, thereby inviting and causing a host for the yeast. If you do like to douche regularly, always use a small amount of apple cider vinegar in the water. Make it fit your comfort level, but vinegar always lowers the PH, so yeast and other infections do not have a chance to take off. Yeast infections can be easily prevented. However, if it becomes severe you may need to see your doctor. Then after you have seen the doctor and all signs of infection are gone, I have a new set of rules that you can do to keep free of the problem. Contracting a yeast infection usually means that you have a compromised immune system. If your doctor prescribes an anti-biotic, you must also take lactobacillus acidophilus (the live culture found in yogurt). When you take an anti-biotic, it destroys most of the beneficial bacteria in the intestinal tract, so it needs to be replaced. I recommend taking anywhere from 6 to 8 capsules of the live culture daily during the time that you are taking the anti-biotic and for a week after you have completed the doctors recommended course for the drug. Also, eliminate your intake of sugar because it feeds the infection.

Now let's look at some alternative treatments that really work, if you have a mild case. Oil of oregano destroys all varieties of yeast regardless of where they reside. A few drops under the tongue and six capsules a day for a week to ten days will stop the infection in its tracks. Do not try to apply it on your genitals, vaginal area, or anywhere near your rectum, as it will cause you to become very uncomfortable causing severe hot sensations. So using oil of oregano undiluted on any sensitive areas of the body is never advised.

Important to know, the oregano that you purchase from the grocery store is not what you are looking for. It is not even oregano. The oregano that you use for cooking things like spaghetti sauce and pizza is usually marjoram and is commonly known as sweet marjoram. It has a mild and pleasant flavor compared to true oregano. Marjoram is also used for fragrances in soaps, cosmetics and perfumes. You can normally find a source of the real oil of oregano at your local health food store. If you don't have, a health store nearby you can purchase a high quality product from a company in Buffalo called AICM. Their phone number is 1-800-243-5242.

Yeast infections such as Candida Albicons are so common that I would like to offer another cure. There is such a high incidence of this pathogen in the United States, that it might affect about one third of the population in the industrialized world. Yeast is a common fungus that we all have, it is only when your immune system becomes compromised, that the problems begin to manifest themselves. Yeast makes poisons called mycotoxins that cause the discomforting symptoms. Candida may settle in the abdomen, urinary tract, mouth or other internal organs. It can also cause acne, anxiety, depression, earaches, headaches, loss of sex drive and dozens of other complications. The manifestation of intestinal imbalance and immune system suppression comes from taking anti-biotics and eating excessive simple carbohydrates e.g. sugar, rice, white bread, pastas, etc. Another direct result is the using of street drugs and sexual promiscuity. When your doctor prescribes the newly introduced broad-spectrum anti-biotics, they can turn the Candida into a pathogen. Here is another treatment that is more effective in the long term then the broad-spectrum mystatin drug commonly used. This natural treatment is olive leaf extract. It can stop systemic and chronic Candida in its tracks. It usually requires about six capsules a day. Olive leaf extract can usually be purchased at your local health food store. However, if you don't have a health food store nearby you can call, 510-770-1215 for information regarding the product or concerning the purchase of the product. Now you have the information that you require to get well if you have been infected, and to stay well if you are not infected. The latter of the two is always preferred and the easiest.

EAR INFECTIONS

There have been several rather conclusive studies about ear infections and its relation to yeast. Therefore, I am covering them sequentially as they manifest themselves in a similar manner. The first thing that I have to mention is that most ear infections can be eliminated by the cessation of milk and dairy products. If writing this sentence 10 times would shock you into action then I would. If you can, substitute the dairy products with soymilk. The use of soymilk by itself might resolve the problem. If you have decided to try the soymilk be sure to consult the label so that you can purchase the brand with the highest protein level you can get. The preferred ratio is 7 grams of protein to 8 grams of carbohydrate. This is about the best that you can hope for and I am sure that there are several brands that have a similar ratio.

Ear infections might possibly be one of the greatest epidemics affecting children today. Here is the major disaster; long-term anti-biotic usage in children leads to yet another problem. Often upon diagnosis, the treatment of choice is an anti-biotic. This often triggers a variety of infections by anti-biotic resistant microbes, particularly candida albicons. It is almost a sure thing that if a child has undergone repeated long-term treatments with an anti-biotic, there will be a moderate to severe infestation of candida albicon. Sometimes an anti-biotic is necessary, but the long-term solution should be a boosted immune system and oil of oregano.

When the mucous membranes become inflamed often, the Eustachian Tube (which acts as a drainage duct) is blocked. When this happens, there is an accumulation of fluid in the middle ear and there will be pain and fever. Now, let's assume that you took an anti-biotic to rid yourself of the ear infection and want to free yourself from ever letting the infection re-appear again. First, let's boost your immune system using vitamin A, (10,000mg) vitamin C, (2000mg) folic acid, vitamin E, (400 IU) and selenium. I will mention this several times in this book but you need to know that vitamin E without selenium is virtually worthless. You must take selenium in order for your body to assimilate the vitamin E. Get your oil of oregano because, not only does ear infection manifest itself in almost the same manner as yeast infection, its cure is also the same. The oil of oregano will cure chronic or acute ear infections. Take two drops of the oil of oregano and two capsules twice daily. Place it under the tongue or in juice to mask the flavor, never put the oil in the ear, for that matter never put anything into the ear during an infection. You can purchase the oil of oregano at your local health food store. If you don't have a health food store in your area, you can call 1-800-243-5242. If you do require an anti-biotic, always remember to follow up with lactobacillus acidophilus to replace the beneficial bacteria in the intestinal tract. Then use half doses of oregano for prevention. You see, preventing an ear infection is not difficult and may save the placement of synthetic tubes in the eustachian canals, which may not prevent further infections. This recommended treatment not only benefits the eradication of ear infections, but it will not cause the undesirable side effects that are caused by anti-biotics. Children are especially vulnerable to the toxic effects of anti-biotics because of their immature immune system. Because of this, they also readily develop yeast infections. The oil of oregano takes care of both problems at the same time. Remember that dairy products are many times the sole problem and sugar also adds to the complications of ridding yourself of these infections.

Hearing Loss

I will try to deal with this subject as briefly as possible. However, I will open the door to several solutions that could begin to reverse the symptoms of deafness. There are many causes e.g.

- Consistent loud noise can damage hearing. Noises such as certain industrial equipment can cause hearing loss. If you have any questions about loud noise causing hearing problems, just go to a rock concert and when you come out, tell me how good your hearing is. Whenever I go to a concert, (even religious concerts now) I bring along a pair of commercial earplugs. I predict that the next generation will have many hearing difficulties at a much earlier age unless "music of extreme volume" ceases to be popular.
- Check for milk allergies, which can be a common cause of deafness and hearing loss in children.
- Your health food store probably carries candles that are very effective in cleaning out earwax that may impair hearing. I have received great response from people who have had a tremendous increase in their hearing capabilities simply by the use of this simple wax removal method. Sometimes you will not believe the amount of wax that this treatment can remove. One person actually avoided getting a hearing aid by the use of this simple procedure.
- You might be deficient in manganese; supplementation could help reverse your hearing loss.
- I also recommend that you contact a company called Natural Care 1448 Business Park Dr. Orem UT 84058 or call 1-800-475-3100 and ask

for a product called Hear-All. This is a great
product and in many instances will help your
hearing loss return to normal.

Allergies

One of the most elusive problems to put a finger on is
allergies. It is always a trial and error situation.
However, to save you a lot of time and money, skin
tests with foreign and antigens are practically
worthless. If you want a test that has some merit
then you need to have an analytical blood test. If
you're primary physician doesn't do this test then
find a physician that can. Here are a few things that
you can take to help reduce some of your allergic
reactions:

- Flax seed oil 3 tablespoons per day.
- Zinc.
- Vitamin C (Ester form) 5000 mg per day.

This subject would take a library of books even to
begin to cover the possibilities of a cure. I will
attempt to cover a few of the more obvious
treatments that may be of value. Clean air and water
free of chlorine and heavy metals are a great start.
There are many excellent water purifiers that are
available to you at a reasonable cost. An air purifier
may be more difficult for you to find so I will suggest
one that is quite efficient in improving the quality of
the air that you breathe. Probably the biggest
offender of indoor pollution is secondary smoke from
cigarettes. The second biggest offender is
formaldehyde which is cancer causing. It irritates

the mucous membranes of the eyes, ears, nose, and throat. Formaldehyde is found in so many items around your home I will just list a few:

- Building materials.
- Carpet and vinyl adhesives.
- Particleboard.
- Cigarette smoke.
- Some molds.
- Cooking fumes.
- Wood burning fireplaces.

Many air purifiers only re-circulate the germs and virus particles. One of the better machines is made by Sun - Pure. To contact Sun - Pure you can call 1-800-211-8562 they will answer all of your questions as well as place your order. In my estimation, this is one of the best air purifiers on the market however I have seen considerable improvement in symptoms with less expensive models that can be purchased at a department store. But if you want, the best at least make a call to Sun - Pure and get some literature about this product.

Now I think that it may be of value to cover some of the traditional treatments that are available to you. Corticosteroids may reduce inflammation in some cases, but the side effects are not worth it. Over a period of time, it may cause bone disease and weaken your immune system. Cortisone does just the opposite of what should be done. It depresses the immune system and increases the risk of bacterial and fungal infection. It may relieve some of the symptoms however, no cure is ever achieved.

Bronchodilators also contain a significant risk for those people with asthma. They should be used for emergency purposes only.

Now, for a few natural treatments that may have value. Please know that I have studied hundreds of cures for allergies and it would take a lifetime for you to try them all, so I can only hope that I may hit on a few things that will bring you some relief. Unfortunately, there is no one solution that works universally. No solution seems to work with consistency for a majority of people. However, there are many times that it seems like a miracle happens when we hit on the right thing. Sometimes we solve the problem by just eliminating a food e.g. citrus fruit, peanuts, wheat, milk or seafood. Some primary culprits include MSG, food dies, sulfites, nitrates and artificial colors. So let's start with a few remedies that might work. I have seen bee pollen cure allergies forever. Always use the granular form not the capsule and take 2 tablespoons per day. There is a good reason for this possible cure. Bee pollen allows your body to make an antibody for the antigens that may be causing your problem. Bee pollen that has been processed in your surrounding area may be the best as it contains samples of variants from your area that may be causing your allergic reactions. I read a testimonial about a senator who tried this and he couldn't believe the results. His allergic symptoms not only cleared up, but vanished for good. Always take it on an empty stomach. You may not experience the same dramatic results that the senator achieved, but it is worth a try. You may also find a marked increase in your energy level. Some herbs that may show some promise in relieving allergies is stinging nettle and rye grass extract.

I would like to recommend once more flax seed and flax seed oil. 3 tablespoons a day should be sufficient. If your allergies are caused by faulty fat metabolism, this might just work for you. Remember; do not let this oil get rancid, keep it refrigerated.

Another product that you may find helpful is oil of oregano and the capsule form as well. Take five drops of the oil twice a day and three capsules. The phone number for the company that supplies the true oil of oregano is 1-800-243-5242. Oil of oregano contains a variety of anti-inflammatory compounds, which reduce swelling. And when rubbed on lesions twice daily there seems to be a considerable reduction in the time that it takes the lesions to heal. I have also seen allergic coughs halted immediately, and within a few minutes, relief from the allergy causing the coughing was arrested.

Very few if any people have had allergic reactions to spices. However, if you find that you are having allergic reactions, discontinue the use of the spices and try ingesting them one spice at a time until you find the one that is causing the problem.

I would like to cover food allergies, but if we did, by the process of mathematical elimination, it might take years. Your health practitioner will be able to save you a lot of time and pain with a simple blood test.

In conclusion, my next book should have a great deal of new information, as the subject of allergies is very exciting as we find new discoveries in DNA research. I can project that soon your DNA may be slightly altered and all of your symptoms will be gone forever. I hope that the few suggestions offered here may help you to be free of the symptoms of your allergies. If I had a simple answer, I would give it to you, not sell it. The future looks exciting in this field, don't ever give up as tomorrow may have the answer you are looking for.

Fungus

Fungal infections are a major cause of disease in the Western world. It is a type of microbe that is known as a saprophyte. A saprophyte, lives off of dead and dying tissue. Fungi (the plural of fungus) commonly infects the skin as well as other organs. The skin constantly adds layers of dead cells, which makes a great feeding ground for the fungi. Our bodies contain some 70 trillion cells and researchers contend, that as many as 3% of those cells may be fungi. We do not have to worry about killing them all because, under normal circumstances, they do little if any harm. However, if they overpopulate, they can cause extensive disease and even death once they become established in the body. Fungi and yeasts are very difficult to destroy. The elderly and young are the most vulnerable and Americans are the most fungally affected people in the world. The main reason for this is because we consume more sugar then any other culture, some 150 pounds per person per year. Now fungi feed primarily on one substance, sugar. Alcohol is yet another stimulant for fungal growth. Alcohol depresses the immune system and makes it more difficult to contain fungal growth. I used to consume a little alcohol (maybe three beers a week) as an aid to heart disease. It may have a few slight benefits, but the down side is much greater then any benefit. Alcohol consumption is the number 1 cause of high blood pressure and causes its own type of heart disease called, cardiomyopathy.

Antibiotics are probably the leading cause of acute fungal infections of the vagina, intestines, and mouth. Here are a few other effects from medications that cause fungal infections: fungal infections are greatly enhanced while taking birth control pills. Cortisone also accelerates fungal growth, especially prednisone which is one of the most potent forms of cortisone. It enhances fungal growth by repressing the function of the adrenal glands which regulates the ability of the body to control fungi. Another interesting observation of the strength of fungi was demonstrated when we first tested nuclear bombs in 1940. After a test bomb was detonated, the one organism, which readily survived, was Candida Albicons. This shows its tremendous ability to mutate and survive even under nuclear radiation.

Please understand that I am not against all antibiotics, as they do have their place in the bacterial world. What I do object to is the indiscriminate use of penicillin, sulfa drugs and their improved varieties. A bacterium has the ability to mutate against these drugs, sometimes in a matter of hours, and produce a super strain that is resistant to the drugs. This super strain is then passed on to the next person. The use of these drugs has saved many lives and still will, but they have little if any use against a virus. Often patients who have a cold or flu demand and antibiotic which offers little if any value to viral infections. Again, there is a place for antibiotics, and I totally agree with the physician who recommends that you take the entire amount of the antibiotic and not stop when you start to feel better. If it does kill the bacteria, you need to kill all of it because if it mutates and comes back, it will only be stronger and more able to withstand further antibiotic treatment. Yes, we have a war against viruses and I pray our researchers will soon find the answer. Until then we may need to refer to some of the natural antiviral substances that have been used for hundreds of years e.g. garlic, onion, cayenne and the normal immune boosters mentioned in other chapters of this book.

Now back to the yeast-fungi problem. In the International Journal of Food Microbiology, the authors observed a complete inhibition of growth of all fungi that was tested, with the use of oil of oregano. This was accomplished with minute amounts of the oil 1% solution. It appears that oil of oregano destroys all varieties of fungi and yeasts regardless of where they reside. Now please do not go to the grocery store and buy some oregano until you have finished reading this whole chapter. If you buy oregano, at the grocery store, you may be buying marjoram which is a spice we add to pizza, but it has few if any beneficial medicinal effects. You may even be able to buy oil of oregano that is commercially available, but it is almost exclusively thyme oil, (labeled oregano oil) which may come from the same plant variety yet it also has no medicinal attributes. In fact, thyme oil may show some toxicity. The true oil of oregano and where to get it will be at the end of the chapter. It comes in tablet form (crushed leaves) and oil form. Even though oregano has been used for centuries for its medicinal properties, it has only been the last few years beginning around 1996 that we have seen it come to prominence again. I have many herbal books, but even books published as recently as 1992, oil of oregano was not mentioned.

GROWING HAIR SAFELY

Hey, is that scalp of yours starting to look like a cue ball, well here's something that might just qualify as a miracle. Re-growing your hair has been a topic of conversation between men in every golf club and health club locker room for quite some time now. The big buzz now days is for Rogaine and other chemical drugs, that really have some severe side effects that you really don't want to deal with. But, long before all of these expensive drugs came along, I came across an article written by a doctor who said that the only thing that he had found to work consistently for the re-growth of hair was capsaicin (red pepper). Well by the time that I had read this article, I was already doing that comb over thing. You know that thing that guy's do letting the hair on the side of their head grow very long and then combing it across the top in a futile attempt to look like they still had hair on top of their heads. Well I was tired of the comb over thing so I decided to try the capsaicin. Within three months, I was starting to see some fuzz growing on the top of my head. Then by six months, I no longer had to do the comb over. My hair definitely isn't as thick as it was when I was a teen-ager but there is enough hair on my head to keep it from getting burned in the summer. It really works. Its use is easy, in the morning right out of the shower after you have dried your scalp, place a small amount of the capsaicin on your fingertips and rub it in thoroughly. I use a formula made by Born Again you can buy it at just about any health food store. There is also another product made by Kal that works well also. Let me give you one small warning. If you buy these products for use on your head be sure to get the formulation that has .025 % capsaicin solution not the one with .075%. The latter formulation is much too strong for your scalp but it works great for arthritis. If you get the .075% solution, you can hardly wash it off of your hands and if you touch any sensitive parts of your body, you will regret it even into the next morning. It lasts from 12 to 18 hours.

That is why it makes such a great painkiller for your back, or anywhere that you would put a heating rub. I will cover this in more detail when we get to the chapter on arthritis. You see, you don't really need to spend $100.00 a month and risk all of those side affects. The above recommendation may cost as much as $3.00 a month and will promote a healthy head of hair.

THE PROSTATE

Prostate protection is probably the most important thing a man can do for his health. Almost all men will face prostate cancer unless steps are taken early to prevent the disease. As of yet, I have never heard of women having prostate problems, so you might want to skip this chapter. However, you may glean some usable knowledge, as many of the factors that cause prostate cancer are also related in some manner to breast cancer and heart disease. Researchers have found a distinct correlation between breast cancer and prostate cancer. If a relative has had a history of breast cancer, it seems to increase the chances of prostate cancer. And for some reason in a marriage where a woman develops breast cancer, the man is also more likely to get prostate cancer. Do you suppose that this is because they share the same diet? The higher your risk of coronary heart disease, the higher your risk for breast and prostate cancer. So when a husband and a wife share the same diet, they may share the same cancer risks. Here is where I will state something that I have believed for some time; prostate cancer is primarily a nutritional disease.

How serious is this disease. Here are some percentages for latent prostate cancers.

- 30 years old – 25%.
- 40 years old – 30 %.
- 50 years old – 40%.
- 60 years old – 60 %.
- 70 years old – 70 %.
- 80 years old – 90 – 95 %.

Younger people who contract prostate cancer seem to have tumors that are more aggressive. So, what is the easy answer? Just surgically remove the prostate and solve all of your problems. Or will it? You will probably survive the operation and will be cured of the cancer; however, as much as I would like to end the story here, it just doesn't end quite that easily. There are two major complications that may occur, incontinence, impotence or both. Special new surgeries may lessen the chances of these catastrophic complications, however if you are persuaded to take the surgical route start off by doing some extensive research on the surgeons that you are thinking of soliciting for the procedure. Check into each doctors credentials, his surgical record, and if possible ask the doctor to talk with a few of his patients that have had the surgery. Believe me; their experience can possibly do more for you in making your decision then anything else. There are several other alternative procedures rather than surgery, radiation therapy and seed implants. But the results of these two procedures may have the same results as the surgical removal.

As I have stated before, after exhaustive research, I believe that prostate cancer is a nutritional disease. This does not preclude the fact that you should always have an annual P.S.A. test. This test is one of the best indicators of a possible serious problem. The results from this test can cause you to take a different direction in your life. Understand that the earlier you know about the existence of a problem, the easier it will be to cure. If all men would just consider the possibility of prostate cancer at an early age, there chances of contracting the disease would be greatly diminished. If only I could get 20 year olds to read about the tragedy of this disease, it may wake them up to the healthier solutions. Thereby not increasing their percentage of contracting the problem as they age, I believe that you can be free of prostate cancer even into your 70s with the knowledge that is being presented here.

Here is where I am going to lose most of you guys, but if you realize that by not following these life choices you might end up incontinent, impotent or dead, it might just change your mind. Well here it is, burgers, fast food, pizza, fries and gallons of sodas are just about the worst thing that you can eat for your health in so many ways that this chapter is just the first place you will here about these foods that are actually just a bullet to your body. Please consider this; Asian men that still live in the orient and continue to eat traditional foods, have a 90% less

33

occurrence of prostate cancer than their American counterparts. Also, consider that Asian women who continue to eat in the traditional manner have 90% less incidences of breast cancer. However, when Asians move to the United States and begin to embrace the convenience of the fast food lifestyle, their cancer rate goes up and reaches the same percentages as their American counterparts. So now you can understand by this comparison, how as I have stated, that diet really does play an integral part in prostrate and breast cancers. Starches, red meat, sugar and refined flour are just part in parcel of the problems that exist in the American diet. The Asian diet by comparison, has more fiber, green leafy vegetables, fruits, soybeans and soybean products. When I was in Japan, their desert was a piece of fruit, not a hunk of pie slathered with whipped cream or topped off with ice cream. Most of the vegetables were lightly steamed or raw. Their primary source of meat is fish, once in a while chicken and on extremely rare or special occasions beef or pork. Another large staple in their diet is soy products e.g. miso soup, tofu and soymilk. Major fast food restaurants like those found in the United States were few and far between. The Japanese form of fast food at the time was rice noodles topped with a sauce that tasted like miso with pieces of tofu. And instead of a high fat, high calorie, listen to your arteries harden while you drink it, milkshake, they served green tea.

In the coming paragraphs we will look into this diet with more scrutiny. First, let's take a look at soy products. I make sure to have several helpings a day.

Soy is a wonderful preventative treatment that also tastes good. If I can convince you of the fantastic properties contained in soy, many of your health problems would be solved. It is this simple; researchers have proven that the more soy products that men consume, the lower their chances of contracting prostate cancer. Likewise, the more soy products that women consume, the smaller their likelihood of breast cancer.

Soy works in many ways to combat tumors and cancers. It appears to stop angiogenesis (growth of new blood vessels). Cancers require a great deal of blood in order to grow, spread and metastasize. Soy inhibits this so it greatly slows the progress that can create a tumors growth. Soy is also a very potent anti-oxidant as it contains a substance known as genistein that prevents cellular migration. So as you can see soy is a fantastic source of the building blocks that will help you with prostate cancer. The product that I normally use is Pure Soy Protein Isolate Powder. You can get it at your local health food store. This product is 50% protein and one serving contains these isoflavones as follows:

- 30 mg genistein.
- 17mg daidsein.
- 3mg glacitein.

For a total of 50mg of isoflavones. It is also low in fat, low carbohydrate and each serving (1 heaping teaspoon) contains approximately 25 grams of soy protein. It is also an ideal source of essential amino acids.

The following is what I consider the perfect health promoting breakfast. It also tests your courage and gag reflex but if you can survive it, you might just learn to enjoy it. Well maybe you will just get it down because of its fantastic health benefits. I have grown to enjoy it through the years. Well here it is, enjoy it for one reason or the other. I mix the following ingredients and drink. Honestly, it won't kill you even if it looks that way. I have been drinking this for breakfast for more than 5 years now and don't plan to change unless after research I find something better.

RECIPE:

- One glass of soymilk and one glass of water.
- 2 Tablespoons of 100% pure soy protein.
- 1 Teaspoon of Nutra Joint a high protein product made by Knox Gelatin can be purchased in most grocery stores.
- One Heaping Teaspoon of barley green. I'll admit this is the one ingredient that separates the men from the boys. If you just can't deal with the taste of the barley green, then use several stems of broccoli.
- 1/2 cup of fresh fruit (not frozen as it contains too much sugar) strawberries, blueberries, or raspberries. A 1/2 of a pear or an apple is a secondary choice.
- 2 Tablespoons of freshly ground flax seed.
- 1 Teaspoon of psyllium seed e.g. Metamucil or any other inexpensive brand.

Now toss all of the ingredients into the blender. Blend thoroughly plug your nose and guzzle it down. I say guzzle because if you stop, you might never start again.

Now that you have forced it down here is why this is such a fantastic breakfast.

- It contains all of the amino acids and is a complete source of protein.
- It is also a great source of flavinoids.
- It contains both soluble and insoluble fibers.
- It lowers the LDL (bad cholesterol).
- It raises the HDL (good cholesterol).
- It tends to attract water to your joints and decreases pain. Great for arthritis.
- Protects bones and reduces the chances for osteoporosis.
- Increases Energy.
- Metabolizes slowly and keeps you from getting hungry.
- It does not raise the insulin level but tends to keep it on an even plane, thus decreasing the buildup of fat. I will cover this in more detail in the chapter on diabetes.
- It contains all of the ingredients that cancer hates.
- Your bowels will move more often, thus decreasing colon problems.
- Your glycemic index will be less than 19 and that makes even oatmeal at 49, look like a chocolate sundae.

- It is highly anti-inflammatory.
- It will clean your intestinal wall.
- It will cause your body to eliminate more cholesterol by increasing the production of bile.

Now another one of the important benefits of this breakfast is in your personal pride. As I will wager that most of you will only try this drink once and say, "I would rather have cancer than drink this crap again". Please listen; it will get easier every time that you drink it. And if you give it a chance you will feel so much better that you won't even hate me anymore for influencing you to try it. I have even convinced my wife to drink it. However sometimes she slips in a banana for flavor, which isn't the best thing to do because of the sugar content. But I am very proud that she sticks with it so I let her get away with a banana or two. I have said many times that I would eat dirt if that is what it would take to stay healthy or to feel good. You may not agree right now but, if you have ever had a relative that has contracted a serious disease and have seen their suffering you will start to drink this concoction every chance that you get. Hey, you can do it! Just keep trying.

Now that you have survived the Marquee De Sade of breakfasts, try to keep the rest of your daily diet as low in fat, sugar and red meat as possible. Switch from cow's milk to soymilk. From cottage cheese to tofu and substitute fruit for that dessert, hey, this one kills me as much as any suggestion I have given so far, as I love desserts as much as you. However, I always remember not to let the food control me, I will control the food.

There are times that I go out to dinner or am invited over to dine with friends. Since I believe that friends are more important than keeping strictly to my diet and lifestyle, I always eat what they are serving for dinner. Not only is this a small treat for me, but food and fellowship are just about the most important links in the human condition. That link can do more for you then any diet. So after a wonderful evening, when I get home, I drink a glass of water with 3 – 4 tablespoons of flaxseed and think flax do your stuff.

Here are some other fantastic supplements to utilize in your fight against prostate cancer.

- Lycopane is a prostate nutrient that is vital. This is, believe it or not, the pigment that makes tomatoes red in color. Experts at Harvard University found that Lycopane reduced the risk of abnormal growths by as much as 34%. That result is amazing. Lycopane is found in abundance in tomato products such as V-8 juice and most other tomato products. Ketchup is full of sugar and salt, which may not be in your best interests. I take an inexpensive supplement that you can get from your local health food store.

- Another supplement that is extremely important in the fight against prostate cancer is zinc. Having overtly low levels of zinc is often responsible for abnormal cellular growth in the prostate. The prostate gland requires more than ten times the amount of zinc than any other organ in the body.

- There are two other nutrients that work in concert with each other to help protect the prostate. I take both everyday. One of the nutrients is pygeum, which will in and of itself be a major contributing factor in alleviating the problems associated with prostate enlargement and restricted urine flow. The other supplement, possibly the most important in your fight against prostate problems is saw palmetto. There have been many conclusive studies that have stated evidence that those persons who began taking saw palmetto realized between 75-90% reductions in the swelling of the prostate gland. Remarkably, in just a few days, a large number of users stopped getting up at night and that urgency to urinate subsided. Saw palmetto prevents testosterone from converting into dihydrotestosterone one of the major problem causes in prostate disease.

- Saw palmetto and the other nutrients can be purchased at your local health food store. I recommend six capsules daily. Three capsules in the morning and three in the evening. If you don't want to take that many pills there is a product that contains most, if not all of the ingredients listed in the previous paragraph.

The product is called Prostata and it can be found in your local health food store. If you don't have a health food store nearby, then you can call 1-800-546-8543 and order the product.

If you follow these suggestions regarding the prostate and if you spend as much time reading studies on the subject of your prostate as you do reading about your favorite sports team, the subject of prostate problems might be solved and very possibly prevented in the future.

Let me explain in more detail the effects of dihydrotestosterone (DHT). Your testicles produce almost 95% of a mans testosterone. Once it gets to the prostate, it has little if any harmful effects. Only when it is converted into DHT does it become a problem. DHT is the most powerful male hormone in the body possibly 10-15 times more powerful than testosterone. As you get older, the problem of conversion is greater. If you have an abundance of testosterone, it does not necessarily mean a large quantity of DHT. This is why saw palmetto is so important in your fight against prostate problems. Saw Palmetto blocks the conversion of testosterone into DHT.

We are just about done with the topic of prostate cancer. However, this should not be the end of your studies. I have given you some healthy choices and some great remedies, but don't stop here. You have made a great start, but continued studies are also part of preventative medicine, possibly the most important part. There is another treatment that is in the works and you should watch. It is so new that you may need to find new information on the Internet. This new treatment is called PC-SPES. This product is something that you will want to discuss with your doctor. Chances are that he might not even be aware about it yet. Here is your chance to help him with the information that you have acquired in order to help yourself and possibly another patient with prostate problems.

PC-SPES is made from eight different herbs. I have read some unbelievable results surrounding this product. One documented case tells of a patient who had cancer that had metastasized into his bones. But after using the PC-SPES, the cancer went into remission within six months, and seven years later, he is still in remission. I am considering this product as a preventative treatment. As a holistic approach, it might possibly be the next new weapon in your fight against prostate cancer. PC-SPES is considered to be 25 times less toxic than aspirin. Please try to learn about this product as soon as possible. If you try this product please write to me with any testimonials or problems as soon as possible, and I will publish them in my next attempt to bring a conclusion to this virulent disease. If you have your doctors blessing to try this product you can get information about this product from 714-514-5513. Now please skip ahead to the chapter on anti-oxidants, as this will be very helpful in your quest for good health.

ADD-ADHD

Don't just accept the first diagnosis of ADHD. Try to get several opinions before you decide on which course to take with your child. It may be a lifelong challenge to help your child. Although the diagnosis of ADHD (attention deficit hyperactivity disorder) in your child may be upsetting at first, it will likely prove to be a relief – for both of you, now that you know what has been causing your child's unruly behavior. And now your child will get treatment to calm down and truly enjoy school, play, friends, and family life. The behavior disorder known as ADHD (attention deficit hyperactivity disorder) is 5-7 times more common in boys than girls and may affect up to 5% of school-age children – making it the most commonly diagnosed childhood behavioral disorder. Children with ADHD typically are impulsive, inattentive, and hyperactive. They may also be easily distracted, excessively talkative, and or prone to temper tantrums. Some children with ADHD also have learning disabilities. Occasionally some ADHD symptoms may continue into adolescence and adulthood. ADHD can be enormously frustrating for both the children who have it and for their parents. But with treatment – of both ADHD and the other treatable problems that can occur, such as learning disabilities, anxiety, and depression – the family frustration level often decreases dramatically ADHD is frequently misunderstood. Not every restless, inattentive, or "jumpy" child has ADHD. The symptoms of ADHD must be frequent, severe, and long lasting for the diagnosis to be made. They include:

- Inattention: The child has difficulty with tasks requiring long-term effort; is forgetful, disorganized, and easily distracted; and may be described as "not listening."

- Hyperactivity: The child fidgets, cannot sit quietly (is "always in motion"), and talks excessively.

- Impulsivity: The child cannot curb immediate reactions, acts or speaks without thinking, interrupts, and has difficulty waiting.

The standard treatment may include any or all of several approaches to calming children with ADHD and improving their ability to focus, work, and learn. Medications are available to reduce the hyperactivity on a day-by-day basis; however, they do not cure ADHD. Beside medications, working with a therapist to learn new ways of behaving is often effective. The different types of therapy include psychotherapy, which helps people accept themselves and their disorder; cognitive-behavioral therapy, which helps people learn to manage their behavior (for example, controlling impulsivity) and social skills training, which teach people to improve their behavior with others. Parents and teachers can also help improve the day-to-day behavior of children with ADHD – for example, in the classroom, the teacher can give the child a place to sit with few distractions, provide extra time to take tests, and give written as well as spoken instructions.

ADHD has taken center stage in just about every schoolchild that has trouble sitting still. Ritalin is still the prescribed drug of choice. But before you administer this drug to your child please consider some of these adverse side effects. Nervousness and insomnia are the most common reactions but are usually controlled by reducing the dosage and omitting the drug in the afternoon or evening. Other reactions include hypersensitivity (including skin rash, urticaria, fever, arthralgia, exfoliative dermatitis, erythemia multiform with histopathological findings of necrotizing vasculitis, and thrombocytopenic purpura) anorexia, nausea, dizziness, palpitations, headache, dyskinesia, drowsiness, blood pressure and pulse changes both up and down, trachycardia, angina, cardiac arrhythmia, and abdominal pain and weight loss during prolonged therapy. Toxic Physosis has also been reported. Although a definite causal relationship has not been established, the following have been reported in patients taking this drug. Isolated cases of cerebral arthritis and or occlusion, leucopoenia and or anemia, transient depressed mood, and a few instances of scalp hair loss. In children, loss of appetite, abdominal pain, weight loss during prolonged therapy insomnia and trachycardia may occur more frequently; however, any of the above adverse reactions listed may occur. Have you heard enough yet, or do you want me to go on? What a travesty this drug is, how can physicians and educators call this the wonder drug. Is this drug really the answer? What is this doing to the physical and psychological welfare of this generation of our youth? Should this drug even be considered? Sure, it makes the child sit still but so will a hammer, and the hammer will probably have less side effects. What are the long-term effects of this drug, no one knows yet! Is there a chance that in our zeal to pigeonhole our kids into that form that fits the so-called ideal child that we are creating a generation of automatons and zombies? Are we possibly hampering the creative processes that could lead to genius? You see ADHD is not a problem cured by drugs.

One of the answers to help fight the powerful urges brought on by ADHD is so astoundingly simple that it devastates me to think that a physician's only choice of action is that drug. 98% of all cases of ADHD can be brought to a manageable level by eliminating one thing from the diet, sugar. It is also important to eliminate as much of the primary carbohydrates as you can. The other 2% can be attributed to food allergies or something else that causes an allergic reaction. Let me try to illustrate what sugar does to the insulin level in the blood and how this can affect mood swings.

Let's use a can of soda pop for example.

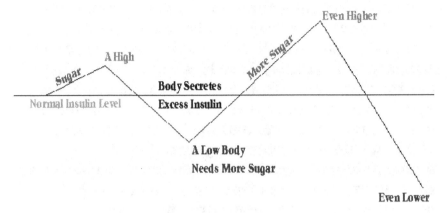

Maybe I can describe it better in words. A normal insulin function as represented by the centerline is the best function of your body and keeps the mood at a norm. But, now we drink a can of soda loaded with sugar. We now have a temporary sugar rush and feel great. As represented by the first rise in the chart. As your body reaches the first plateau, your pancreas gets the message and kicks into overdrive. It begins producing insulin in large quantities in order to move back to the normal insulin level. However, the pancreas always over compensates and brings your sugar level below the normal insulin level as represented by the first valley in the chart. Now you feel slow and sluggish, your mood is also depressed. So what's the cure? Have another soda or a candy bar. Well here you go again for another ride to the top of the charts, even higher now see the second peak on the chart. Of course, you have just started the cycle again; the body secretes even more insulin than the first time. And guess what, the low goes even lower than before. And here it is the fastest roller coaster in existence and you don't even need to leave the house. Now add that to your ADHD affected child. As hard as it is for the child to concentrate when the sugars are at a normal level, now the devastating effects of the peaks and valleys, the ups and downs in energy, the elation and depression of moods, makes anybody a ticking time bomb. As an adult, these reactions are hard enough to deal with, and the affects on a normal child are serious enough and you begin to see the changes very quickly. As the sugar rises, they start to bounce off of the walls full of energy. And as the sugar levels drop you see them fighting over the game that they are playing with their friends or siblings and then comes the unruly behavior. The effects of ADHD are like an amplifier; these children are affected by a factor of about 3 times that of a normal child so you can just imagine the results. How can you expect them to react in a normal fashion? Their bodies are fighting with them physically and mentally! Frustration becomes depression, then anger, fear, self-loathing and a myriad number of devastating and sometimes debilitating reactions.

Instead of setting your child on that roller coaster of desperation, just feed them correctly. It might be difficult to control this in a school setting, but as a good parent, it is not only your job but also your life's work. You need to be creative in the education of your children, their nutritional education should be as important to them as learning to ride that bike or to catch a ball. Discuss with them how much better they behave without that candy bar. Tell them how proud you are of their abstinence from sugar.

The other alternative and the only reason that I call this an alternative, is that we are woefully behind in researching new drugs that have far less adverse side affects then the one that is so often applied. There have been several studies involving the taking of these drugs and violence in schools. These drugs only create more problems not answers. I am often asked to speak to children in juvenile detention centers and talk to violent and drug addicted kids from every walk of life. And do you know what I really see? Kids whose bodies' minds and spirits have never been nourished properly. Kids who live on soda, junk food, and television. Sometimes for the first time in their life during their incarceration, they receive a nourishing meal and an ear to listen to their problems. Without doubt, ADHD is fueled by an improper diet. You can help your child with a little time to listen, to cook a hot meal, and a hug. Let them know that you are there, and that you love them no matter what. I know that this takes a little more creativity then just handing them a pill but, remember what the rewards will be, you see it really doesn't amount to much effort when you think about the joy you and your child will feel in the long run.

Bedwetting

Bedwetting can be a complex problem that is experienced by a high percentage of children and even teenagers. It can be a very debilitating psychological disadvantage to those who experience it. the problem of bedwetting can be exacerbated when the person affected uses simple sugars e.g. highly sweetened carbonated beverages, sweetened juices e.g. apple juice, grape juice, highly sweetened breakfast foods or to much candy.

You will never cure the disorder by keeping your child from drinking water. The first lesson I ever learned, as a parent was during the time my son was about nine years old and his bedwetting was out of control, I gave him a spanking for wetting his bed. This is one spanking that I would like to take back 100 times over if I could. This is a case where parents must learn along with their children. The problem of bedwetting is almost never cured with drugs. The problem stems from the person sleeping too deeply making them unable to feel the need to urinate. However, the solution is so simple it is almost beyond belief. Just purchase a simple device that is activated by just the slightest amount of urine causing it to make a noise that awakens the child. Here is where the parent comes in. If your child sleeps so deeply that he or she does not feel the natural urge to urinate, it is also quite possible that the alarm will not awaken your child either. Talk to your child and make a game out of the situation or just call it a sleep over to make them feel comfortable with your sleeping in the same room. At first, you will need to get up with your child four to five times a night. Make sure the child is awake. Try something like a cold damp towel placed on their forehead to make sure that they are wide-awake. Take the child to the toilet even if it is too late. Always try to make a game out of the situation use whatever innovations you can think of. Keep a chart on your child's progress and always place stars or something else that your child will recognize as a reward on the chart so they can follow their own progress. Praise is also extremely important, as this is a fantastic psychological booster for your child. After about a week, you will begin to notice dramatic changes in your child's habits and by the second week, you will only need to get up maybe once or twice a night, within three to four weeks it is usually over forever. No spankings, threats, or embarrassment, all you are left with is a happy child. During this treatment, you may also want to include chromium and vanadium 50-150 mg per day along with calcium and magnesium. If you cannot find the wetting machine locally, you can get more information or purchase it from Pacific International Nekoosa Wisconsin 555 Bert St. 54457-1397 or call 1-800-477-2233.

Even though the initial cost of the equipment for this treatment may be somewhat expensive, its value far outweighs the cost. Even after forty years of research, I have never found anything to equal the results of this program. Our son could now stay overnight with his friends, go camping, visit with relatives and never again have that fear of a mistake. The psychological value to your child alone is beyond description, and the bond that you have built with your child by helping them through this situation will last a lifetime.

My advice to you is not to spend several years trying to use drugs that may be harmful to your child's health. This treatment has no side affects only the peace of mind that the problem is solved. Again, I have never seen the problem solved with drugs because drugs do not get at the cause of the problem. You may slow down the amount of urine with drugs, but that is ultimately not the answer.

COLDS AND FLU

The only thing that you need to cure that nasty cold or flu is to watch all of the goofy ads on television and then pick out one of the fine products i.e. the feel good drugs. O.k. now for the real truth these so-called remedies don't cure a thing, they aren't intended to. They are meant to dull your senses and numb the aches and pain until the symptoms are over. I suppose that is not such a bad thing until you realize that for the most part you could get the same results with a shot of heated whiskey, a tablespoon of honey and a few drops of eucalyptus oil. You see that mixture will also clear your stuffy nose and definitely dull your senses and it costs a whole lot less then those other remedies.

There is no best way to get rid of a cold or flu; the key is to prevent them. Keeping your immune system at its peak form is the best way to stay healthy during that cold and flu season. A virus almost always causes these illnesses. Antibiotics have little if no effect on a virus and can only do harm to you down the road if you take them for a cold or the flu. Then if you get a bacterium and that bacterium has mutated and become resistant to the antibiotic, look out! Let's take a stab at boosting that immune system first. Again, let me recommend the great value of soy products. Not only are they great for their nutritional value but they also give your body a fantastic boost of anti-oxidants. Well we will cover this list of anti-oxidants many times in this book, so get ready to feel redundant. Or figure out just how important anti-oxidants are in your fight for health. Here is a suggested daily intake.

- **Magnesium Citrate- 600mg.**

- **Beta Carotene-25000IU.**

- **Grape Seed Extract-100mg.**

- **Folic Acid-1600mcg.**

- **B12-5000mcg.**

- **B100-Multiple B Vitamins.**

- **E-1200IU.**

- **Selenium-200mcg.**

- Alpha Lipolic Acid-200mg.

- Garlic-3000mg.

- Lycopene-5mg.

- Ester C-3000mg.

- Cayenne-40,000 units.

- MSM-1500mg.

This will keep your immune system at a full charge and will help you to fend off almost anything that comes your way. Now you're looking down that grocery list and thinking to yourself, "How can I swallow all of this stuff"? It isn't as hard as it sounds, I can do it in about three handfuls. Think of it this way, how many times do you run through the kitchen and stop to grab a few handfuls of chips they aren't hard to get down are they? And here's the bonus, I can't remember the last time that I had a cold and I almost never get the flu, even if I do it doesn't last very long and the symptoms aren't severe. Now, do you think that the pill popping is worth it? As I have stated before, prevention is always better than cure. The only problem with this thought is that we are lazy, so doctors don't spend much time studying nutrition as we won't pay them for a consultation when we are healthy and we are to lazy even when we know about the benefits of these nutritional items. So as they are only consulted when the illness arrives, that's where they put forth most of their energies and studies. Understand that I do not criticize the medical profession because they saved my life for the tidy little sum of $40,000 simply because I was not wise enough to follow my own advice on prevention instead of cure. So for my laziness I not only spent a large sum of money, but I will be harnessed with the problem for the rest of my life. Now here's the toughie, even with your immune system boosted to its peak level there is still that one little buggie that wants to give you a hard time. And there it is, a cold. Now what, well here's the quickest way to get rid of that cold. At the first indication of the symptoms of a cold, you need to drink a half-cup of colostrum, or take, and this isn't fun, 25 colostrum tablets. Then repeat the process in 5-6 hours. And presto the cold is gone. What is this miracle substance anyway? Is it a miracle drug? Is it even a drug at all? Did aliens beam it down? No, it's probably the most natural thing on the planet, and very possibly the first thing that you ever consumed. It is one of the ingredients found in mother's first milk. This is one of the things that start a babies immune system functioning. This substance is so important that in the animal world, if it weren't introduced within hours of their birth, calves and horses would very possibly die in just a day or two. Without it, your baby will suffer the consequences of a weakened immune system for the rest of his or her life. You see it is nature's way of preventing disease. I use bovine colostrum because it is much easier to get than human colostrum and has eight times the IgG that human colostrum has. You cannot take to much colostrum so enjoy it. It is not expensive but it should be kept on hand in your refrigerator at all times. Colostrum is probably one of the best immune system boosters you can get. It also has many other advantages that you will hear about later in this book. Another thing is in the event that you catch a cold increase your intake of vitamin C from 2000 mg to 5000-7000mg. Always take the ester C form as it will not cause additional acid in your stomach. The answer to the cold and flu season is now in your hands. Colostrum is so simple that I missed it in 20 years of research and study. I can save you thousands of pages of reading and study if you can just accept the value of this almost magical substance. I take it two or three times a week just to keep my immune system in top form. The liquid form is the best. If you have, any questions about colostrum please call the people at Cuprem and they will be glad to give you any information that you need. You can call Cuprem at 1-800-228-4253. There may be other companies producing colostrum but I have found Cuprem to be the best. They follow very stringent guidelines in producing their product, and they always make sure of the quality and potency of the ingredients. You can also purchase the human form of colostrum but it can only be found in Germany and it doesn't come close to the amounts of IgG that the bovine formulation has. Since the two products are exactly the same by comparison on a chemical level, Why would you want to purchase a product that is about 10 times more expensive than the bovine formula and isn't nearly as potent.

Now a little bit about the chemistry of colostrum. Colostrum has four classes of immunoglobulins or immune factors are IgG, IgA, IgM and IgE. IgG accounts for about 80% of the total antibodies in human serum. The protein content of colostrum contains 80% immunoglobulins also called immune factors or antibodies. Bovine colostrum has 10-20 times more immunoglobulins than human colostrum. IgA antibodies account for about 10% of the antibodies in humans and are prevalent in saliva, tears and breast milk. Please note: IgA is most prevalent in human serum, while IgA antibodies are more prevalent in the body. IgA antibodies prevent the attachment of viruses and bacteria to tissue in the body e.g. IgA would prevent the strep bacteria from attaching to the tissue in the throat, thus stopping the formation of colonies from forming and causing the throat to inflame. Now you can see why colostrum is so affective and is such an important addition to boosting your immune system.

So there it is, if you don't want to try colostrum, I understand. I know how much everybody likes to suffer for a week to ten days with a cold or the flu. Not to mention the missed work and the chance to spread it to your children or others, you know how misery loves company.

INSOMNIA

There are many negative effects on thinking and performance. In a 1999 survey, people with insomnia reported dramatically worse waking behaviors including reduced concentration, decreased memory, impaired task performance, and less enjoyment of other people. One study reported that missing only two to three hours of sleep every night for a week significantly impaired performance and mood. Some experts report that deep sleep deprivation impairs the brain's ability to process information, and one study indicated that healthy sleep is important for learning certain perceptual skills related to visual patterns as well as repetitive skills, such as typing. Some studies reported no difference in test scores between people with temporary sleep loss and those with full sleep, although a Canadian study found that students who slept after cramming for an exam did better than those who stayed awake.

The effects on emotions, stress and depression can cause insomnia, but, in turn, insomnia also increases the activity of the hormones and pathways in the brain that can produce these emotional problems. Sleep abnormalities are an integral part of depressive disorders, with more than 90% of depressed patients experiencing insomnia. Even modest alterations in waking and sleeping patterns can have significant effects on a person's mood. Abnormal sleep patterns often have preceded the first episode of depression. Studies indicate that in some cases persistent insomnia may actually be a symptom of impending emotional disorders, including anxiety and depression. One 1997 study suggested that young adults with stress-related insomnia were at an increased risk of developing depression later in life, although sleeplessness unrelated to stress did not appear to be an important factor in causing later depression. Another study of male medical students found that young men who experienced insomnia were twice as likely to suffer from depression at middle age. Genetic factors may play a role in the association between sleep disorders and depression. In one study of patients diagnosed with depression, family members with certain sleep abnormalities were found to be at greater risk for depression than those with normal sleep patterns. Individuals with normal sleep patterns who are from families with abnormal sleep habits also appear to have an increased risk for mood disorders. Some investigators, in fact, are exploring the possibility of preventing psychiatric disorders by early recognition and treatment of insomnia.

Alcohol and substance abuse is also a major contributing factor. A 1999 survey reported that 14% of American adults use alcohol within a month to help them sleep, with 2.5% reporting frequent use of alcohol to induce sleep. Some medications, such as the benzodiazepines, used to treat insomnia can become habit forming and even addictive, although the risk is low.

Accidents caused by insomnia are on the rise and studies continue to report that drowsy driving is as risky as drunk driving. An Australian study reported that 17 hours of sleep deprivation causes impaired performance levels comparable to those found in people who have blood alcohol levels of 0.10%, a level that defines intoxication in many states. A large 1997 survey indicated that accidents involving motor vehicles or machine tools occurred twice as often in persons with moderate or severe daytime sleepiness, compared with those without daytime sleepiness. As many as 100,000 automobile accidents in the U.S. and 1,500 deaths from such accidents are caused by sleepiness. Estimates on fatigue as a cause of automobile crashes range from 1% to 56%, depending on the study. In a major 1995 poll, 33% of those surveyed said they had fallen asleep while driving and 10% of these people had accidents because of this.

Some studies have associated a higher risk of heart disease with shift work. This has been reported in only two studies, however, and more research is needed to confirm this finding. Another study reported signs of heart and nervous system activity in people with chronic insomnia that might place such individuals at risk for coronary heart disease. If it exists, however, this increased danger is modest compared with other risk factors for heart disease. Yet another report suggested that sleep complaints in elderly people without coronary artery disease predicted a first heart attack. Sleep disorders in such cases may have been a marker for depression, a risk factor for heart attacks in elderly people. A study of elderly women reported that insomnia had no effect on survival rates.

Headaches that occur during the night or early in the morning may be caused by sleep disorders. In one study, patients who had these complaints were treated for the sleep disorder only and over 65% reported that their headaches were cured.

Insomnia costs the U.S. approximately $100 billion each year in medical costs and decreased productivity.

All of us have experienced the inability to get a good nights sleep. Sleep is as you have probably now assumed is an absolute need for your health. Physicians try to solve this problem and often do by prescribing too often, by my thinking, some of these drugs. Halcyon, Librium, and Valium. However some of these drugs could and often do have serious side affects. If you are prescribed one of these sleep medications you should always consult the Physicians Desk Reference. I have rejected many medications after going home and reading about their possible side affects. There are many times that the cure is many times worse than the disease. Here are just a few of the serious repercussions that can be awaiting you if you decide to take one of the above listed sleep medications. Some people become extremely irritable and aggressive, while others become nervous and confused. The real disaster is when you actually wake up feeling more tired than before you went to sleep. This causes depression, and depression can lead to a host of other physical and mental problems.

Of the sleep drugs listed above, Valium is probably the least offensive to your body. It is, like all of the other drugs, extremely habit forming. It should never be used as a replacement for regular sleep, but if you are confronted with a serious inability to sleep, it can be used safely for a short period of time. At least until your regular sleep cycle adjusts itself and you can go it on your own again.

Here are some non-drug remedies that I have found to be helpful.

- Magnesium Citrate: You need magnesium for your muscles to relax. You cannot relax without it. In My opinion, 90 % of people in the United States are deficient in this mineral. I recommend 3 capsules of this form of magnesium. Remember to always use magnesium citrate. Other forms of magnesium are not nearly as effective.

- The proven remedy of the ages is that old standby, chamomile tea. A cup or two of this tea may in and of itself have little or no effect but it might just be enough to let you relax and reflect on your day so that you won't go to bed with all of the days problems on your mind. Also, it is compatible with all of the other suggestions, but if you need to miss one of these suggestions then this is the one.

- Probably the most effective substance to induce sleep is valerian root. For many people that suffer from insomnia, the extract from valerian root is by far one of your best choices. Clinical studies continue to show this to be a safe remedy and almost as effective as small doses of tranquilizers, but with no side effects. I recommend 3-4 capsules (150-300mg.) 30 minutes before retiring. If you have that groggy feeling, the next morning then just adjust your dosage the next time that you are having a sleepless night. However, as with the sleep inducing drugs you need to stop taking this remedy after a short term so your body can take over its normal sleep cycle. If you are having long-term problems with your sleep then you might want to consult a physician, as there may be other physical problems that are causing your sleeplessness.

Here are some other important recommendations that will help you find your proper sleep cycle again. When your sleep is being interrupted, try to avoid these things as they are directly attributed to sleep loss.

- Caffeine e.g. coffee sodas.

- Black Tea.

- Chocolate.

- Hot Cocoa.

- Alcohol, sometimes a glass of wine, may actually produce a soothing effect and give you some temporary relief. But here is the problem- and it is a big potential problem. Almost all wines contain sulfites. Sulfites will cause a headache and other side affects that you don't need. If you can find a brand of wine without sulfites, then go ahead and give a glass a try before bedtime. However, using wine to help you get to sleep, as with other remedies shouldn't be used more than once or twice a week. It is also possible that wine may be of some benefit to your heart. But make sure that you purchase a wine that you hate the taste of, because I would hate to be the cause of your beginning to enjoy to much wine consumption. If you try wine for help in sleep and you find, that after drinking one glass that you want two, then leave it alone completely. It's a bad road to go down.

- Eliminate sugar especially before going to bed. This will raise your insulin level. I recommend that if you feel that you need to have something before bed then have a glass of soymilk. It has a 50% ratio of protein to carbohydrates. This will stabilize the blood sugar throughout the night.

With these ideas, you should have a sufficient amount of information to help you get that sometimes-elusive nights sleep. If these remedies don't have the desired effect, be sure to contact your physician, as there may be other health problems that are causing your normal sleep cycle to be interrupted.

HIGH BLOOD PRESSURE

Hypertension has been aptly called the 'silent killer, because it usually produces no symptoms. It is important, therefore, for anyone with risk factors to have their blood pressure checked regularly and to make appropriate lifestyle changes. Such recommendations are urged for individuals who have overall high normal blood pressure, mild or above systolic pressure with normal diastolic, family histories of hypertension, are overweight, or are over forty years old.

Untreated hypertension increases slowly over the years. In rare cases (less than one percent of hypertensive patients), the blood pressure rises quickly (with diastolic pressure usually rising to 130 or higher), resulting in malignant or accelerated hypertension. This is a life-threatening condition and must be treated immediately. Symptoms may include drowsiness, confusion, headache, nausea, and loss of vision. Hypertensive individuals should call a physician immediately if these symptoms appear.

High blood pressure, also called hypertension, occurs when the bodies smaller blood vessels (known as the arterioles) narrow, which causes the blood to exert excessive pressure against the vessel walls. The heart must therefore work harder to maintain this higher pressure. Although the body can tolerate increased blood pressure for months and even years, eventually the heart can enlarge and be damaged (a condition called hypertrophy), and injury to blood vessels in the kidneys, the brain, and the eyes can occur.

Two numbers are used to describe blood pressure, the systolic and diastolic. For example, optimal blood pressure is less than 120/80 mm Hg (systolic/diastolic). The systolic pressure (the higher and first number) is measured as the heart contracts to pump out the blood. The diastolic pressure (the lower and second number) is measured as the heart relaxes to allow the blood to flow into the heart.

Blood pressure is categorized as normal, high normal, mild, moderate, severe, and very severe. Normal pressure is below 130/85 and should be everyone's upper goal. High normal is considered to be 130-139/85-89 and hypertension is above 140/90. Any blood pressure above normal should be attended to with appropriate treatments; even high normal puts one at higher risk for heart events and stroke.

Hypertension itself is further categorized into four stages: mild (140-159/90-99) moderate (160-179/100-109) severe (180-209/110-119) very severe (over 210/120). If there is a disparity in these ranges, the higher category of either measurement should be used to determine severity. For example, if systolic pressure is 165 (moderate) and diastolic is 92 (mild), the patient would still be diagnosed with moderate hypertension. Mild systolic hypertension, in fact, may be a warning sign for more severe hypertension, even if diastolic pressure is normal. A child's blood pressure is normally much lower than an adult's. Children are at risk for hypertension if they exceed the following levels: 116/76 for ages 3-5; 122/78 for ages 6-9; 126/82 for ages 10-12; and 136/86 for ages 13-15.

Most of you are probably in the first phases of hypertension and your problems can be easily corrected with a few simple procedures. After forty or more years of hamburgers, fries, x-rays, smoking and sodas, your arteries begin to narrow and your blood pressure increases.

First, please note that if your blood pressure is anywhere near normal, I don't recommend taking drugs to lower your blood pressure. Here is where the cure can be worse than the disease. Some of the most common drugs used for this disease are beta-blockers. Here are just a few of the popularly prescribed beta-blockers listed below.

- Inderol.

- Lopressor.

- Normodyne.

- Corgard.

- Blocardren.

- Sectral.

- Tenormin.

- Trandato.

- Visken.

Beta-Blockers work by suppressing the electric process that governs the heartbeat, thus slowing the heartbeat creating less force. This will lower the systolic reading. Here is where you need to own your own physicians desk reference and see the side effects for yourself. But let me list a few:

- Fatigue.

- Impotence.

- Loss of energy.

- Dizziness.

- Congestive heart disease.

- Elevated cholesterol.

- Depression.

- Nightmares.

- Loss of appetite.

Beta-blockers should only be used in emergency situations – and there are some emergency situations. If you do not take the necessary precautions and the advices offered to change your lifestyle then drugs are not only a possibility, they are a certainty! Not only will you have to face the consequences of the disastrous side affects, the mortality rate is significantly higher for you when you use blood pressure medications.

Another commonly prescribed blood pressure medication is diuretics. Here are just a few of the most common diuretics that are prescribed today.

- Diuril.

- Enduron.

- Hydro diuril.

- Meta hydrin.

- Oretic.

- Renese.

- Anhydron.

- Aquatag.

- Zestril.

Diuretics cause the body to eliminate excess fluids, which in turn reduces the volume of blood and lessens the load on the circulatory system. Side effects caused by diuretics can be very severe. Here are some of the possible complications listed below.

- May worsen diabetes.

- May cause kidney problems.

- May cause impotence.

- May increase cholesterol.

- Causes a loss of potassium.

So what do you think? Well, sit down and have a burger and some fries while you're reading the next paragraphs. Why, what's a little more plaque forming and getting stuck to the sidewalls of your arteries going to hurt? Just kidding, well by now you have probably decided that you want to do something that's not quite so possibly harmful to your body as the above listed medications so, I will try to approach hypertension from many different angles because what will work great for one person won't even dent the problem for somebody else. The main goal is to provide the heart with nutrients that will help to restore oxygen-rich blood through re-expanded, more flexible arteries.

First of all, let's take a look at some of the things that you can do every day if you have been diagnosed with hypertension and could possibly reverse the problem if you have a mild case and help to lower it if you have a more severe problem.

1. Lose weight

2. Reduce stress – good luck, this is far and away the most difficult thing to reduce in today's runaway lifestyle. Most of us like stress and eat it like candy, we thrive on it. Here is where you might want to think of a major lifestyle change.

3. Exercise – at least 20 minutes a day 3-4 times a week. I remember attending one of Zig Ziegler's lectures when he told the audience that his main form of exercise was to pull the plug in the bathtub and to fight the current to get out. Zig has trimmed down considerably since then but he really had to change his lifestyle and his attitude towards the amount of exercise that he was doing, and I don't mean taking more baths.

4. Take magnesium citrate 3 tablets twice daily.

5. Use coenzyme Q10- at least 2 300mg tablets daily. This allows the heart to operate more efficiently with less oxygen. Please do some of your own research on this product study, read and then study some more. Only then will you begin to realize the tremendous effects that this product will have on your heart. It is a rather expensive product but its benefits outweigh the expense and your heart will love the wonderful changes that will occur. It also might save your life someday.

6. Purchase and use a product called grape seed extract. The value of this extract is that it strengthens the walls of your arteries and helps to restore elasticity. This can be very effective in lowering blood pressure as well as making your circulatory system much stronger. I recommend at least 2 capsules daily.

Now let me give you some information about a procedure that few people know about and most doctors won't recommend because they know little if anything about it. I had one very knowledgeable cardiologist tell me about one test on the peripheral circulatory system where it showed little effect.

Let me tell you that if you want to save yourself some time, understand that I have read hundreds, if not thousands of pages on the subject as well as had the procedure done on myself, and still do regularly. However, the rest of this chapter should convince you of its effectiveness.

EDTA chelation is very effective in removing heavy metals from your blood. Chelation will virtually strip your arteries of toxic metals and calcium deposits; it also emulsifies fatty acids from the lining of your arteries. In order for this almost miracle cure to take effect you, need to take 20 treatments. After that have a treatment every other month to keep your arteries clean and flexible. Chelation in and of itself may very well be the key to normal blood pressure. I was having a treatment and was sitting by a nurse who was also there for a treatment, and she informed me that before chelation her carotid arteries were 90% plugged before she began taking the treatments. And after taking the first series of treatments there was such an improvement, that there wasn't even a sign of a problem. This isn't the only testimonial that I could give to you. There haven't been very many double blind studies on the subject of chelation therapy, and for the most part, what I know about chelation is from what has happened to me in my own personal life and from the many lives that it has changed including people with serious problems. Here is the small catch, you will probably need to call a lot of doctors to find one that will know about the treatments, let alone administer them to you. There are a few Do's out there that will do the procedure for you and if you find one that is knowledgeable enough to know the advantages of EDTA and chelation therapy don't let him go.

The treatments consist of a small needle inserted into your arm for 1-2 hours. You need to eat protein and drink large amounts of water during and after the treatment because the EDTA will combine with the heavy metals and you will eliminate the toxins through your urine. There is no discomfort and I usually do business as usual while the procedure is being administered. I read, make phone calls, plan my day etc. The only fear that I have is not doing the therapy. Heavy metals such as lead, mercury, cadmium, aluminum, iron, nickel and radioactive particles are all very toxic and they embed themselves in the walls of your arteries resulting in your life being shortened by years. One of the reasons that women live longer is because of their menstrual cycle. They have a chance to get rid of the heavy metals and then make new blood every month. However, as soon as they have gone through menopause and their menstrual cycle ceases, their incidence of heart disease increases. It is also a healthy thing for you and the national blood supply to donate blood once in a while. Not only is it great for the national blood supply in case of emergencies, but it is also wonderful for you to allow your body to remove some of the metals from your system and make new blood. Men, never take a supplement if it has iron in it. Look at the labels; try to limit the iron in every way possible. There are few if any times where iron does not have serious side effects for men. Now back to chelation, let's consider comparing chelation therapy to calling the roto-rooter man to clean out your houses plumbing. EDTA restores the structural integrity of your arteries. I can never begin to cover the value of this treatment in this book, but I strongly recommend that you go to the library or the health food store and do some serious reading on the subject of chelation therapy. There are many kinds of chelation therapies on the market but I don't believe that any oral chelation is even remotely in the ballpark with EDTA that is given intravenously. However if you are not able to find a doctor that will give you a chelation treatment then you may be forced to take one of the oral treatments. There are several oral chelation treatments available. One is called The Royal Arterial Flush. There is also another product called OCC, you can contact the company that sells OCC at (1-800-546-8543) OCC has chelating agents that are heart friendly. This product contains cysteine, Irish moss, alutatrione, zinc, alphalfa, manganese, selenium, garlic, potassium and other anti-oxidants such as vitamin C and E.

Liver Flush

There is another therapy that is extremely effective and may be one of the few things that will work for you. This therapy isn't a fun thing to recommend or for you to do, but it works many times when nothing else will. This therapy is called a liver flush. The liver contains such a great deal of blood that if it is not functioning properly, high blood pressure is just one of the complications that can result. This procedure, if you follow it closely, could really change your life. Here are the ingredients and the procedure, lets start with the ingredients first.

- 10 Tablets Niacinamide.

- 10 Tablets Choline.

- 10 Tablets Orcex.

- 10 Tablets Beta Food.

- 10 Drops Phosfood in juice.

Now for the procedure, take the above ingredients 5 times fifteen minutes apart. During the process drink Gatorade and eat small amounts of food that are easy to digest e.g. toast with butter, rice, and broth. Do not take any supplements for 2 days after the procedure. You might not feel as good as you should for a few days and will probably get symptoms similar to the stomach flu. It is best to tackle this procedure when you have 2 full days off to do the liver flush, one day to do it and one day to rest. Here are some things that you might want to do before you start. Get some magazines and put them into the bathroom, if you don't have two bathrooms you had better send the kids to the neighbors for several hours as you are really going to be spending some quality time on that toilet of yours. Once the effects begin to happen you are going to see things that you have never seen before, but don't be scared, this is why you are doing it. I have never really had too much discomfort during the process and have usually felt great the next day, but how you feel depends on how contaminated your liver is. You will want to take 2 B6 tablets and 2 Zypan tablets to help you with digestion for about a month. Eat light foods for a few days, and avoid alcohol during the next month – be kind to your liver. If you have trouble finding some of the items above contact Jen at Natures Assets 3023 362 Se. Fall City Washington 98024 (425) 222-6753 or 1-800-609-2160 and she will help you with all of your needs. This is probably the only place that you will read about this wonderful treatment but that is exactly the reason that I am writing this book. My cousin was having trouble with her blood pressure and most of the prescribed medications were not working. I offered this treatment to her and it worked almost immediately. I have, and still plan to do this treatment yearly. My reason for doing this treatment was to clean out one of the most important organs in the human body, the liver. Believe me it truly works. If you think of your liver as resembling a sponge, because it is very much like a sponge as it scrubs all of the impurities from your blood. But just as the sponge you use to clean the dishes gets dirty from constant use, so does your liver. Pretty soon, it can't clean as well as it used to. Well you don't want dirty dishes to eat off of, and you certainly don't want dirty blood coursing through your veins, so this is the best way to clean it up. You will probably hate me at first after you have tried this treatment because of the way that you will feel for the next few hours, but just think about the last time that you stubbed your toe and remember thinking "This is gonna feel great right after it stops hurting". Well the same holds true here also, but the rewards in doing this are much better than stubbing your toe, think about the return of lower if not normal blood pressure and more.

Because the liver plays such a major role in your health, I am going to add one more liver flush and cleanser of the body's major detoxifier. There are so many contaminating agents in our environment ranging from cosmetics, detergents and solvents that are accumulative over a long period. When the liver ceases to function properly because of its inability to do its critical job, the elimination of toxins in producing bile your health goes down drastically. If there are gallstones that block the functioning of the liver to produce bile, it not only impedes digestion, but also prevents cholesterol from leaving the body thereby causing a rise in the LDL (bad cholesterol). I have just researched this new formula for a liver flush that I believe to be equally as effective as the one that I recommended earlier. The ingredients required for this liver flush are:

- Three quarts of apple juice natural not from concentrate no added sugar.

- One-cup pure virgin olive oil.

- 1-12 ounce can of Coca-Cola Classic.

- One lemon freshly squeezed.
- Super phos 30, 90 drops, one level Teaspoon.

Instructions

Note: Best results are obtained with a healthy, clean colon and 2 to 3 normal bowel movements daily. Use Jim Foley's Colon Pills and Colon Cleanser.

DAY 1: Mix 90 drops (level teaspoon) of Super Phos 30 in one quart of apple juice and drink.

DAY 2: Mix 90 drops (level teaspoon) of Super Phos 30 in one quart of apple juice and drink.

DAY 3: Mix 90 drops (level teaspoon) of Super Phos 30 in one quart of apple juice and drink.

You do not have to drink it all at one time, but throughout the day. Eat normally. This is not a fast. Super phos 30 contains orthophosphoric acid, and apple juice contains pectin, which helps soften stones in the gall bladder and liver.

For diabetics or if you cannot tolerate so much apple juice, use one quart of distilled water per day, and increase Super Phos from 90 drops to 120 drops daily.

DAY 3 EVENING: Eat dinner. Wait minimum three hours after dinner. Now prepare and drink the following liver flush mixture.

The liver flush mixture: Thoroughly mix juice from one squeezed lemon and one cup of Coke Classic and one cup of pure virgin Olive Oil.

Quickly drink the mixture! Do not wait or the oil will settle to the bottom. You will feel very full. If you have an oily feeling on lips or teeth, use lemon 'rind on them to relieve the oily feeling. The coke is used to lessen the nauseous feeling.

Immediately lie down after drinking the flush mixture. Lie down on your RIGHT SIDE for a half hour

(30 minutes) not less! It is best to draw your knees up to your chest (fetal position) so the oil will force the gall bladder and bile duct to contract and throw off the stones. If you cannot do this, then lay stretched out full length. Stay in either position for 30 minutes.

After 30 minutes, you can move around, resume normal activity, and then go to sleep. It usually will take up to 8 hours for the flush to work.
 It is a good idea to take an herbal laxative (Jim's Colon Pills) that evening or the next morning.

WHAT TO EXPECT there will be considerable soft stool the first time. This will decrease and a more formed stool usually comes about the fifth time. Stones are not usually found with the first stool. Most will come out with the second stool, maybe 5 to 8 hours later. Less stones will be noticed with each additional stool. Reports range from under hundred to as many as one thousand stones being discharged. The stones will be somewhat soft and waxy green (like cooked peas). Stones have been reported to be anywhere from pea size to the size of a golf ball.

Optional: Ozonate the olive oil for 20 minutes before preparing the liver flush mixture. You need to buy a small Ozonator. Ozonated olive oil can kill live bacteria and viruses in the bile ducts.

Optional: Epsom salt can help relax the liver bile ducts. On Day 3, in the afternoon, mix one tablespoon of Epsom Salt in One cup of water and drink. You may repeat this the next morning.

How to Keep Liver Bile Ducts Clean and Prevent Future Stones from Forming! A teaspoon of Olive Oil a day will keep the liver bile ducts clean and prevent new stones from forming. It is that easy and works! Use pure virgin olive oil. Mixing it with juice from a lemon makes it easier to drink. Drink it in one shot or with meals, salads, etc. In Greece, they devour olive oil and the incidence of cancer is minuscule in comparison to America.

If you cannot find Super Phos at your local health food store it can be ordered by calling 718-871-1363 or you can write NMS Publishing Company Dept. JF 5711 14th Avenue Brookline, New York 11219.

This treatment is consistent with the chemistry I have studied and I believe it to be extremely effective in removing the stones and allow your liver and gall bladder to function normally again. Now for a caution, do not substitute and do not use too much Super Phos 30 in the apple juice. You only need 90 drops-one level Teaspoon. Follow the instructions to the letter and you will be amazed at the number and size of the stones that you will eliminate. They may be green or a lighter color, ranging from about the size of a cherry or as small as a pin head. I know that after doing the treatment myself my blood pressure went down, and I felt much better. You may pass from 0 to over 1000 stones. This process can be repeated if necessary several times a year to keep your liver functioning properly. Do not forget to use your fresh ground flax seed, milk thistle and L cysteine to strengthen the liver function in between cleanses.

On another note, I need to stress again the value and importance of coenzyme Q10 (at least 200 mg). Enzymatic Therapy also makes a product called Rogenic. If you try this product, take 2 tablets three times daily. Now please forgive me for not giving you more of the chemistry, which is my favorite thing, but if I filled this book with all of the chemical terminology to describe all of these wonderful procedures, this book would be thicker than War and Peace and you would probably be snoring after the first chapter. Just understand, that I have done exhaustive research on all of these treatments and have found them to be not only safe but effective. The above suggestions are alternative plans and you should consult an experienced health professional on such subjects as the liver cleanse. You now have the necessary information to make choices other than standard drug treatments. However, if you have severe hypertension you should consult your physician immediately and employ any or all of the measures above. Very few patients with uncomplicated marginal hypertension ever require drug treatment – you can fix it! Remember before doing the liver cleanse, I strongly recommend that you check with your health professional first.

THE HEART

HOW THE HEART FUNCTIONS

Every 60 seconds your heart pumps over five quarts of blood. When sitting or doing non-strenuous work your heart will beat 60 to 100 times each minute. The heartbeat is divided into two main phases called "diastole" (when the heart relaxes and fills with blood) and the "systole" (when the heart contracts and pumps out the blood). The heart typically spends about two-thirds of its time in the resting phase and one-third of its time in the pumping phase. Keeping this activity in perfect time is the job of the heart's electrical system.

The signals that begin the contraction in the atrium, the top region of the heart, start in the "Sinoatrial (SA) node". The atrial contraction pumps the blood down into the ventricles. The next signal that activates the ventricles comes from the "atrioventricular (AV) node". The (AV) node delays its signal just long enough to allow the atria to finish contracting and fill the ventricles with blood. The ventricles contract from bottom to top and pump the blood up and out into the lungs and body. This ends the cycle, and the ventricles relax and the process will soon begin once more. Your heart is the most efficient pump known to man. During an average lifetime, your heart will beat approximately 2.5 billion times. It is more reliable and much more energy efficient than any pump ever created.

To sustain life, the heart must beat continuously to circulate blood and oxygen throughout the body. We previously discussed the two atria, which receive the blood returning to the heart and the two ventricles, which pump the blood back out. We now must account for the function of the four chambers, each having a one-way valve to insure that the blood always flows in one direction. The heart consists of two pumps that are in series. With each beat, the right ventricle pumps the deoxygenated blood to the lungs. The left ventricle pumps the oxygenated blood from the lungs throughout the body. The left ventricle works much harder than the right ventricle, so it is much thicker and stronger. The left ventricle and right ventricle always pump the same volume of blood. The reason for this is that the resistance of blood flow to the lungs is much less than that of the rest of the body so the left ventricle must work harder and contract more forcefully to keep up with the right ventricle. Now, let's explain the course of a red blood cell, which incidentally last about four months before it wears out and must be replaced. When the red blood cell has used its oxygen, it returns from the body and enters the right atrium. From there the right atrium contracts and pumps the blood across the tricuspid valve into the right ventricle. The right ventricle then pumps it across the pulmonic valve into the pulmonary artery where the blood can then go to either the right or left lung. When in the lungs, the blood discharges carbon dioxide and re-invigorates itself with oxygen. Now the oxygenated blood goes to the left atrium where it is pumped across the mitral valve to enter the left ventricle. Now the left ventricle sends the blood across the aortic valve out to the whole body. It takes about two minutes for this cycle to be completed, and then it starts all over again. Maybe now you are starting to appreciate the complexity of your wonderful heart.

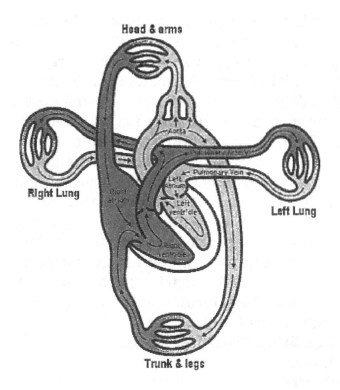

Now that you understand the basic functions of the heart, I would like to show you through some of the cause, effects and treatments of several heart diseases. The perfect heart is one of normal size and has all of the oxygen and nutrients that it needs to do its job. There are some risk factors that we all have to deal with during our life, some have simple solutions and sometimes we make decisions based on a lack of knowledge and the solutions become more difficult. I am a living example of some very wrong decisions. It is not difficult to correct things before serious problems have to be dealt with. That is the reason for this book. Some of these things have never been heard of and possibly never will, because television is not going to provide you with the answer. First, in part, because medical information isn't "good television," so there goes the ratings and second, divulging that information would make all of the pill peddling advertisers go crazy and then there goes their revenue. So for your sake and the health of your family it's time to return to an older form of assimilating information... reading. Whether from a book like this or from the Internet, reading is still the best way to get up to date learning materials.

Here are some of the risk factors that contribute to heart disease, and you will need to deal with them in order to keep a healthy heart. They are as follows:
1. Elevated Cholesterol.
2. Trigliceride Levels.
3. High Blood Pressure.
4. Diabetes.
5. Obesity.
6. Smoking.
7. Lack of Exercise.
8. Genetics.
9. Stress in excess.

Let me deal with cholesterol first. Today the opening words to a conversation aren't "How are you?" but what are your cholesterol levels? Let me first explain that cholesterol in and of itself is not necessarily the problem. Many Eskimos have extremely high cholesterol levels, yet they have no bad effects whatsoever. Their arteries stay clear and supple throughout their whole life. Could it be their diet? They eat a lot of fat and fish, so let's try to diagnose our western diet and see if we can find a solution to our problem. First of all, we need to look at beneficial fats and harmful fat diets. The HDL (high density lipids) is the beneficial cholesterol and the LDL (low density lipids) is the harmful cholesterol. You may have a cholesterol level of 250 but if your LDL is 225 and your HDL is 25 you are at a high risk and had better continue reading this book until you understand that there is a fix for your problem. If your HDL is 150 and your LDL is 75 or better you are in a much lower risk factor. There is another risk factor of importance and that is your Trigliceride blood fat level. This may be as important, if not more so, than your cholesterol. The same things that fix the cholesterol levels also fix the triglycerides. Before I explain some of the conventional treatments, I would like to comment on several things that may have bypassed your knowledge in the past. Here are several things that are absolutely horrific for your heart and its function:

1. Homogenized milk is very destructive to the surface of the arteries. Xanthine oxidase is an enzyme in homogenized milk that irritates the inner surface of the arteries and may cause cracks in the arterial walls. These cracks may then be sealed by cholesterol, triglycerides and calcium, which may cause clots and blockages. I have a difficult time trying to find non-homogenized milk so I always use soymilk. I try to find one that has a 50/50 ratio of protein to carbohydrates. You can purchase any number of soymilk products that has this ratio. Please make sure to read the label, I use a

brand called Silk but there are other fine products also.

2. Never, use margarine – Never. Never use any hydrogenated fats e.g. candy bars, cookies, cakes, shortening. All hydrogenated fats are a problem. Some companies will try to fool you by saying that they contain no cholesterol, DON'T FALL FOR IT! Read every label and if the word hydrogenated is used, then throw it away. In actuality, butter is much better for you than margarine. Does this surprise you? What are the differences between fats and oils and what do the terms saturated, monounsaturated and polyunsaturated mean? This is a complex question and a full understanding requires some knowledge of fat chemistry. The answer provided here attempts to avoid the more difficult aspects of the chemistry involved. The Appendix below provides a more detailed answer and may be worth reading if you are reasonably familiar with organic chemistry.

Fat and oils are similar chemically, but the subtle differences that do exist have major effects on health. Fats and oils both consist of molecules that have backbones of long chains of carbon and hydrogen atoms chemically bonded together. These molecules are called fatty acids. Fats and oils in the diet and most fat in the body contain three fatty acids chemically bonded to form one fat molecule.

A fatty acid may be saturated with hydrogen i.e., all the carbon atoms along the fatty acid backbone have the maximum possible number of hydrogen atoms attached, monounsaturated two adjacent carbon atoms have less hydrogen atoms or polyunsaturated more than two carbon atoms along the fatty acid backbone have less hydrogen atoms –See diagram

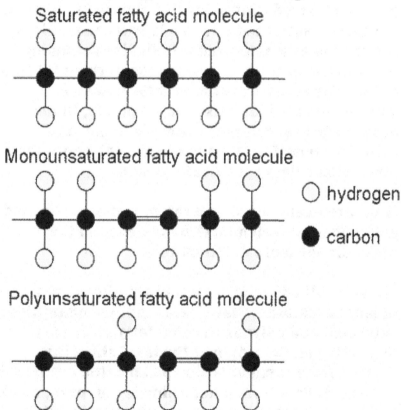

Saturated fatty acid molecule

Monounsaturated fatty acid molecule

○ hydrogen

● carbon

Polyunsaturated fatty acid molecule

The most obvious difference between a fat and an oil is that a fat is solid at room temperature while an oil is liquid. A fat is usually solid because it consists mostly of saturated fatty acids. Oils usually have mostly polyunsaturated fatty acids. All edible oils and fats also contain monounsaturated fatty acids. Margarines and other semi-solid fats will have a mix of mostly monounsaturated and polyunsaturated fatty acids. Although there are no naturally occurring fats that contain only saturated, monounsaturated or polyunsaturated fatty acids, for simplicity, a fat that has mostly saturated fatty acids will commonly be referred to as a saturated fat. Similar reasoning leads to use of the terms 'monounsaturated fat,' most of the fatty acids are monounsaturated and 'polyunsaturated fat'. Also for simplicity, in the answers below, reference is made to 'fat' as a collective term for fats and oils except where the discussion refers specifically to oils.

What are examples of saturated, monounsaturated and polyunsaturated fats? Read ahead in the Appendix for more detail on this.

Virtually all-edible fats contain significant quantities of monounsaturated fatty acids, but the quantities of saturated and polyunsaturated fatty acids vary depending on the origin of the fat. Animal fats derived from ruminants sheep and cattle are largely saturated. Fats from other animals e.g. pork, chicken are less saturated than ruminant fat and contain some polyunsaturated fatty acids. Fats from game meat e.g., elk, deer tend to be lower still in saturated fatty acids and often contain significant quantities of a range of polyunsaturated fatty acids. Fats from fish are generally highly unsaturated and contain a form of polyunsaturated fatty acid known as omega-3 - see Question 3 in the Appendix for details.

How do edible fats and oils differ in the amount of energy kilojoules they provide and how does this affect weight gain? Any pure, edible fat will provide about 37 kilojoules kJ per gram. This is more than twice the energy level of one gram of protein or carbohydrate. Because butter and margarine both contain some water, about 20%, they provide 30 kJ per gram. Cream contains even more water, so the energy content of 1mL, 1gram of cream is 14 kJ. Cooking oils and fats generally contain little or no water, so they provide the full 37 kJ per gram. Although all pure fats provide about the same amount of energy, there is some evidence that the effects of fats on weight gain differ according to their chemical composition. It appears that the degree of saturation influences the amount of weight gained or lost on an otherwise similar diet. That is, consumption of a diet that is high in saturated fat seems to be associated with increased risk of putting on weight, while polyunsaturated fats may be less fattening and may even be protective against obesity. The evidence for this is strong in animals and preliminary studies suggest that the same effect may occur in people too.

What effect do saturated fats have on blood cholesterol? Because they are derived from a ruminant animal, lard, drippings, butter and cream contain far more saturated fat than do the polyunsaturated or monounsaturated margarines and cooking oils. In the body, cholesterol production can be increased in response to the consumption of foods rich in particular saturated fatty acids. High blood cholesterol is associated strongly with increased risk of heart disease. Coconut and palm-kernel oil also contain the saturated fatty acids found in butter, so they can promote higher blood cholesterol too. These two plant-derived oils are similar to butter in their ability to raise blood cholesterol. Most other plant oils have little saturated fat - e.g., avocados and peanut (and other nut) oils are largely monounsaturated and or polyunsaturated and are therefore considered to be relatively heart-friendly.

What effects do polyunsaturated fats have on blood cholesterol? Many of the polyunsaturated fats are believed to have cholesterol- lowering properties, particularly those rich in omega-6 fatty acids (see Question 3 in the Appendix for details), e.g. safflower, sunflower, soybean and cottonseed oils. The other major polyunsaturated fats - the omega-3 series (found in significant quantities in fish, but also in canola, linseed and walnut oils) - are also believed to be helpful in reducing the risk of heart disease, but by means other than lowering cholesterol. Currently, omega-6 fatty acids predominate in the diet. The National Health and Medical Research Council recommend a moderate increase in intake of omega-3 fatty acids.

What about the monounsaturated - how do they affect blood cholesterol? Oils and margarines that are rich in monounsaturated fat e.g. canola and olive oil are also believed by many nutritionists to be heart-friendly. In fact, high consumption of olive oil has been suggested as a possible major component of the Mediterranean Diet that is believed to be protective against heart disease. That is, people who live near the Mediterranean Sea, where olive oil is widely consumed, have much lower rates of heart disease than people in the USA, UK, Australia and other countries where olive oil is not eaten in large quantities. Of course, this could be coincidence.

Some nutritionists believe that olive oil and other monounsaturated fats are simply neutral with respect to cholesterol. That is, it may be that any cholesterol lowering that follows replacement of saturated with monounsaturated fat is the result of reduced saturated fat consumption rather than due to a positive effect of the monounsaturated fat. The relationship of olive oil and other monounsaturated fats to health, especially heart health, deserves and is receiving more investigation.

I have heard that there are new margarines that are supposed to help lower blood cholesterol - what do these contain and how effective are they? A new spread containing compounds called phytosterols was released onto the market recently. It is claimed by the manufacturers that this spread is more effective than the existing monounsaturated and polyunsaturated margarines in combating high blood cholesterol. Studies are being conducted to test the validity of this claim and to ensure that these products have no undesirable long-term effects. All the scientific studies so far conducted demonstrate a cholesterol-lowering effect and animal studies indicate that toxicity is very unlikely in people. The product has been accepted by the United States Food and Drug Administration as being safe for human use.

Should we reduce intake of fat, and if so, of which fats? The National Health and Medical Research Council's dietary guideline number 2 recommends that we should eat a diet low in fat and, in particular, low in saturated fat. Switching to low- or reduced-fat milk is one simple way of reducing total fat (and saturated fat) intake. Replacing spreads and cooking fats derived from ruminant animals with polyunsaturated and or monounsaturated spreads and cooking oils will also assist in reducing intake of saturated fat.

APPENDIX

ADDITIONAL MATERIAL FOR PEOPLE WITH A BACKGROUND IN CHEMISTRY

1. What do fats and oils consist of and how do they differ chemically? Fats and oils in our diet and in our body fat deposits commonly consist of three fatty acids chemically combined with a molecule of glycerol to form a Trigliceride. Each fatty acid consists of a methyl group CH_3 at one end, a carboxyl group $COOH$ at the other, and a chain of

carbon atoms connecting these ends. The degree of saturation of each fatty acid depends on how many atoms of hydrogen the backbone of the fatty acid molecule contains. If every carbon atom has nothing but hydrogen bound to it, that fatty acid molecule is saturated i.e., saturated with hydrogen so there are no double bonds along the molecule. A monounsaturated fatty acid molecule has one double bond. Polyunsaturated means that there is more than one double bond along the fatty acid molecule. The greater the degree of saturation, the harder the fat is likely to be. That is, predominantly saturated fats are usually solid at room temperature, while polyunsaturated fats are liquid oils. Fats with mostly monounsaturated fatty acids will generally be semi-solid. (See diagram above).

2. What forms do fats take in the body and in food? All fats contain a variety of fatty acids - that is, there are no naturally occurring fats containing exclusively saturated, monounsaturated or polyunsaturated fatty acids. Some fats will have mostly saturated fatty acids, in others monounsaturated fatty acids will predominate, while oils have mostly polyunsaturated or a combination of monounsaturated and polyunsaturated fatty acids. For convenience, fats that contain mostly saturated fatty acids are commonly called saturated fats, those with mostly monounsaturated fatty acids are referred to as monounsaturated

fats and oils in which polyunsaturated fatty acids predominate are called polyunsaturated oils.

3. Are any fats or oils essential in our diets, and, if so, what foods are they found in? Only two types of fatty acid are essential in the human diet - the polyunsaturated omega-6 and omega-3 fatty acids. An omega-6 polyunsaturated fatty acid has the first of its double bonds on the sixth carbon atom from the methyl (CH_3) end. An omega-3 polyunsaturated fatty acid has its first double bond on the third carbon atom from the methyl end. Polyunsaturated margarines and seed-based cooking oils are the major sources of omega-6 fatty acids in the American diet. In addition, sunflower seeds, sesame and pumpkin seeds, walnuts and oats are moderate sources. Fish and other seafood's are the main sources of omega-3 fatty acids. Canola oil is the second most important source. Linseed and walnut oils are moderate sources of omega-3 fatty acids.

4. What percentages of polyunsaturated, monounsaturated and saturated fats occur in edible fats and oils?

The percentages of polyunsaturated (P), monounsaturated (M) and saturated (S) fatty acids in common margarines, cooking oils and fats are (in the order P:M:S:):

Canola oil 30:63:7
Safflower oil 77:14:9

Sunflower oil 66:23:11
Olive oil 10:76:14
Soybean oil 62:23:15
Peanut oil 36:45:19
Cottonseed oil 58:16:26
Palm oil 30:39:51
Monounsaturated margarine* 22:63:15
Polyunsaturated margarine* 41:40:19
Table margarine* 33:33:34
Animal frying fats 5:45:50
Butter 7:36:57

*Percentage content varies depending on the raw materials. Although saturated fat has the reputation for increasing blood cholesterol, this applies only to a few saturated fatty acids, specifically the C12 (lauric), C14 (myristic) and C16 (palmitic) fatty acids the C-number refers to the number of carbon atoms in the fatty acid molecule. Butter, palm oil and coconut oil contain appreciable quantities of these fatty acids, so these fats and oils can increase blood cholesterol.

5. Trans fatty acids - polyunsaturated or saturated fat? A complicating factor is the existence of trans fatty acids. These are technically unsaturated fatty acids, but their structure has been altered so that they now behave in the body more like saturated fats. Small quantities of trans fatty acids will be found in many margarines that have undergone partial hydrogenation (to make them spread able). The National Health and Medical Research Council recommend that trans fatty acids be considered as

equivalent to saturated fats. American margarines generally contain only small amounts of trans fatty acids. Current intakes of trans fatty acids are relatively small in this country and they are not considered to represent a nutritional hazard.

The word trans refers to the orientation of the carbon chains around a double bond - in this case, the carbon chain ends are oriented on opposite sides of the double bond. It is thought that this actually makes the molecule behave like a saturated fat because it is relatively straight in character. The other form of the isomer is in the cis orientation where the carbon chains occur on the same side of the double bond giving them a V-shaped character.

2. Here is one reason to avoid hydrogenated fats e.g. margarine – it   melts at 114 degrees. The body temperature is only 98.6 degrees. Therefore, it should be easy for you to deduct that if it cannot be broken down by the body's temperature then it will leave a residue behind that will clog your arteries. When double bonds are hydrogenated it is no longer a natural product, you might as well drink a can of motor oil from your car. If it didn't have all of the additives in it for your car, it might not do your body any more harm. Now don't get any ideas about drinking motor oil, as it is very toxic. I was just trying to represent the seriousness of this subject.

3. Now for one more major fallacy that I would like to expose. The yoke of an egg may have

cholesterol in it, but it also contains lecithin. Eggs do not raise your cholesterol levels (especially if they are cooked at a low heat) and the lecithin might actually lower your cholesterol. I know of one M.D. that has treated some 65,000 patients, and he recommends 2 eggs a day for people with a mild heart disease and up to 6 eggs a day for people that have a serious condition. I always eat at least 2 lightly poached eggs every morning.

Sometimes some of these medications are necessary and I do not want to condemn in any way your physician's efforts to help you, but I do want to provide you with some knowledge, so that you can make an informed decision about your treatment. Please know that I highly recommend that you purchase a book called the Physicians Desk Reference (PDR) because it gives you a descriptive analysis on the drugs that your doctor has prescribed for you. You can find out about the reactions and side effects of the drugs that are prescribed by your doctor, discuss it with him, and see if there are any better alternatives. You might just be criticized for speaking up about your situation, and if you are, find another doctor. However, you must realize that the side effects, though not desirable, are sometimes necessary for the recovery of your health. What I am suggesting here, is that you are aware of some of the side effects that are associated with the drugs that are prescribed for you. Remember to take charge of your health, it's your life, not there's. They are your employees, you have paid for their services and you should be able to ask any question when it regards your health.

Now let's cover some of the conventional treatments for heart disease. Conventional treatments may include the following:

1. Cholesterol lowering drugs e.g. Mevacor (Lovastatin) or Provastatin (Mevastatin). These drugs have a significant risk. Any drug in this category can cause a high percentage of liver damage. It has been conclusively shown through research with rats, that after being fed Lovastatin for 2 years, they developed liver cancer. None of these drugs have been shown to retard progressive arteriosclerosis, much less, reverse the process.

2. Now for diuretics which are intended to reduce the amount of fluid in your system in order to relieve pressure on the heart. This causes an overproduction of urine, which leads to a loss of electrolytes such as calcium, magnesium, sodium and potassium. They should never be taken without a potassium supplement. Some of the more common diuretics are Esidrix (Hydrochlorothiazide) and Diuril (Chlorothiazide). These are two of the better diuretics. If they are used properly used in conjunction with a potassium supplement, they may prove to be of some value with little danger.

3. A.C.E. inhibitors lower the body's adrenalin level as it inhibits its production. One of the better ones is Monopril (Fosinopril). Some that

may be used for limited use are Vasotec (Enalapril) and Capoten (Captopril). It may be to your advantage to use these products if your adrenalin is excessively high to the point that your heartbeat is faster due to an overabundance of adrenalin.

4. Calcium channel blockers hold back calcium from the heart muscle thus preventing too strong a heart contraction. It may also control angina by relaxing the artery muscles thereby dilating the lumen and increasing the supply of blood and oxygen to the heart and reducing its workload. Here are some possible side effects of the common calcium channel blockers e.g. Cardizem (Diltizen), Calan (Verapamil) and Brocardia (Nitedipone). If you have the following side effects while taking any of the above listed beta channel blockers contact your physician immediately.

- Difficulty breathing.
- Chest Pain.
- Pounding heartbeat.
- Leg swelling.
- Headache.
- Heartbeat less than 50.
  Note: with these drugs, try not to miss a dose, if you do, don't double up on your dosage, and don't stop taking them suddenly.

5. Beta-blockers interfere with the nerves beta fibers, lowering the sympathetic nerve functions, which may decrease stress. Beta-blockers also seem to reduce the incidence of

second or third heart attacks but seem to have little if no effect on reducing the incidence of first heart attack. Here is just a short list of some of the adverse side effects to look for.

- Difficulty in breathing.
- Anxiety.
- Itching.
- Diarrhea.
- Sleeping problems.
- Diminished sexual activity.
- Cold feeling.
- Slow pulse – under 50.
  Some of the beta-blockers include Lopressor (Metoprolol), Inderol (Propanolol), Atenolol (Tenormin) and one that you should be very careful of Trandate E (Labetalol). Again, as with the channel beta-blockers, you should never try to double up if you miss a dosage and don't smoke (smoking eliminates the effectiveness of these drugs). Do not stop taking this drug without checking with your doctor as it takes some time to wean the medication out of your system.

6. Aspirin is said to reduce cardiac failure. I agree that it may reduce the likelihood of death should a heart attack occur. It has been proven that aspirin reduces blood platelet clotting. If taken on a regular basis a low dose (baby aspirin-enteric coated) may be very beneficial. In this case the more the better does not fit at all. Taking larger doses over a period of time has been linked to kidney damage, liver

damage and macular degeneration. Red wine and red grape juice (without sugar- real juice not a juice flavored drink) also reduces the stickiness of blood platelets. Aspirin can be a very good preventative as long as you aren't aspirin sensitive, have ulcers, or any internal bleeding (which can be diagnosed by noticing black spots in your stool). As with any medication you should:

7. Check with your care provider and pharmacist for any problems or drug interactions. Garlic is also a good blood thinner with only one downside and that is bad breath.

8. Nitroglycerine improves the supply of blood and oxygen to the heart and may prevent angina pain. However it may cause:

- Headaches.
- Nausea.
- Flushing.
- Dizziness.

9. Sometimes a blood thinner may be needed especially if you are suffering from atrial fibrillation. Coumadin that was originally used as a rat poison, which caused internal bleeding until it resulted in death. Patients on this drug must be monitored constantly, to be sure that their blood isn't to thin or too thick. It is very effective in preventing blood clots and reduces the bloods ability to coagulate. I have been using this drug for 5 years now with no adverse side effects. However, you must watch out for any excessive bleeding e.g. nose, mouth, stool,

coughing up blood or any other unusual bleeding. If you cut yourself, just prepare to put on a band-aid to stop the bleeding. While taking this drug, you need to have a fairly consistant diet. A diet high in green vegetables is fine as long as you keep it constant. You need to eat a regular diet so your blood can be kept at a normal thickness because changes in your diet will change how the drug will react to your blood.

Now for some supplements that help to enhance your heart function:

- Vitamin C (Ester Form) 4000 mg daily.
- Beta Carotene 25,000 I.U.
- Vitamin E with Selenium 1200 I.U. note: Vitamin E without selenium is not metabolized properly.
- Magnesium Citrate 400 mg 3 times a day. This is of extreme importance, if you are dealing with atrial fibrillation or arrhythmia.
- Potassium may not be necessary if you eat lots of fruits, vegetables, beans, nuts and seeds. However. if you take medications to remove water from your system, potassium is always necessary.
- Co Enzyme Q10, take at least 200 mg a day. This is a magic heart enzyme, as it provides oxygen to a damaged heart, as well as prevents further heart attacks.

- L-Carnatine strengthens the heart muscle. Use 250 mg 3 times a day. Hawthorn (an herb) also acts to strengthen the heart muscle.
  Here is a short list of some wonderful cholesterol lowering supplements:
  - Flax seed.
  - Garlic.
  - Psyllium.
  - Lecithin 3 tablespoons of granules daily.
  - Fish oil 1000 mg daily.

Now I would be derelict if I did not give you a little information on Cayenne, which is an herb that sometimes has remarkable effects on heart problems. Cayenne (Red pepper) dissolves clots, opens arteries, and stimulates the heart. Cayenne does not raise your heartbeat or blood pressure. But it does improve circulation all over your body. Now you can understand why I am writing this book, if you don't know about natural alternatives you have no choice but to join the world of drug therapies. If you have the knowledge you also have a choice, without it you are deprived of the right to choose.

There are two things that are synergistic (remember that word) with cayenne, and that is garlic and ginger. Used together these supplements lower the level of fibrin, the material that causes clotting. Garlic seems to soften the hardened deposits, softening them so that the cayenne can remove them, thus cleaning your arteries. This allows the arteries to heal and become more elastic. Researchers in

Loma Linda School of Medicine have found that cayenne fights cancer as well. It also makes weight loss easier as it can cause your body to burn up to 25% more calories a day. I take 3 450 mg tablets a day along with 2 garlic tablets and some ginger tea. You might feel a slight burning sensation in your stomach when you first start, if you do, try to either lower your dosage and work your way back up to the three capsules a day or, take one capsule 3 times a day. Some health food stores have a form that causes no burning feeling at all. Cayenne has been proven to help the arteries and veins regain the elasticity that you had in your youth. It boosts the overall health of the entire cardiovascular system.

Now for the part that no one wants to even have nightmares about, surgical procedures. Coronary Bypass surgery is bypassing the blocked arteries that feed the heart. Here a vein is removed from another part of the body to bypass a plugged artery. However if you do not change your lifestyle and your diet drastically, another blockage will soon occur. The way that this procedure is done is that they have to stop your heart and attach a mechanical device called a heart lung machine. It is used to send blood and oxygen from the body through the machine and back. As the blood flows through the machine it picks up heavy metals, which are toxic and can cause memory problems, but hopefully these problems are just temporary. Here are just some of the complications that can happen after this surgery:

- The death rate is 2%-6%.
- 5% have immediate heart attacks.

- **5% have strokes.**
- **20% have mental disorders.**

Angioplasty is the insertion of a catheter with a balloon attached and inserted into a blocked artery. The block is then opened up so as to increase the flow of blood; however angioplasty has failed to live up to its expectations. Again, I will not leave you hanging out there on a limb. There are new devices that improve on the original balloon. They include a type of device that looks like a small drill that loosens the plague and then sucks it out.

I have certainly never intended to put down all of the conventional treatments, but I do intend to help you with better cardiac health with as many ideas (old or new) as I can.

Chelation

If you have found that you are experiencing any symptoms of heart disease, even at its earliest stage, you need to become very familiar with this treatment, as it may reverse your problems completely, if not save your very life. This therapy is called chelation therapy. It is a non-invasive outpatient procedure that consists of a series of (maybe 20 or more) intravenous infusions of a synthetic amino acid called (Ethylene Diamine Tetraacetric acid). This is a man made protein called EDTA. Over half a million people have experienced chelation therapy over the last 30 years but less then 1% of the population has ever heard of it. Chelation therapy has been tested in some of the best labs in the world. During testing many patients got well, including those who weren't achieving success from other conventional treatments, however, they have returned to health after chelation. Adverse reactions are practically non-existent. The substance EDTA is not new; it was developed in Germany in 1935. They found that this substance successfully removed heavy metals from the blood by uniting the proteins along with the heavy metals and excreted them through urination. Those heavy metals include lead, cadmium, mercury, aluminum, chromium, iron, cobalt and copper. Iron and copper, the two most potent free radical catalysts are removed by EDTA. This will diminish the destructive free radical activity by a million fold according to H.B. Demopoulos M.D. professor of pathology at NYU Medical Center. Please re-read the last sentence, understanding what those last few words describe, should in and of themselves convince you to try chelation for yourself. EDTA chelation has the ability to clear out plugged arteries. You will probably learn the most from people who have been treated. Please re-read the testimonial from the nurse in the chapter on high blood pressure. But for you guys here is another testimonial that might be of interest to you. At another treatment I was talking to a gentleman who was also taking a treatment, and I asked him why he was there. He told me that he had badly impaired circulation in his genital area, so impaired that he was impotent. That was before chelation treatments, after just a few treatments he was delighted (as you can well imagine) to find an almost immediate improvement. P.S. so was his wife.

The benefits of EDTA chelation are so important for you to understand that I will give you just a partial list of some of the benefits and you can decide if any of these will fit your condition:

- Reduction of cholesterol.
- Increase of good cholesterol (HDL).
- Reduced need for diuretics.
- Cold extremities will feel warmer.
- Overcome chronic fatigue syndrome.
- Improved memory.
- Reduced blood pressure.
- Normalized arrhythmias.
- Leg cramping is relieved.
- Allergies relieved.
- Weight loss is much easier.
- Lessened varicose vein problems.
- Age spots begin to disappear.
- Fewer arthritic problems.
- Less pain.
- Reversal of hair loss.
- Better sight, hearing and taste.
- Better skin tone.
- Normalization of atrial fibrillation.
- Slows effects of Alzheimer's disease.
- Stroke related incidences decreased.
- May reverse hypertension.
- Impotence is often diminished.

If any of the above fits you, it is imperative that you study further your knowledge of chelation. If you have access to the Internet search for chelation, and read everything that you possibly can on the subject. I have listed several books in the bibliography on many of the subjects covered in this book to help you in your quest for health. Go to health food stores and the library to find even more information on the subject. It just might mean the reversal of your high blood pressure.

Now you might ask what this treatment is and how is it done? The doctor will seat you in a comfortable chair and put a bottle with about a pint of fluid above you. Then he will insert a small needle into one of the veins in your arm. I have never felt any discomfort and you might not even feel it. You should take along some protein with you to eat during the process. Something like nuts, cottage cheese, soymilk or something like that. As the EDTA drips slowly into your vein you can read, rest, work, or just about anything that you want. The procedure takes about an hour maybe a little more. I like to talk to the other people beside me that are having the procedure done to find out what caused them to choose chelation therapy and how it is affecting their condition. You should also drink several glasses of water or Gatorade either during, or just after you are done with the procedure. This is to facilitate the transport of the toxins from your body. The reason for eating the protein is to give your body the extra amino acids that facilitate the chelation process. In order for the treatments to be effective you must take at least 15-20 treatments initially. Is it really worth it? Well let's see, 15 treatments at

$75 equals about $1,500. Pretty high you say, well lets try a bypass operation with no complications at $35-$50,000. Or how about a heart transplant for hundreds of thousands of dollars with the probability of reaching the million-dollar stratus. But how can you compare any invasive surgery with possible devastating results, with the ease and effectiveness of chelation therapy. If I had the knowledge that I do now I never would have subjected myself to the permanent heart damage that is now a painful lifelong illness. If I had known about chelation therapy my heart disease wouldn't even be an issue. Please don't just shrug off the knowledge that I am giving you here! Use it, and prevent the problems that can destroy not only your life, but even if you survive, it make the quality of that life not worth living. I have seen almost miraculous recoveries from stroke victims. As your arteries begin to clean themselves up the transformation is amazing. It has such a beneficial effect on so many diseases, that by the time I write the next book I will have hundreds of testimonials. If you go to your doctor and consult with him about chelation therapy and he tells you that chelation is of no value –find another doctor. Here is the problem; you see EDTA is not a patented product. Therefore the drug companies can't get rich on it. Still wondering why you haven't heard about it? Well I'm very sorry to say that most of our society is driven by financial gain. This is not just the driving force in the medical profession but in most of our endeavors. So you can't blame it on the medical profession. Now as remarkable as chelation therapy is, I need to list some lifestyle changes that you will need to make in order to allow your arteries to recover.

1. Stop smoking, you already know the rest of the story. Once you stop smoking your body quickly recovers and you don't need to worry about all of those cigarettes that you smoked. After you have been smoke free for few weeks, your body quickly adjusts to a healthy pattern of eliminating toxins. Chelation is greatly hindered by smoking but will quickly help your body eliminate the toxins and free radicals that smoking generates. This applies even if you have smoked 30-40 years. If you do smoke and can't stop, I will encourage you to do some other beneficial things to lessen the damage e.g. take 4-10,000 mg ester C tablets along with all of the other anti-oxidants.

2. You need to drastically change your eating habits concerning fat. No hydrogenated fats. Get your fats from flax seed, flax oil, fish oil, or maybe virgin olive oil. No margarine or foods containing margarine or hydrogenated fats. This is almost all store purchased cookies, candy, French fries, most ice creams, white bread, rice that is converted into sugar by the body, corn products again sugar conversion, all sugar products, chocolate and the rest is up to you to find. Do not be fooled by

contains no cholesterol, that is only a ploy to confuse the issue. Let me give you a few examples. How about that wonderful FAT FREE French Vanilla Non Dairy Creamer. Makes you just want to make a pot of coffee, sit back, relax and read a good book doesn't it? Right up until you read the label. Its contents are water (if they stopped there it would be a healthy product), sugar, corn syrup, partially hydrogenated soybean oil, natural and artificial flavors, sodium casseinate, artificial color, cellulose gel, cellulose gum, sodium stearoyl, lactylate, polysorbate 60, dipotassium phosphate, mono and diglycerides, carrageenan and salt. You don't need to get a degree in chemistry to realize the damage what this goop will do to your arteries. Does it taste good, you bet. It really makes a great cup of coffee, but it can stay in your system for a long time and really do a number on your circulatory system. Here are some other things to watch out for, preservatives such as BHT, BHA and TBHQ. These preservatives are made from petroleum (no wonder it never spoils) but it probably should. These derivatives should be used to lubricate your car rather than lubricate and clog your arteries. If you will follow some of these simple rules you will be able to eliminate 90% of the chemically laden, nutritionally bankrupt foods on your supermarket shelves. Now try this one for example -- I used to think this was one of the safest pies made. Well, let's try this for safety; dextrose, citrate acid, partially hydrogenated soybean oil, carrageenan, pectin, potassium sorbate, mono and diglycerides, calcium lactate, agar, calcium propinate, whey solids, ammonium bicarbonate, sorghum grain flavor, and BHT (butylhydroxytoluene). Doesn't that sound appetizing, but who cares as long as it tastes great right? This wonderful tasting goop is doing fantastic things for your taste buds but disastrous things to your arteries. Oh I forgot to tell you, I am talking about lemon meringue pie. There are no lemons, no cream, just a disgusting amount of chemicals and soap like fats. It is designed to extend shelf life but it certainly does not extend your life. If only we really knew what we were eating. A good rule of thumb might be to never eat anything that we can't pronounce, spell, or understand. Spend most of your time in the fresh fruit and vegetable area of your grocery store. When you get to the meat counter, look at the fish first. Fish with fins and scales e.g. salmon, mackerel, trout, bluefish, mullet, pompano, are good choices because of their high content of fish oils that lower blood fat (triglicerides). Next, lean toward turkey instead of ground beef, chicken is good if you remember to remove the skin, I enjoy cornish game hens. Always purchase water packed tuna, feed the oil packed tuna to your cat, and he will appreciate me for that suggestion. Use very little oil in your cooking. A poached egg is much better then an egg fried in oil.

3. Now for the good stuff, fiber. I have mentioned in several chapters about the wonderful properties of fiber. It must also be represented here as we deal with cardiovascular problems. The form of fiber we will be dealing with is flax seed. Flax seed contains omega 3 oils. Remember that flax seed, in the seed form, remains fresh almost indefinitely. Considering the speed with which the ground flax seed goes rancid, it is always best to use it immediately after grinding. Omega 3 oils help prevent arteriosclerosis. It also makes the platelets less sticky as well as lowering blood pressure. Along with the ground seed add some psyllium seed (Metamucil). This will cause your liver to induce your gallbladder to excrete more cholesterol out of the blood. The fiber will grab the cholesterol and take it out of your system. If you do not want to go through all of the trouble of grinding

your flax seed, you can get similar results with flax oil. You can purchase flax oil at your local health food store. Remember that you should always refrigerate the flax seed oil and use it as soon as possible. You will know when it turns bad, as lipid peroxides are formed and there is a bitter taste as it starts to turn rancid. When it has a bitter taste discard it because it is forming lipid peroxides which may he harmful to your body. Here are a few other suggestions as you try to modify your diet. Most experts agree that when you are cooking you should use canola oil and olive oil which are monosaturated oils and are more resistant to the damaging effects of heat. Polyunsaturated oils such as corn, Safflower, and soy, when exposed to heat have a chemical change which may go to toxic derivatives such as lipid peroxides. If you decide to take the flax oil you should expect 20 grams a day to lower your serum cholesterol by 9% and you could expect it to lower the LDL (bad cholesterol) by 18%.

Now just a small note on exercise, it is extremely important for you to do aerobic exercise the e.g. walking, swimming, stair stepping, jumping rope, etc. is much better then anaerobic e.g. lifting weights as the anaerobic exercise will tend to raise blood pressure.

Now if I failed to convince you of anything else in this heart chapter except chelation, I will feel successful. This may be the single key to your cardiac health. It would be the last thing in this group of suggestions about the heart that I would give up. No matter what, find a physician that will perform chelation therapy for you. This is probably the safest, most effective non surgical way to treat coronary artery disease, heart arrhythmias, and possibly avoid strokes and heart attack. I know some people who drive 200-300 miles in order to be treated. But, with the knowledge that I have now, I would drive twice that far. However, your chances are good that you will find a qualified physician much closer to you. When you have found a doctor that will give you chelation therapy, be sure to discuss heart medications with him. Facing heart conditions of any kind can be a very stressful situation. So if you have been diagnosed with a particular condition, read about it, study and learn everything that you can. Have a consultation with your physician, surf the internet, learn about the possible medications that may be prescribed for your condition. Then get out your PDR and read about their possible side affects. Then go back and reread the chapter on chelation, it won't take long for you to understand how much better chelation therapy is for you instead of prescription drug use.

For a current updated fairly complete listing of chelating physicians send $2.00 and a self addressed

stamped envelope to: Health Savers P.O. Box 683
Herndon VA. 22070

Please feel free to write me and advise me about the
options that you have chosen based on my advice. My
next book might just have your testimonial published
along with that of others.

STRESS

Stress comes in all shapes and sizes, and has become
so pervasive, that it seems to permeate everything
and everybody. There is job stress in lawyers,
doctors, CEO's, police, taxi drivers, housewives,
children, teen agers, senior citizens, etc. There is the
stress of bereavement, divorce, poverty, social
isolation, moving, retirement, attending school, child
rearing, etc., etc., etc. And there is also heightened
media attention because of growing confirmation of
the role of stress in heart disease, hypertension,
sudden death, depression, anxiety, smoking, obesity,
alcoholism, substance abuse, cancer, arthritis,
gastrointestinal, skin, and a host of infections and
immune system disorders.

It's hard to get through a day without hearing or
reading something about stress. Time magazine's
June 6, 1983 cover story referred to stress as "The
Epidemic of the 80's", as if it were some kind of new
plague. However, numerous surveys confirm that the
problem has progressively escalated since then. It's
hard to get through the day without reading or
hearing something about stress. Why all the

commotion? After all, stress has been around since Adam and Eve were in the Garden of Eden.

Is it because there is more stress today? Is today's stress somehow different or more dangerous? Is the frenzy of media attention due to our increasing ability to explain the mechanisms of many stress induced disorders, and scientifically confirm what were previously dismissed as old wife's tales? Are unions and workers jumping on the stress bandwagon because of the growing financial awards for job stress related injuries? Are corporations attracted because they have increasingly been held liable for such awards? Or is it because they recognize that stress management training can be extremely cost effective, not only by reducing litigation and health expenses, but also absenteeism and worker turnover, thus improving productivity - and the all important bottom line?

The answer to all of these questions is a very resounding "YES!" Stress is an unavoidable consequence of life. Without stress, there would be no life. However, just as distress can cause disease, there are good stresses that offset this, and promote wellness. Increased stress results in increased productivity - up to a point. However, this level differs for each of us. It's very much like the stress on a violin string. Not enough produces a dull, raspy sound. Too much makes a shrill, annoying noise, or causes the string to snap. However, just the right degree can create magnificent tones. Similarly, we all need to find the proper level of stress that promotes optimal performance, and enables us to make melodious music.

How Vulnerable Are You To Stress?

In modern society, most of us can't avoid stress. But we can learn to behave in ways that lessen its effects. Researchers have identified a number of factors that affect one's vulnerability to stress - among them are eating and sleeping habits, caffeine and alcohol intake, and how we express our emotions. The following questionnaire is designed to help you discover your vulnerability to stress and to pinpoint trouble spots. Rate each item from 1 (always) to 5 (never), according to how much of the time the statement is true for you. Be sure to mark each item, even if it does not apply to you - for example, if you don't smoke, circle 1 next to item six.

	Always		Sometimes		Never
1. I eat at least one hot, balanced meal a day.	1	2	3	4	5
2. I get seven to eight hours of sleep at least four nights a week.	1	2	3	4	5

3. I give and receive affection regularly.	1	2	3	4	5
4. I have at least one relative within 50 miles, on whom I can rely.	1	2	3	4	5
5. I exercise to the point of perspiration at least twice a week.	1	2	3	4	5
6. I limit myself to less than half a pack of cigarettes a day.	1	2	3	4	5
7. I take fewer than five alcohol drinks a week.	1	2	3	4	5
8. I am the	1	2	3	4	5

appropriate weight for me height.

9. I have an income adequate to meet basic expenses.

1   2   3   4   5

10. I get strength from my religious beliefs.

1   2   3   4   5

11. I regularly attend club or social activities.

1   2   3   4   5

12. I have a network of friends and acquaintances.

1   2   3   4   5

13. I have one or more friends to confide in about personal

1   2   3   4   5

matters.

14. I am in good health (including eyesight, hearing, and teeth).   1   2   3   4   5

15. I am able to speak openly about my feelings when angry or worried.   1   2   3   4   5

16. I have regular conversations with the people I live with about domestic problems - for example, chores and money.   1   2   3   4   5

17. I do something for fun at least once a week.	1	2	3	4	5
18. I am able to organize my time effectively.	1	2	3	4	5
19. I drink fewer than three cups of coffee (or other caffeine-rich drinks) a day.	1	2	3	4	5
20. I take some quiet time for myself during the day.	1	2	3	4	5

To get your score, add up the figures and subtract 20. A score below 10 indicates excellent resistance to stress. A score over 30 indicates some vulnerability to stress; you are seriously vulnerable if your score is over 50. You can make yourself less vulnerable by reviewing the items on which you

scored three or higher and try to modify them. Notice that nearly all of them describe situations and behaviors over which you have a great deal of control. Concentrate first on those that are easiest to change e.g., eating a hot, balanced meal daily and having fun at least once a week, before tackling those that seem difficult.

As we have seen, positive stress adds anticipation and excitement to life, and we all thrive under a certain amount of stress. Deadlines, competitions, confrontations, and even our frustrations and sorrows add depth and enrichment to our lives. Our goal is not to eliminate stress but to learn how to manage it and how to use it to help us. Insufficient stress acts as a depressant and may leave us feeling bored or dejected; on the other hand, excessive stress may leave us feeling "tied up in knots." What we need to do is find the optimal level of stress that will individually motivate but not overwhelm each of us.

There is no single level of stress that is optimal for all people. We are all individual creatures with unique requirements. So, what is distressing to one may be a joy to another. And even when we agree that a particular event is distressing, we are likely to differ in our physiological and psychological responses to it.

The person who loves to arbitrate disputes and moves from job site to job site would be stressed in a job that was stable and routine, whereas the person who thrives under stable conditions would very likely be stressed on a job where duties were highly varied. Also, our personal stress requirements and the amount which we can tolerate before we become distressed changes with our ages.

It has been found that most illness is related to unrelieved stress. If you are experiencing stress symptoms, you have gone beyond your optimal stress level; you need to reduce the stress in your life and or improve your ability to manage it.

Identifying unrelieved stress and being aware of its effect on our lives is not sufficient for reducing its harmful effects. Just as there are many sources of stress, there are many possibilities for its management. However, all require work toward change: changing the source of stress and or changing your reaction to it. How do you Start?

- Become aware of your stressors and your emotional and physical reactions.
- Notice your distress. Don't ignore it. Don't gloss over your problems.
- Determine what events distress you. What are you telling yourself about the meaning of these events?
- Determine how your body responds to the stress. Do you become nervous or physically upset? If so, in what specific ways?
- Recognize what you can change.
- Can you change your stressors by avoiding or eliminating them completely?

- Can you reduce their intensity (manage them over a period of time instead of on a daily or weekly basis)?
- Can you shorten your exposure to stress (take a break or leave the physical premises)?
- Can you devote the time and energy necessary to making a change (goal setting, time management techniques, and delayed gratification strategies may be helpful here)?
- Reduce the intensity of your emotional reactions to stress.
- The stress reaction is triggered by your perception of danger...physical danger and or emotional danger. Are you viewing your stressors in exaggerated terms and or taking a difficult situation and making it a disaster?
- Are you expecting to please everyone? Are you overreacting and viewing things as absolutely critical and urgent? Do you feel you must always prevail in every situation?
- Work at adopting views that are more moderate; try to see the stress as something you can cope with rather than something that overpowers you.
- Try to temper your excess emotions. Put the situation in perspective. Do not labor on the negative aspects and the "what ifs."
- Learn to moderate your physical reactions to stress.
- Slow, deep breathing will bring your heart rate and respiration back to normal.

- Relaxation techniques can reduce muscle tension. Electronic biofeedback can help you gain voluntary control over such things as muscle tension, heart rate, and blood pressure.
- Medications, when prescribed by a physician, can help in the short term in moderating your physical reactions. However, they alone are not the answer. Learning to moderate these reactions on your own is a preferable long-term solution.
- Build your physical reserves.
- Exercise for cardiovascular fitness three to four times a week (moderate, prolonged rhythmic exercise is best, such as walking, swimming, cycling, or jogging).
  Eat well-balanced, nutritious meals.
- Maintain your ideal weight.
- Avoid nicotine, excessive caffeine, and other stimulants.
- Mix leisure with work. Take breaks and get away when you can.
- Get enough sleep. Be as consistent with your sleep schedule as possible.
- Maintain your emotional reserves.
- Develop some mutually supportive friendships relationships.
- Pursue realistic goals that are meaningful to you, rather than goals others have for you that you do not share.
  Expect some frustrations, failures, and sorrows.

Always be kind and gentle with yourself, be a friend to yourself.

Crohn's Disease And Ulcerative Colitis

Crohn's disease and ulcerative colitis are major inflammatory bowel diseases. These diseases may cause malabsorption of nutrients as well as intestinal pain and possibly severe diarrhea. And this is another case and where the drugs cure, which may include prednisone and some form of antibiotic may be as bad or worse than the disease. Prednisone is a glucocorticoid. It is used primarily as and anti-inflammatory measure. Here is some information that I culled from the Physicians Desk Reference, so you could look at the possible side effects. Corticosteroids may mask signs of infections as well as cause the inability to localize infections. Prolonged use may produce cataracts, glaucoma with possible damage to optic nerves and may enhance ocular infections, due to fungi or viruses. It should not be used during pregnancy. Children who are on immunosuppressant drugs are far more susceptible to infections and chickenpox and measles may take a fatal course when the corticosteroids are used. Steroids should be used, with caution in nonspecific ulcerative colitis, if there is a possibility of perforation, abscesses, diverticulitis, latent peptic ulcer, renal problems, hypertension and osteoporosis. Here are some more adverse reactions (to list just a few) are as follows:

- Sodium retention.
- Fluid retention.

- Heart failure.
- Potassium loss.
- Hypertension.
- Muscle weakness.
- Osteoporosis.
- Vertebral compression fractures.
- Ulcer problems.
- Pancreatitis.
- Impaired wound healing.
- Thin fragile skin.
- Convulsions-especially if mixed with other drugs.
- Headache.
- Menstrual problems.
- Suppression of growth in children.
- Manifestations of latent diabetes.
- Cataracts.
- Increase in intraocular pressure.
- Glaucoma.

When you add some of the above side effects to the problem, it is possible that you will want to look at some alternative methods. I believe Crohn's disease is diet oriented, therefore the cure must also be diet oriented. The high sugar, high fat, fast food diet is again the culprit that appears to exacerbate these diseases. Crohn's disease and ulcerative colitis are completely nonexistent in most primitive cultures that do not have access to fast foods. Again, it is our own fault, as long as we patronize these places; they will continue to be in business. Why we do not demand a healthier diet is anybody's guess. If we did, there would be a lot of healthier food choices.

The old recommendation for these diseases was to use a low fiber diet. But there are many fiber options that should be utilized. You should use a lot of ground flax seed, psyllium seed, broccoli and other forms such as pectin and sometimes oat bran. Animal fats should be reduced and fish oil (EPA) should be used instead. Research shows that a large amount of fish oil is beneficial e.g. some 20 grams a day. That is a lot of capsules but it is worth it. You should also try some barley green juice twice a day. I mix it with Willard's water and try to enjoy it, good luck it will never happen.

Now comes the most important solution to Crohn's disease. Isn't it interesting that most of the things presented here also apply to most other diseases? You will probably read the same things over and over again. Now something that also works well for colds and flu really seems to have a beneficial effect here. Colostrum is the most potent immune booster known to science. It helps strengthen you against a wide variety of bacterium and viruses. It is completely safe. It has two properties that make it work its wonders on Crohn's disease and inflammatory bowel disease. First, it is a powerful anti-inflammatory and second it works to control and destroy bacterial and viral infections in the colon. Colostrum's qualities have a high content of immunoglobulins, including IgG, IgA and IgM. It also plays a major role in halting allergic reactions to food and other antigens.

This may be of some interest; scientists in Finland have done research that confirms that bovine colostrum kills heliobacter pylori, the bacteria associated with duodenal and peptic ulcers. Colostrum is in mother's first breast milk. It comes before the milk sets in and is the oldest form of protection. Nature made this substance to help regulate and support the immune system. Antibacterials may wipe out sensitive bacteria leaving behind the smart ones that have learned to mutate against the antibiotic. Future attempts to kill the bacteria again will fail. Colostrum is very wide in its spectrum of antiviral and antibacterial substances. It does not allow for mutations like antibiotics. It is also protective for the following:

- Esterichra coli.
- Pseudomonas.
- Aeruginosa.
- Salmonella.
- Candida albicon's yeast.
- Staphylococcus epidermis.
- Streptococcus.

Let me try to establish the advantage of using colostrum. Not only does it destroy pathogens, but prevents them from attaching to the intestinal walls, it also helps prepare and regenerate the critical skin surface of the intestinal wall at the cellular level. Partly because it contains many growth factors, notably epidermal growth factor. It also destroys harmful organisms in the intestines and encourages the colonization of beneficial bacteria in the bowel.

Now let me summarize the recommendations for Crohn's disease and colitis:

1. Colostrum, take 3-5 tablets or 1 tablespoon of liquid three times a day on an empty stomach.
2. Two glasses a day of barley green, 1 tablespoon in each glass.
3. 5-10 tablets of EPA-fish oil, at first you may have an aftertaste, but it will soon go away.
4. Use several forms of fiber at least twice a day. The best ones to use are finely ground flax seed (4 tablespoons a day in water) 1 tablespoon of psyllium seed (Metamucil type), oat bran, guar gum and or pectin (a great form of pectin is Nutra-joint).

You should begin to see an almost immediate and long lasting support from the above suggestions.

Ulcers

Ulcers have more than one cause, so there may be multiple solutions with some of the solutions providing a cure. And others will only help treat the condition and make living with them much easier to bear. Some ulcers may be relieved by lessening stress. However a high percentage of ulcers are caused by a germ that lives in the lining of the stomach. The bacterium is spiral shaped and lives best in an environment that prefers less oxygen. This bacterium is called heliobacter pylori. This bacterium has the ability to neutralize acids and create an environment conducive to its growth. Now let's add an antacid to the situation. The less acid in the stomach the poorer the digestion. And an antacid is one of those feel good things that only escalates the situation. If you take enough antacids, you will stop the normal digestive process. Heliobacter pylori has not only been named as a cause of gastric and duodenal ulcers, but it can lead to stomach cancers and some forms of lymphomas. It is classified by some research centers as a class one carcinogen. Now an ulcer is defined as a lesion on the surface of the stomach lining. Heliobacter pylori eats at the stomach lining, this exposes delicate tissue of the stomach to the very strong acids necessary for digestion to take place. Therefore the symptoms are very predictable, a burning pain in the stomach or abdomen. If the stomach is empty it is usually worse. However, I have seen it so bad that some people are unable to eat. Severe cases bleed, may cause anemia, vomiting, or blood in the stool. If the blood in the stool is dark, it comes from causes higher in the intestinal tract or stomach. If the blood is red, it may be from hemorrhoids or other causes close to the anal passage. Now here are some solutions. Allopathic treatment consists of one or two weeks of antibiotics. If you do not opt for the traditional treatments I suggest the following which may cause the body to create its own defense mechanisms. It does this without destroying the friendly intestinal flora.

1. The first line of defense is colostrum, three to five times daily, preferably on an empty stomach. It is a broad spectrum antibiotic as well as a great anti-inflammatory agent. It is very effective against heliobacter pylori. It can provide passive immunity by naturally destroying the pathogens. Colostrum also inhibits the ability of a pathogen to bind to the stomach lining thereby causing it to be unable to colonize and reproduce itself. I like using the liquid, taking a tablespoon five times a day on an empty stomach. Why take it on an empty stomach? Because it is a large molecule and is not easily passed through the epithelial lining of the digestive tract. When it is by itself, it does much better than when mixed with food, colostrum contains antibodies that seek and destroy the pathogens.
2. One of the things that will make you feel better but have no adverse side affects is aloe vera. This remedy is very inexpensive and you can take a swallow of it every hour of the day, it is very soothing and is synergistic with colostrum.
3. If the cause of the ulcer is not bacteria, there is a form of licorice that provides a healing coating to the stomach lining, it is called, deglycyrrhizinated licorice. This should be taken several times a day.

If you go to a health food store, just ask for the licorice that helps to prevent ulcers. This form of licorice has been used throughout Europe for years to treat stomach ulcers. To my knowledge there are no known side affects. The chewable form is the one I recommend. There is a reason for this recommendation; it appears that when the licorice is chewed, it mixes with the saliva which also stimulates the growth and regeneration of the cells lining the stomach. This should be chewed about an hour before meals. It also enhances the normal defenses of the stomach and intestinal walls and seems to increase the lifespan of the intestinal tract cells.

4. If you take vitamin C, use the Ester form, this will not increase the stomach acid.
5. You should also take one tablet of magnesium citrate with each meal.

You may find any or all of the above to be helpful. Please, should your condition persist always consult with your health practitioner. It will probably be a lot more convenient for you to take a product like Tagamet, Zantac, Pepcid or Axid. However, these products are debilitating to the activity of the protective cells in the intestinal tract. The success of these drugs depend on the disruption of natural digestion. However without stomach acid food may not be assimilated properly. All of these products are H 2 receptor antagonists. I am very sorry to have to do this to you, but just for a laugh you should know the chemical name of Zantac: N[2-[[[5-|(dimethylamino)methyl |]-2 furanyl |methyl|]thiolethyll-N' methyl-2-Nitro |,| ethenediamine,HCL. Now would you please repeat that back to me. The Physicians Desk Reference evaluates the adverse reactions as follows (I will only list a few):

- Dizziness.
- Insomnia.
- Rare cases of mental confusion.
- Agitation.
- Depression.
- Hallucinations.
- Rare reports of arrhythmias e.g. tachycardia.
- Constipation.
- Diarrhea.
- Nausea.
- Rare reports of Pancreatitis.
- Occasional reports of hepatitis, however these events are usually reversible but in very rare cases death has occurred.
- Occasional cases of Impotence and a loss of libido however, the incidences of the above do not differ from that in the general population.
- Rash.
- Fever.
- Increases in serum creatinine.

The above-mentioned side effects may be very rare, and it is probably one of the safest antacids you can take. The alternative treatments listed here may not solve all of your problems for you but it is my sincerest of hopes that they do, as I feel that they will be quite beneficial without the possibility of side effects.

Drinking milk is an age-old home remedy that could actually be doing you some harm. Milk is a highly allergic food that may greatly increase stomach acid production and cause ulcers to be aggravated. This natural remedy should be discarded. If you want to drink a milk like product in order to sooth the burning sensations, I would like to suggest that you try soymilk.

Kidney Stones

This is a condition that only those who have gone through it can ever describe the pain. You will probably not be very concerned about this chapter until you have passed a kidney stone for yourself, then you will consider this chapter to be the most important in the whole book. Thank God there are some very sophisticated treatments e.g. altered sound therapy which may break down the stones so that they might pass through the ureter where if it becomes stuck, it will cause extreme pain. Some experts recommend drinking plenty of water, reducing calcium in the diet and taking a thiazide diuretic. But if you follow these directions you will only make things worse (with the exception of drinking large amounts of water). There has never been any research to substantiate the fact that decreasing calcium will solve the problem. If you are an older woman and decrease your calcium intake you would not only be wasting your efforts on kidney stones, but you would increase your propensity for osteoporosis. Kidney stones may be as small as a grain of sand and you will wonder how something so small could ever cause so much pain. The stones are usually formed from calcium and oxalic acid -- calcium oxalate. The people who are more susceptible to getting kidney stones are as follows:

- Heavy users of alcohol.
- Family history of stones.
- Men or women over the age of 40.
- Sedentary people.

Now that you have experienced the pain caused by calcium oxalate, let us look at some possible preventions:
- The single most important prevention is to drink plenty of pure water.
- A high intake of vitamin D may tend to over absorb calcium.
- You certainly can not restrict calcium from your diet, but you can restrict oxalates: here are a few foods that should be restricted by those who have or have had kidney stones. Carefully look at the following foods, many of

which are great when it comes to heart disease or cancer, but when you have kidney stones, it is worth considering eliminating them as much as possible.

- Rhubarb * *.
- Strawberries.
- Blackberries.
- Cranberries *.
- Beets.
- Beet greens * *.
- Cooked spinach * *.
- Parsley *.
- Almonds *.
- Cashews *.
- Pepper *.
- Poppy seeds *.
- Chocolate * *.
- Cocoa *.
- Cola beverages.
- Coffee * *.

The * is an indicator of the items that you should avoid, no indicator, least problem. * * indicators should always be avoided.

- Take at least 1000 mg of magnesium citrate daily. Magnesium and manganese will tend to react with the oxalates to keep it in suspension and stop the formation of stones.
- Vitamin B 6 will also reduce the production of oxalates.

- Avoid all dairy products fortified with vitamin D.

Before we leave this subject it is worth honorable mention to note some dietary patterns that tend to exacerbate the problem:
- Low fiber diets.
- Sugar.
- Refined carbohydrates.
- High alcohol consumption.
- High fats.
- High salt.

With this information, you should be able to say goodbye to kidney stones forever. If you only choose one thing from the suggestions above, you're best bet is to take lots of magnesium and add manganese. These chemicals do their job very well and you have a good chance of solving the problem even if you are unable to eliminate all the oxalates from your diet. I will admit it would be very difficult for me to give up strawberries and almonds, as these foods are beneficial for so many other things, so if I to eat them, I often take extra fiber (ground flax seed and or psyllium seed), and magnesium. Some diseases are very difficult to prevent, thank goodness this is one that can usually be controlled with a simple dietary fix.

Glaucoma

Glaucoma is caused by increased pressure (intraocular) in the eye, due to and imbalance of production and outflow of eye fluid. Some of the symptoms may be a loss of peripheral vision (tunnel vision), and as the condition gets worse there may be pain, redness of the eyes, blurring of vision, inability to adjust from light to dark areas and or have halos around lights. If the situation is acute, it may be very serious and the patient should go immediately to an ophthalmologist. If therapy is not started within 12 hours, permanent loss of vision may occur in just a few days. It is the second leading cause of blindness. Some possible causes are aging, infection, genetic predisposition, tumors, trauma, hormone disorders, nutritional problems, stress, and allergies. Conventional treatments may be in the form of drug therapies such as acetazolamide and pilocarpine, prescription eye drops, epinephrine compounds, surgery or laser treatments. Some things you must avoid are caffeine in all forms as caffeine is a vasoconstrictor and raises eye pressure. Here are several things that you can use in your fight against glaucoma; they have proven to be extremely beneficial:

1. Vitamin C (ester formulation) if your body can assimilate it use up to 10,000 mg a day or more. If this begins causing diarrhea lower the dosage a little and that will solve the problem.
2. There is sometimes a very quick response to EPA (fish oil). You should take 3-4 tablets 2-3 times a

day. At first you may taste fish, but that will go away in a few days.
3. Beta carotene 25,000 units a day. Beta carotene is the raw material for vitamin A
4. Querectin is a bioflavonoid that is synergistic with the metabolism of vitamin C.
5. Eye bright is an herb that strengthens the eye and provides elasticity to the nerves and optic devices for sight.
6. The good thing about bilberry may help increase your night vision.

Now I am going to give you an easy assignment. It may sound unscientific, but try it, it works. I have been doing this simple exercise for over 20 years. Shut your eyes; place your hands gently over your eyes so there is no light. Now try to picture something in detail, a waterfall, a house, a lamp, but see every detail you can imagine. Do this for several minutes, then when you are through, look at a bright light with one eye covered for 15-20 seconds, then cover the other eye and let the light shine in. if you do this several times a day you may find an almost miraculous improvement in your vision. Some people have even been able to discard their glasses when they perfected this procedure.

Macular Degeneration

As we get older our eyes begin to fail. For over ten million Americans, it means macular degeneration, a deterioration of the retina that leads to permanent blindness. This is another disease where prevention is much easier than trying to reverse the process of deterioration. The origin of this disease appears to be related to damage caused by free radicals (an oxygen atom looking for an electron). So a diet high in antioxidants is the first step to take in stopping macular degeneration. There is no medical treatment to date for the most common form of macular degeneration. Here are some of the steps you can take to prevent this debilitating disease:

1. Read and study everything you can on antioxidants and make sure you have and use vitamin A (Beta carotene form), vitamin C (Ester form), and vitamin E with Selenium. Another super antioxidant is Alpha Lipolic acid. I began using this product about a year ago and have seen favorable results. Some scientists believe that it chelates certain metals from the eye, thus preventing cataracts as well.

2. The two organs in your body that have a high concentration of zinc are the eye and the prostate gland. Since the eye has such a high concentration of zinc, it is extremely important that you take 25-100 mg of zinc everyday. Zinc supplementation has been shown to be of benefits in improving and visual function of people with macular degeneration.

3. The single most exciting product that you can take is bilberry. During World War II, British military officers discovered that fighter pilots who ate bilberry jam had better night vision then those who did not. Since that time a multitude of studies have been conducted and the results are simply astounding. Bilberry extract improved the

condition of patients with macular degeneration, retinitis, diabetic neuropathy, retinitis pigmentosa and in some cases greatly improved on the progression of cataracts. If you want to protect your eyes, there is no better way than to heed the above recommendations. However, if you only choose one of these recommendations then treating your eyes with bilberry may be the most important. You will get better results if you take the extract rather than the whole berry. The formula should contain 25% anthocyanosides. Then take 160 mg 3 times a day. This information may be the key to protecting your eyes for many years to come.

Hormone Replacement - The Fountain of Youth

The new hot topic of the day is the fact that diseases caused by aging such as heart disease, stroke, cancer, diabetes, osteoporosis, senility, impotency and a host of other diseases are all a part of the normal aging process. That is a natural process as we grow older. However, the good news is that aging is becoming a preventable disease that can be controlled with hormones which have amazing anti-aging benefits. The best solution for any disease is to prevent it before it happens. Research is proving that by maintaining our hormone levels close to what they were in our youth (latter teen years) we can prevent the debility and illness that go along with the aging process. The goal of this technology is to enhance the quality of life in latter years.

Hormones are amino acids which form a long chain called polypeptides that are manufactured by the endocrine glands which include the following:
- Testes.
- Pancreas.
- Adrenal glands.
- Ovaries.
- Thyroid gland.
- Pituitary gland.
- Pineal gland.

As we age, the levels of hormones these organs are able to produce diminishes. This results in the decreased ability of your body to repair the cellular damage done by free radicals and the normal degeneration of the organs which normally shrink with age. After age 40 the organs will become smaller and their ability to rid the body of toxins decreases in proportion to these effects.

Now you may be ready for a little good news. Genetic engineering has made it possible to produce natural hormones that are a perfect match to those produced by your body. We now no longer have to accept the fact that we will grow frail and feeble. The really good news is that the key hormone HGH which in the 1980's cost around $25,000 a month and had to be extracted from the pituitary gland of cadavers and then purified. Now, it is genetically engineered and the costs are from $250 to $500 monthly. Much of the medical community has ignored the extreme value of hormone replacement and I strongly recommend to every reader that they find a physician who is either familiar with these procedures or wise enough to recommend you to someone who "is in the know". When my life had virtually ended at the age of 62 I went to a physician who helped me in every way he knew how and when I inquired about hormone replacement he had the wisdom to say, "Let's try it, it might just be your only hope". I practically owe my life to this doctor. He could have ridiculed the suggestion and watched me die. His wisdom and understanding told him that all of his conventional methods weren't going to work, so he knew that it was time to try something unconventional. For that, I will be eternally grateful. If you are going to a physician that ridicules your suggestions just because you aren't a professional, I have only one suggestion for you, Find Another Doctor!

The person who recommended that I try hormone replacement wasn't even in the medical profession, he was a mining engineer. I remind him quite often that I would not even be here had he not cared enough to try and help me with medical advice.

Hormone replacement is not a cure all. We will all someday meet our maker as each cell in our body can only replicate itself so many times as the process of telomere shortening takes over. The hope of an extremely long life such as is mentioned in the early biblical days, may someday come into play once we are able to control the telomerase enzyme which is responsible for the shortening of the telomere (tail) section of the DNA molecule. Then we will be able to stop the aging process even further. Once we find a way to keep the DNA molecule reproducing itself in exact likeness over and over, you can forget about getting older. You should be able to be playing tennis at the age of 90, produce children, play basketball with them and even compete in sporting events. If you like these ideas, just keep reading. I enjoy writing about the possibilities that are before us as they may be closer then you can possibly imagine. We never thought that we would walk on the moon until a former president dreamed of it and gave us the tools to make it happen. Society should give thanks to a man by the name of doctor Daniel Rudman, who published an article in the England Journal of Medicine, where he discovered that the activity of the human growth hormone was responsible for:

- An increase in lean body mass.
- An increase in muscle strength.
- A decrease in adipose (fat) tissue.
- An increase in bone density.
- An increase in skin thickness.
- An increase in proper organ function.
- An improvement in lipid profiles.

Dr. Rudman's results were so overwhelming that they could no longer be ignored and the search for wellness took a giant leap forward. Doctor Rudman's investigators are now combining growth hormones with sex hormones, DHEA, melatonin, thyroid hormones and pregnanalone, all of which will be discussed as you continue to read this chapter. At the end of this chapter I will give you several excellent clinics that you can deal with. It can now be concluded that by raising the levels of these hormones we can reduce the incidences of disease and therefore prolong life. Please know that it is not just longer life that we are after, but we are also interested in the quality of life that allows you the freedom to painlessly do the things that you always wanted to do.

The true reversal of the aging process requires a considerable amount of research in genetic engineering and proper manipulation of these genes. Unfortunately this technology is not quite perfected yet so we must take advantage of the knowledge that we now have in anti-aging techniques e.g.

- Avoidance of risk factors of disease
- Optimal nutrition.
- Adequate exercise.
- Calorie restriction.
- Antioxidant therapy.
- Hormonal replacement.

Some of the obvious changes that result from reduced production of the growth hormone are shown by the catabolic changes in normal aging such as:

- Osteoporosis.
- Muscle atrophy.

- Sleep disorders.
- Decreased sociability.
- Decreased sexual function.
- Increased body fat.
- Mental atrophy.

Within 12 months or less (with me it was less than 90 days) hormone replacement will reshape your body, you will see fat disappearing, increased muscle tone, your height may even increase to that of your younger years, sexual improvement and a sense of well-being that you have not known in years. I will now discuss the individual hormones and how they may affect your future.

Human growth hormone (HGH), until recently, the supply of this hormone was scarce and extremely expensive. Those days are now over. It is now available in large supply due to genetic engineering. It was developed through recombinant DNA technology. It is now obtained from bacteria that have been engineered to produce HGH in exact likeness to what your body produces or produced in the past, during your younger years. Some of the signs of a lack of HGH are as follows:
- Decreased cardiac output.
- Osteoporosis.
- Loss of muscle strength and tone.
- Increase fat especially around the waistline.
- Decreased physical performance.
- Poor sleep.

- Poor libido.
- Thinning of hair.
- Thinning of skin.
- Poor self image.
- Lack of confidence.
- Poor memory.
- Lack of energy and endurance.
- Sagging breasts.
- Sagging abdomen.

HGH not only has the potential to counteract these effects, simply by stopping them, but in many cases, even reversing them completely.

Let's take a look at the muscle to fat ratio for a moment. There is usually a 10% increase in lean body mass along with a 10% decrease in body fat. The fat loss is greatest in the abdominal area. There may not be a large amount of weight loss because of the muscle mass increase. I have seen abdominal measurements decrease from 38" to 32" with a corresponding increase in chest measurements. Now for the exciting part, HGH affects a favorable response in the kidneys, liver, spleen, skin and bones as well as protecting against atrophy by causing regrowth of tissue. As you age, the organs decrease in size approximately 10% for every 10 years over the age of 40. HGH has the potential to bring the organs back to their original size and function. Your metabolism is increased thus affecting a lowering of cholesterol. The skin is restored to its youthful appearance because HGH will replenish the extra cellular water which makes skin thicker and wrinkles disappear. There is also a normalization of the kidney function.

Concerning bone density, HGH is the only substance that I know of that reverses the effects of osteoporosis. Several studies have shown an increase in bone density of over 2% a year. This is done without the side affects that taking Fosamax has. You still need calcium and magnesium in the citrate form, other forms may be worthless. Citrical is a good product as long as you add magnesium in the citrate form. HGH increases your muscle capacity thus allowing you to exercise and enjoy it again. There is also increased cardiac output. My output increased about 20% even with a damaged heart.

Now how HGH is administered. I do not know of many oral treatments that are of any significant value. There are lots of oral precursors that make great claims but you can forget about them entirely. If your pituitary gland is not producing HGH now, it is not likely to start up again, so it is of little value to take a precursor. However, there are some oral HGH products that contain recombinant HGH. Check the label Carefully. Some researchers have used HGH injections twice daily, but recent research shows that a once daily injection at night is the most effective. The correct amount of HGH can only be determined by a well-trained physician. I will not explain the determining factors here as that is a question of sophisticated testing and analysis. I will tell you that I take (by injection) 8 units per week. You may require more or less depending on your age and blood analysis. When the above procedure is done correctly, you can forget about any adverse side affects as there are none. Again, I caution you that the only effective methods of increasing HGH is through daily injections, or oral tablets that contain recombinant HGH.

DHEA

DHEA is a steroid like hormone which is the most abundant hormone in the bloodstream. It is found in extremely high concentrations in the brain. As the levels of DHEA decline you can expect to see increased symptoms of aging e.g.:

- Senility.
- Sexual dysfunction.
- Diabetes.
- Obesity.
- Elevated cholesterol levels.
- Arthritis.

DHEA shows exceptional promise of enhancing memory and improving cognitive function. It is also converted over to estrogen, testosterone and progesterone. DHEA actually reverses much of the deterioration that occurred since reaching middle age. It not only makes you feel great, but it also improves the immune system as well as brain function, it relieves stress and has proven to be a very potent anti-cancer drug. If you look at the above list of symptoms and just reverse all of the deleterious side effects of aging, you will have a picture of where this hormone can take you. It not only protects you from the symptoms of aging above, but it has the ability to actually reverse those effects. It also increases the insulin sensitivity which may lower the amount of insulin required for diabetics. Not only does it protect against diabetes, it also helps control the problem once you have it. It has the tremendous ability to stimulate protein synthesis which in turn results in cellular regeneration. DHEA is one of the most powerful anti-oxidants you can take to prevent free radical damage. By the time you reach the age of 40, you produce about 1/2 of the DHEA that you did at the age of 20. Some people produce no DHEA whatsoever and in this case the quality of their life becomes much more unpleasant, as fatigue, muscle weakness, inability to sleep and deal with stress sets in. DHEA was proven to be so effective, that the FDA has criticized its use based on the fact that it may cause liver damage. They based their conclusion on one study where rats were given 3000 mg of DHEA over an extended period of time and sustained some liver damage. However, 3000 mg of DHEA given to a creature the size of a mouse is 1000 times more than the average human would take. This is about as ridiculous as saying that 1000 cans of soda could kill you. Of course it would, your sugar levels would go out of sight and your stomach would burst. Based on this way of making conclusions, the FDA could say that saliva causes stomach cancer also. However, only if it is swallowed in small quantities over a long period of time. How many wonderful medications have been thrown by the wayside based on claims as ridiculous as these? Millions of patients have taken DHEA over the last 25 years and my research shows absolutely no side affects when taken under the supervision of a competent physician. It is a good idea for men to take an annual PSA test when taking DHEA and testosterone to assure that there is no abnormal increase in these values. DHEA is available over the counter, but I recommend that you take a pharmaceutical grade, as the half life of DHEA is only six hours which would require you to take it four times a day. I will list several sources at the end of the chapter that I recommend as it has a sustained release in the micronized form which allows you to take only one capsule a day.

Pregnenolone

Pregnenolone is a steroid hormone that has been known to be a precursor to the DHEA hormone. It has many independent and significant biological functions of which the most important is to keep the brain working at its peak efficiency. This hormone has been shown to be the most potent memory enhancer of all time. The brain concentrations peak at around the age of 30 and later may decrease with age to about 5% of that value thereby increasing the need to supplement pregnenolone. Of all hormones, pregnenolone is very efficient in improving memory, mental function, concentration and overall well-being. Research has extensively documented that this hormone has such great memory enhancing affects that it can improve post learning memory function at a dosage of 100 times lower than other memory promoting steroids. The City of Hope Medical Center in Los Angeles California conducted tests on animals that concluded that pregnenolone may actually restore impaired memory. Their findings reported that pregnenolone will restore normal levels of memory hormones which decline during the aging process and is several hundred times more potent then any memory enhancer previously tested. This hormone is synthesized from cholesterol and is the precursor to DHEA and other sex hormones. It is produced both by the brain and the adrenal cortex. By the time we have reached the age of 40, we produce less than half of the amount that we produced when we were in our 20s. It should also be noted that pregnenolone does have a short half-life and should be obtained in a sustained release micronized form. I will list several good clinics and a supplier at the end of this discussion. Pregnenolone also has the ability to repair enzyme activity. Is also has anti-inflammatory effects and when administered immediately after a spinal cord injury, has aided in the restoration of motor function. The anti-inflammatory effects were used to treat rheumatoid arthritis but when cortisone was discovered it replaced pregnenolone however, the side effects of cortisone are many and severe e.g.:

- Euphoria.
- Insomnia.
- Hot flashes.
- Osteoporosis.

- Adrenal atrophy.

Pregnenolone was never found to have adverse side affects, and can be used to withdraw from cortisone therapy because of its normalizing affects on the adrenal gland. I am 67 years old and personally take 200 mg. of the sustained release, micronized form of pregnenolone. You will need to check with your physician or one of the clinics that will be mentioned at the end of this chapter to find out what dosage is the best for you. The results are almost immediate and within a couple of days you will begin to see a big difference in your ability to function at a higher level of thinking and memory retention. This is one time you will not need to wait several months to see the results.

Pregnenolone is also a God send for diabetics as it has been shown to rejuvenate the beta cells of the pancreas in animals and is synergistic with HGH in its effects of the pancreas. It also is very effective in helping the latter to reduce the ravages of stress through its impact on the adrenal function. Its also affects the repair of the myelin sheath membrane, that protects the brain and the nervous system. Pregnenolone also enhances the DHEA levels and plays a role in balancing the estrogen levels in women. The lower your pregnenolone level, the greater the rewards you can expect. The proper amount that you need can the determined from a blood test. This is one hormone that can easily be missed unless you are dealing with a specialist in longevity.

Melatonin

Melatonin is now beginning to generate strong
scientific interest as one of the body's most powerful
anti-aging, anti-oxidant, immune system boosting,
cancer fighting, heart helping, and mood elevation
known to man. In fact, pineal gland transplant
studies in mice have shown that old mice receiving
Pineal glands from young mice increase their life
span to the span of the younger mice, while the young
mice who received the Pineal gland from the old mice
grew old and died prematurely. Melatonin is
secreted by the Pineal gland, which is a small organ
set behind and between the eyes. The initial and
clinical studies of melatonin focused on problems
related to sleep and daily cycles, as it is the
timekeeper of the brain that governs the daily
rhythms such as the waking and sleeping cycles. If I
haven't peaked your interest by now, try this on for
size. A research scientist by the name of Pierpaloni
extended the life span of mice by as much as 25%
with melatonin supplementation. The treated mice
appeared younger and more vigorous. It rejuvenated
their sexual desire and appeared to regenerate their
sexual organs so that the organs were comparable
with those of the younger animals. Now imagine that
you are 75 or 80 years old, all you need to do is find
an 18 yr. old who is through using his Pineal gland
and we will have new evidence to support what
happens to an 80 year old when he competes with the

world's best athletes. Now back to some of the other advantages of using melatonin:

- It enhances the immune system.
- It is one of the most effective free-radical scavengers yet discovered.
- It lowers cholesterol.
- Shows promise in preventing and treating cancer.
- It has a dramatic beneficial effect on the thymus gland.
- It induces restful sleep.
- It helps overcome jet lag.
- It inhibits prostate cancer.
- It protects the brain from a variety of degenerative diseases
- It prevents cataracts in some scientific trials.
- It is harmless to the body, no matter how high the levels, it apparently causes no side affects other then a natural drowsiness.

Each one of the 11 points mentioned above could have a book written exclusively discussing its cause and effect. However, I will choose a few to comment on further concerning how much your dosage should be. You may do fine on 1 mg. 20 minutes prior to sleep. The average dose is 3 mg. It is sold over the counter and is very inexpensive. The amount that I take is 24 mg and it achieves excellent results for me. Sublingual tablets are also available as are time release capsules. There are a few cautions that must be noted. Do not use melatonin if you are pregnant, nursing, or trying to conceive (very high doses act as a contraceptive but please, don't rely on it as being 100% effective). Also people on steroids, anti-depressants or have immune deficiencies such as lymphoma or leukemia should avoid melatonin.

Now for a few suggestions that will help. When you go to sleep, do not leave a light on. Sleep in a darkened room as leaving a light on will tend not to give you a restful nights sleep. When morning comes and you are ready to go, roll up the blinds, have a good stretch, soak up some sunlight and have a wonderful day. Melatonin and free-radicals also deserve further comment. Free-radicals are atoms that have an unpaired electron and it is highly reactive. This atom (mostly oxygen) is looking for an electron and will get it regardless of the cost. It may attack your genetic material, causing an aberration and the results may be cancer, heart disease, auto immune diseases and the list may never end. Anti-oxidants are able to supply this wild atom with an electron maybe before it can do any damage. Some of the popular anti-oxidants are vitamin C, vitamin A, vitamin E, alpha lipolic acid etc. But melatonin is one of the most powerful free-radical scavengers yet discovered and is capable of penetrating every cell of the body, and works both inside and outside of the cell. In one study with rats at the University of Texas Health Science Center they gave melatonin to rats before feeding them food laced with carcinogens and found that melatonin treated rats had from 41 to 99% less genetic damage then the untreated rats.

Another intriguing sideline to melatonin is the reduction of nocturnal urinary frequency. Many men think they have prostate problems because they awaken several times a night to urinate. Melatonin usually abolishes this nighttime awakening to urinate, which stops the concern about prostate problems. This problem is solved in an equally effective manner with women. Now my final comment before proceeding is to ask you this question, why would anyone not want to take this safe, natural, effective, cheap, cancer preventative, immune system enhancing therapy that has stood the test of time. It is completely harmless to the body and regardless of how much you take there are no serious side affects other then natural drowsiness.

Estrogen

Estrogen is the miracle hormone that could either help you in many ways or destroy you just as easily. It all depends on your knowledge of the subject. This hormone has been used for over 40 years for women who have suffered menopausal symptoms. Estrogen has vastly improved the quality of life for women, making them feel more youthful, energized and healthier. Women using estrogen had far better muscle tone, fewer wrinkles, stronger shinier hair and a more enjoyable and satisfying sex life after menopause. They also stood taller and straighter and did not suffer typical bone loss associated with osteoporosis. Estrogen users had half of the risk of heart disease and stroke. They had an extremely low incidence of Alzheimer's disease and senility. They were not subject to genital atrophy and contaminant infections. Estrogen is produced by the ovaries and adrenal glands. Men also produce a small amount of estrogen from the conversion of testosterone. If men used estrogen they could receive many of the same health benefits as women do, however, I am not willing to see my breasts grow or my voice change.

Before I discuss the three forms of estrogen I would like to list a few characteristic symptoms of menopause:

- Hot flashes.
- Insomnia.
- Vaginal dryness.
- Bladder problems.
- Difficulty concentrating.
- Anxiety.
- Cardiovascular disease incidences increase.
- Stroke.
- Osteoporosis.
- Alzheimer's.

The National Menopause Foundation makes the following conclusive statement, "Estrogen, progesterone replacement therapy is almost like women immunizing themselves from the two most prevalent diseases that can affect postmenopausal women, heart disease and osteoporosis. The intelligent use of hormone replacement therapy will be the greatest boon ever to women's health". Please reread one important word in that last statement "intelligent". Intelligence requires research and I pray that you do not stop your research with this book alone. I am only trying to open the door to your knowledge on this subject. Let me draw you a simple chart that you may always remember. It shows the progression of heart disease by comparison to men and postmenopausal women:

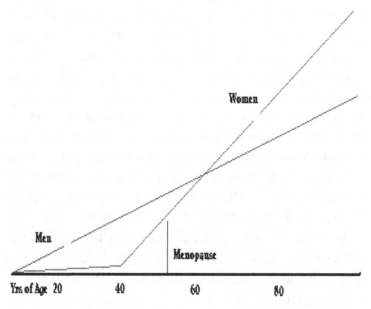

There are three forms of estrogen, estradiol, esterone, and estriol. Estradiol is by far the most biologically active form and some gynecologists do not believe the last two play a very effective role in female physiology. Estradiol is frequently prescribed in a conjugated form such as Premarin which is derived from sources such as horse urine. It is not well absorbed by mouth, as the gastrointestinal tract destroys much of it before it enters the bloodstream. However, the micronized form allows it to be taken orally. It is well absorbed through the skin and can be used in patches or gel which is the preferred method since it delivers a natural form directly into the bloodstream without going through the liver. Esterone has the capability to relieve hot flashes but may promote endometrial or breast cancer if taken without progesterone. Please do not read this chapter alone because the most important is yet to come when we discuss the topic on progesterone. Estriol is a weak form of estrogen and may require a dose large enough to create nausea and discomfort. However it is the only form that has been shown to have an anti-cancer effect. It inhibits the breast cancer promoting effect of estradiol in mice. It was shown to inhibit the development of breast cancer in rats when given a carcinogen. In several instances women with breast cancer showed a 37% change of either remission or the complete cessation of further progression. It may be ideal for women at risk of either uterine or breast cancers. It must be noted: that one of the most brilliant doctors that I know, Dr. Jonathan Wright recommends a combination of:

- 80% estriol.
- 10% esterone.
- 10% estradiol.

This combination is called Triesterone. I will give you a list of functions unique to estrogen only but you must read the list concerning the functions of progesterone and then you will understand the synergistic effects of these two hormones together. Progesterone is the key piece of the puzzle that makes it all work. Listed below are the functions of estrogen only:

- Decreases mood swings.
- Coronary heart disease is reduced by 60%.
- Stroke death rates reduced by 70%.
- Decreases cholesterol (HDL ratio).
- Prevents Alzheimer's (lowers incidence rate).
- Interferes with thyroid function.
- Provides defense against free-radicals.
- Decreases libido.
- Improves memory.
- Increases salt retention.
- May increase body fat.
- Causes a loss of zinc and copper.
- Causes gallstones and liver dysfunction.
- Causes depression and headaches.
- Increases blood clotting.
- Impairs blood sugar control.
- Increased risk of breast and uterine cancer when not balanced with progesterone.

Now you know the good news and the bad news, but before you even consider throwing estrogen replacement away you need to read the following chapter on progesterone and compare the chart above with the one in the next chapter. Always remember the estrogen you take must be in the form of natural estrogen. The dosage will be determined by age and medical history. The physicians and clinics mentioned at the end of this chapter are very competent and I am thankful that they have allowed me to use their expertise to help me help you. I am very grateful to them, and always will be.

Progesterone

One of the safest hormone supplements that can be used by both men and women is natural progesterone which can raise depleted levels of DHEA and improve the mood and libido. Let me start with a list of functions, which are unique to progesterone only (now remember the comparison that I asked you to do on the list in the chapter on estrogen:

- Protects women against cancer.
- Restores libido.
- Helps normalize blood sugar.
- Normalizes zinc and copper levels.
- Precursor to estrogen and testosterone.
- Increases breakdown of fat therefore promotes energy through fat loss.
- Increases the breakup and removal of small blood clots.
- Increases thyroid hormone efficiently.
- Protects against fibrocystic breast disease.
- Maintains the endometrium of the uterus and protects against both breast and uterine cancer.
- It is a natural diuretic.
- It is a natural antidepressant.
- May be effective in stopping migraine headaches.

- Urinary tract infections are rare in women using natural progesterone.
- Fibroid tumors cease growing and usually decrease in size or disappear with the use of natural progesterone.
- Progesterone stimulates new bone formation.
- It can be used to help regulate menstrual cycles.

The question now is, why not use natural progesterone? Many women have complained about the side effects of the synthetic version progestin and now demand the natural progesterone. Research has shown the tremendous health benefits of the natural progesterone, however, the administration and use is usually consumer driven, demanded by well educated, and well informed men and women. This is because natural progesterone allows you to feel much better than any of the synthetic progestins, besides the fact that it is also much safer. Even though natural progesterone is better, many in the medical community do not seem to accept this. Natural progesterone cannot be patented; therefore there is no financial incentive for the drug companies to promote it. Natural progesterone has a very mild tranquilizing effect and enhances overall well-being.

Progesterone is the most versatile hormone in the human body. It is manufactured in the human body by both men and women. Natural progesterone can be compounded by a pharmacist and I prefer the cream to the capsules or sublingual tablets. It has a half life of about eight hours so should be used twice daily. The levels should be measured by a physician to assure the level is within your therapeutic range. It is a major regulator of estrogen, testosterone, and cortisol. As with most hormones, progesterone is manufactured from cholesterol. There are precursors to progesterone e.g. wild yam (dioscorea) a vegetable steroid that when added to hydrochloride acid and warm water converts to natural progesterone. However wild yam is not always dependable and some cannot convert it to the usable form. There is little evidence that wild yam by itself can be converted to progesterone. The daily production of progesterone in a menstruating woman rises from 2-3 mg. per day to 30 mg. per day a week or so after ovulation. If an egg is not fertilized, progesterone production falls rapidly back to 2-3 mg level. It is that sudden drop in progesterone that causes menstruation. Progesterone produces no secondary sexual characteristics and it causes neither feminization nor masculinization. It is carried through the circulatory system into the liver where it is eventually excreted through the urine. A woman should regulate her menstrual cycle by adding natural progesterone cream on days 10-12 through days 26-28 of her cycle. Use at least 1/4 Teaspoon twice a day transdermally (applied to the skin). It can be applied under the breasts or in the vaginal area.

Now let's move on to a deeper level of knowledge. Progesterone levels are much higher in adult men then they are in postmenopausal women. There are progesterone binding sites on the sperm, however; infertile males have defects on the progesterone sites of their sperm. If you examine the chart and compare the differences between men and women you will see the definite advantages that progesterone plays in men. It is that advantage that causes the more gradual increase based on the timeline. Remember that progesterone has no feminizing effects on men like estrogen does. Progesterone regulates the calcium uptake in the sperm as well as playing a very important role in the strength of bones. When males go through andropause (the male equivalent of menopause), there is a decrease in progesterone production. The adult male should apply natural progesterone to the scrotal skin and there will be marked improvements in mood, libido and DHEA levels. Males should also use 1/4 teaspoon twice daily. Natural progesterone does not interfere with the body's ability to produce it; there is simply an additive factor. Natural progesterone is the only hormone that does not suppress the body's own production. I personally use it and find the same advantages that we are discussing right now.

As you know, prostate cancer is strongly associated with testosterone when the body converts it into dihydrotestosterone. This conversion can be largely prevented by the following:

- Saw palmetto six tablets daily depending on concentration. I never recommend taking the minimum amount. Take at least 160 mg twice daily if you start this regimen early in life, at

the latest by the age of 50 you will prevent and abundance of problems later on in life.
- Pygeum also tends to alleviate prostate problems.
- Lycopane is the active part of the tomato.
- Extract of pumpkin seed oil.
- Zinc.

Progesterone may increase the amount of testosterone significantly. That is why the above becomes very important and if you choose to take only one of these supplements listed above, then make it saw palmetto. It is inexpensive and is proven to show dramatic results. Now for the best news about progesterone and men. Progesterone blocks the conversion of testosterone to dihydrotestosterone. Progesterone also helps to prevent prostate enlargement.

Now back to the discussion about women. The major cause of uterine cancer is excess estrogen without the constant use of natural progesterone. Natural progesterone may not only prevent cancers of the breast and uterus but may also prevent the return of cancer and or the spread of cancer. Dr. John Lee believes "Having an adequate level of natural progesterone balances the excess estrogen and may prevent up to 90% of breast cancers".

Endometriosis is often an extremely painful disorder. Medical treatments using synthetic estrogen and progesterone have brought little success. In fact it

could even aggravate the condition. The best
treatment for endometriosis is pregnancy after which
the problem usually subsides. However, having
children is a life choice that you should make
because you want children, not because you want to
solve a health problem. Another treatment that
works well is to use natural progesterone from the
10th to the 28th day of the menstrual cycle in
adequate doses. This usually relieves the problem.
Very few times will you need to resort to surgical
procedures. Antioxidants such as coenzyme Q10
(100-200 mg daily) L-Carnatine, alpha lipolic acid,
vitamins A, C, E, and selenium may have beneficial
effects. I also recommend four capsules of
magnesium citrate. Another interesting note that you
may want to consider is the fact that during
menstruation, coitus can push secretions back
through the fallopian tubes into the pelvic cavity
aggravating the incidences of endometriosis.

Many women have a small to moderate amount of
fibrocystic breast disease. It may show itself in the
form of tenderness or soreness of the breasts. This
to may be caused by the imbalance of estrogen and
progesterone, especially the over activity of two types
of estrogen, esterone and estradiol. The major
treatments include:

- Avoidance of any caffeinated products i.e.
  coffee and any caffeinated sodas.
- Discontinue the use of natural progesterone, it
  may take several months for the fibroids to
  disappear. Then you can resume its use at a
  lower dosage.

Uterine fibroids are the most common form of tumors in the female urogenital tract. They have been known to grow to huge proportions. "Believe it or not," the largest uterine fibroid ever recorded was in the range of 100 pounds. They may also cause excessive bleeding and irregular bleeding. As many as one-half of all women have fibroids. After menopause most fibroids shrink providing the woman does not take estrogen. Some of the causes of uterine fibroids are:

- Late pregnancy (after the age of 35).
- Too much estrogen.
- Imbalance of estrogen and progesterone, excess fat and fatty tissue produces estrogen, augmenting the imbalance.

Some of the common treatments for uterine fibroids are:

- Surgical removal of the uterus.
- Removal of the fibroids by surgery.
- Anti-hormone therapy to reduce estrogen e.g. Tamoxifen.

Surgery may increase the risk of heart disease by 300%, because the uterus produces prostacyclin, which protects a woman against heart disease. Sexual pleasure may be impaired and it opens the door for the bladder to prolapse. These tumors are usually the result of estrogen dominance, so when treated with natural progesterone, the fibroid tumors usually cease growing and decrease in size. It is a clear cut decision that the treatment for all fibroids should be natural progesterone cream. Other suggestions that may be very beneficial are as follows:

- Try to lose excess weight as fatty tissue produces estrogen.
- Exercise as much as possible because inactivity allows the overproduction of fat which stimulates estrogen production.
- Have a thyroid test because an under-active thyroid allows the overproduction of fat which stimulates estrogen production.
- Take a good B complex without PABA or folic acid.
- Take two tablets of milk thistle (silymarin) three times per day. This will increase the liver function enabling the liver to break down toxins and estrogen.

Testosterone and Andropause

Allow me to begin with a case illustration. One of my best friends is in his early 40s. He was a champion boxer and has kept his body in almost perfect condition. You would almost think that he was a candidate for a body building competition. His heart just began hurting, so he began a series of all of the diagnostic heart tests that were available. He had CAT scans, thallium tests, ultrasound tests and everything looked great. He had no cholesterol deposits and all of his veins and arteries were clear. There wasn't a diagnostic test that even showed the

slightest sign of a problem. Still the pain. Finally,
they recommended a psychiatrist. He was in to good
a condition and diagnostic tests showed no sign of a
problem, so in their estimation, it must be a mental
condition. One of his friends casually recommended
that he go to Palm Springs California and have them
look at the possibility of hormone replacement.
When he arrived in Palm Springs, he went to the
Palm Springs Life Extension Institute, which was run
by Dr. Edmund Chein M.D.. After an examination, Dr.
Chein found that his testosterone level was at an
extremely small percentage of what it should be. In
fact, it was so low, that Dr. Chein didn't even
understand how his heart was beating at all. The Dr.
wouldn't even allow him to leave the office before
administering testosterone. Within hours, the pain
was gone. The pain and heart problems were solved
and remain so even today. He didn't need a
cardiologist, or a psychiatrist, neither of which could
help him. Just a note for you to remember, you can
function fine sexually on a very low testosterone
level, but your heart can not functioning properly, if
at all. This gentleman is back in top form, free of
pain and thanking the creator that there was
someone out there who could help him. He now has
his hormone levels restored to that of a 25 yr. old
and he looks like a 25 yr. old also.

Testosterone levels are easily correctable. It is
administered in the form of injections or oral
supplements. These two methods of testosterone
replacement are prescribed as synthetic testosterone
or natural testosterone. The preferred choice is

natural testosterone gel applied to the skin. Do not use testosterone on the scrotum, but rather on the inside of the upper leg (inner thigh). Never use testosterone if you already have prostate cancer. It has never shown to cause prostate cancer but it may cause the over accelerated growth of a tumor. That is the reason for an annual PSA test when using testosterone. Here are just some of the advantages of the use of testosterone:

- Increased energy.
- Increased sexual capacity in both men and women.
- Increased strength and libido.
- Restoration of muscle tone.
- Improvement of moods and overall well-being.
- Improved cardiovascular health and function.
- Beneficial effect on glucose tolerance.
- It may stop angina pectoris.
- Restores positive nitrogen balance causing a positive protein synthesis in the liver decreasing the production of hormone binding globulins.
- It stimulates the erythropoietin in the kidneys. Erythropoietin is a hormone that stimulates red blood cell production.
- Testosterone has a protective effect against auto-immune diseases e.g. lupus, Crohn's disease, and rheumatoid arthritis.
- It can lower cholesterol.
- Testosterone can normalize abnormal heart arrhythmias.

- It can improve diabetic retinopathy.

As the first testimony proved, the most significant role of testosterone is protecting men against cardiovascular disease. Testosterone is responsible for the sex drive in both men and women. Women will use considerably smaller amounts of testosterone, but diagnosing the proper amount is simple for your physician to determine. Women will experience many of the same physical results as men do when taking testosterone. It is extremely important for women who have auto-immune diseases to supplement their testosterone levels. Your local physician may not have researched testosterone use for women and will tell you that, "It will just grow facial hair". If you get an answer like that, I recommend that you visit one of the clinics listed at the end of this discussion on hormone replacement. These people are experts in this area and have dedicated their lives to making you happy and healthy through natural means.

Now, here is a little history on testosterone that may be of some interest to you. Since the beginning of time, scientists have known that the removal of testicles takes away the vitality of men and animals. Male servants of the Chinese Empress were castrated to make them into eunuchs, which made them more submissive. In biblical times (the Old Testament) the Kings servants were eunuchs, thus leaving no possibility for them to be a problem to the Kings many wives. In 1934 a scientist isolated the testosterone molecule and won the Nobel Prize in

1935. Then in 1935, research revealed testosterone was able to stop angina. In 1951, it was proven to increase nitrogen balance. This discovery proved testosterone benefited cardiovascular disease through protein synthesis. Bone, ligament and muscle are all made up of protein and can be repaired with positive protein synthesis. Here are some interesting statistics:

- At forty years of age 2% of the male population becomes impotent
- By age 50 – 5%.
- By age 60 – 18%.
- By age 70 – 27%.
- By age 80 – 75%.

Research has shown that men with high testosterone levels live longer, healthier lives and maintain sexual potency. Stress is also significant, in that it reduces testosterone secretion. This reduction is caused by stress induced release of hormones e.g. cortisol, adrenalin and non-adrenalin which have opposing catabolic reactions. This can cause an imbalance that can affect cardiovascular disease. So in order to solve a lot of problems, try to avoid stress as much as possible, Good Luck.

Now, recent data suggests that testosterone is not the cause of prostate cancer. There are some things that you can do to protect yourself from prostate cancer. As men age, their body turns the testosterone (beneficial) into dihydrotestosterone which is the risk factor in cancer of the prostate gland. Here are some other known risk factors:

- Smoking.
- Obesity.
- High fat intake.
- Poor nutrition.

Here are some treatments that you can use to aid in stopping the conversion of testosterone into dihydrotestosterone:

- Eat as many soy products as possible. Mix 2 tablespoons of pure soy powder in a glass of water twice a day.
- Use antioxidants such as vitamin A, C, E, along with Selenium and zinc.
- Take at least six tablets of saw palmetto every day. This is probably the most important treatment as it blocks the conversion of testosterone into dihydrotestosterone. It is very effective, and you will see the results almost immediately. It will almost completely eliminate the need to get up for nocturnal visits to urinate.
- Take 4 tablets of Lycopene each day.
- There is an extract called pygeum that is extracted from the bark of an African tree that has a healing effect on the prostate gland. This extract can actually shrink the size of the prostate through an anti-inflammatory action. I have been using this product with excellent results for over 10 years. Take 2 - 4 tablets daily.

The alternative medical treatment to the above is a prescription drug called Proscar, which is very costly and produces some very serious side effects. However, there are three natural substances, Pygeum, Lycopene and Saw Palmetto. They are synergistic and give you a great deal of relief regarding problems associated with the prostate gland with no known side affects. Consider the word synergistic in this instance, when all of the above substances are taken together they have a much greater effect then if they are taken separately. Each drug taken by itself will produce a factor of 1, but if they are taken together they produce a factor of 10, that is the synergistic effect.

Before we leave the subject on testosterone, I want to discuss with you further the value of testosterone replacement for women, as it is also a female hormone. Even though women take estrogen and progesterone, they still may not feel completely normal because as they lack testosterone, they may lack energy and not have the physical and emotional health that they deserve. Upon starting testosterone replacement you can expect to see some of these wonderful changes:

- Enhancement of sexual drive.
- Relief of menopausal symptoms.
- Increase in energy.
- Strengthening of bone structure and the prevention of osteoporosis.
- Sense of well-being.

- A renewed zest for life. Improvement of the skin.
- Improvement of the musculature.

Many women have been given the wrong information about testosterone, thinking that it might make them more masculine. This can not be further from the truth, it increases libido and when it is administered under the supervision of a knowledgeable physician, you do not have to worry about it causing you to grow facial hair, or any other side effects. To conclude, testosterone is produced by the ovaries, and adrenal glands which will tend to decrease fat, and give you more energy and a feeling of well-being. It also extends life and decreases diseases associated with aging, such as heart disease. It also enhances your memory and tends to protect against Alzheimer's disease. I hope that I have convinced you to contact your physician or one of the longevity clinics. I have only opened the door for you, it is entirely up to you to step through.

Thyroid Hormone

The thyroid gland functions to supply thyroxine which to a large degree controls one's metabolism. Thyroxine regulates the oxygen content of the cells. Hypothyroidism means the patient is a slow oxidizer and there is insufficient oxygen. Hyperthyroidism means there is an abundance of oxygen and the thyroid gland is overactive. Insufficient thyroxine causes clotting and thickens blood, which is a leading cause of heart attacks. Too much thyroxine thins the blood and could cause hemorrhaging. It can also cause anxiety, high body heat, rapid pulse and loss of hair. Hypothyroidism may cause low body temperature, dry skin, mental sluggishness and dark circles under the eyes.

The conventional treatments for hypothyroidism is replacing the missing hormone with levothyroxine (a synthetic hormone). This can have side affects e.g. headache, digestive problems, and tremors, rapid heartbeat and bone loss. Anti-thyroid medications may cause allergies in humans and cancer in lab rats.

Radioactive iodine is a very exact science in which too much thyroid tissue can be destroyed or possibly not enough. Iodine from kelp, seaweed, sea salt (only use sea salt) and fish balance thyroid function. Soybeans and their products e.g. tofu and soymilk contain thyroid-depressing elements and tend to alleviate overactive thyroid problems. An effective natural thyroid replacement is Armor Thyroid but it must be prescribed by a physician. I must warn you that you need to do all of these suggestions under the strict guidance of a physician. A physician who specializes in complete hormone replacement therapy.

An early indication of thyroid problems is, if your early morning temperature before getting out of bed is below 97.6, you should definitely be evaluated. A temperature less than that indicates thyroid deficiency. Supplementation with a natural thyroid product, which is a combination of T3 and T4 hormones might be used. The synthetic thyroid replacements are not nearly as effective as their natural counterparts. Patients who switch from the synthetic form to the natural form notice marked improvement in their symptoms. To help you to understand a little of the chemistry here, I will try to conclude my observations with the fact that the thyroid hormone initially produced is a storage form called T4. Then the body converts the T4 form into the active form called T3, by an enzyme. As we age, the production of T4 diminishes, therefore,T3 also diminishes. The mitochondria needs thyroid hormone T3 to burn oxygen and produce ATP, which is your energy fuel. No ATP, no energy, it's just that simple. Now, ATP goes through what is known as the Kreb cycle. As energy is produced, ATP is turned into ADP and the energy is spent. It is revitalized as it goes through the Kreb Cycle which is driven by enzymes that convert the spent energy (ADP) back to ATP and you are now ready to go again. This cycle is largely controlled by hormones, that is why I recommend hormone replacement. Let's get you going and feeling like you did 20 or 30 years ago, it can happen.

Thymic Hormone

The thymus gland is located in the thorax behind the sternum or breast bone. Its function is to produce thymic hormone, which is essential for normal immune function. Its size is large at birth but atrophies completely by the second decade of life. Its function is to nurture the lymphocytes and it does so by secreting a hormone. The T lymphocytes, which are programmed by proteins from the thymus gland, are white blood cells which fight viral infections including cancer cells. This protein has been scientifically proven to stimulate T4 helper, while blood cells which locate and recognize foreign bodies e.g. viruses, cancer cells, hepatitis, and most other virus caused diseases. Once the T4 cells locate the foreign virus, or bacterium, it sends out an army of T8 cells to destroy them. Most of us have abnormal cells such as cancer or tumor cells, but only 1 in 25 or so develops cancer. Those that do not develop cancer have a strong immune response which destroys the abnormal cells. This immune response is programmed by the thymus gland. Without specific thymus protein, the T4 cells can not do their job and the T8 (killer cells) are not called in to do battle. In the last few years, four distinct thymic preparations have been identified. They are Thymosin, Thymulin, Thymopoietin and Thymic Humeral Factor. Thymosin is extracted from bovine (cow) thymus. It has displayed very strong stimulant affects on T-lymphocyte mediated immunity. Thymulin is a protein extracted from pig thymus tissue. This thymic hormone stimulates T8 (killer cell) activity. This hormone requires zinc in order to be fully activated. Thymic Humeral Factor is an extract of Thymus. Hepatitis B seems to respond to this hormone. Thymopoietin is a protein from the cow thymus gland.

In conclusion, thymus produced protein appears to be a key to good health and immunity. It will positively affect longevity and the quality of life. I use a product called Biopro-protein A. It is packaged in single doses and is sublingual. I use one packet a day. This product might require a prescription. Some companies may produce a thymic hormone that does not require a prescription.

I would like to summarize the values of hormone replacement. Most of the symptoms of aging are drastically reduced by total hormone replacement. Despite all of the evidence available, hormone replacement is often overlooked, misdiagnosed, given inadequate treatment, or no treatment at all. The last 10 years have shown drastic improvement in the affects of hormone replacement. The price of hormone replacement has gone down considerably in the last few years. This science is not commonly practiced and physicians need collaborative practice arrangements to meet the patient's needs. Individuals are being seriously untreated, even though effective treatments are available. Many of the treatments are not paid for by your insurance companies or Medicare. I spent a great deal of time dealing with physicians that represent insurance companies and was commended for a great presentation, but was still told, "Sorry, you will still have to pay". I thought that I had adequately presented the facts that would save insurance companies a great deal of money. I guess that you can deduce that I truly won the battle, but lost the war.

With the hope of not being redundant let me again review the advantages of hormone replacement:

- Increased breakdown of fat.
- Increased cardiovascular function.
- Increased energy.
- Improved quality of life.
- Increased muscle size and strength.
- Prevents osteoporosis and in some cases reverses osteoporosis.
- Increases bone growth by about 2% per year.
- Increased lung function.
- Increased renal function.
- Improved skin thickness.
- Improved memory.
- Increases immunity to most diseases.
- Improves wound healing.
- Increases life expectancy.

Exercise drastically benefits from hormone replacement. It also enhances your sense of well-being and decreases weight which is one of America's worst plagues. We live in a country where some 25-30% of the population borders on obesity and that is one of the games that hormone replacement will help you to win.

I like to keep my diet high in:

- Protein.
- Fiber, fiber and more fiber.
- Fresh uncooked vegetables and fruits.

In the next few pages I will cover what my diet largely consists of. For those of you, who have read the whole book, feel free to skip the breakfast portion as it was already listed in the chapter on the prostate.

The following is what I consider the perfect health promoting breakfast. It also tests your courage and gag reflex, but if you can survive it, you might just learn to enjoy it. Well, maybe you will just get it down because of its fantastic health benefits. I have grown to enjoy it through the years. Well here it is, enjoy it for one reason or the other. I mix the following ingredients and drink. Honestly, it won't kill you, even if it looks that way. I have been drinking this for breakfast for more than 5 years now and don't plan to change, unless after research I find something better.

RECIPE
One glass of soymilk and one glass of water.
2 Tablespoons of 100% pure soy protein.
1 Teaspoon of Nutra Joint a high protein product made by Knox Gelatin can be purchased in most grocery stores.
1 Heaping Teaspoon of barley green. I'll admit this is the one ingredient that separates the men from the boys. If you just cannot deal with

the taste of the barley green, then use several stems of broccoli.

1/2 cup of fresh fruit (not frozen as it contains too much sugar) strawberries, blueberries, or raspberries. A 1/2 of a pear or an apple is a secondary choice.

2 Tablespoons of freshly ground flax seed.

1 Teaspoon of psyllium seed e.g. Metamucil or any other inexpensive brand.

Now toss all of the ingredients into the blender. Blend thoroughly, plug your nose and guzzle it down. I say guzzle because if you stop, you might never start again.

Now that you have choaked it down, here is why this is such a fantastic breakfast.

1. It contains all of the amino acids and is a complete source of protein.
2. It is also a great source of flavinoids.
3. It contains both soluble and insoluble fibers.
4. It lowers the LDL (bad cholesterol).
5. It raises the HDL (good cholesterol).
6. Protects bones and reduces the chances for osteoporosis.
7. Increases Energy.
8. Metabolizes slowly and keeps you from getting hungry.
9. It does not raise the insulin level but tends to keep it on an even plane, thus decreasing the buildup of fat. I will cover this in more detail in the chapter on diabetes.
10. It contains all of the ingredients that cancer hates.

11. Your bowels will move more often, thus decreasing colon problems.
12. Your glycemic index will be less than 19%, and that makes even oatmeal, at 49%, look like a chocolate sundae.
13. It is highly anti-inflammatory.
14. It will clean your intestinal wall.
15. It will cause your body to eliminate more cholesterol by increasing the production of bile.

Now another of the important benefits of this breakfast is in your personal pride. As I will wager that most of you will only try this drink once and say, "I would rather have cancer than drink this crap again". Please listen, it will get easier every time that you drink it. And if you give it a chance, you will feel so much better that you won't even hate me anymore for influencing you to try it. I have even convinced my wife to drink it. However, sometimes she slips in a banana for flavor, which isn't the best thing to do because of the sugar content. But I am very proud that she sticks with it, so I let her get away with a banana or two. I have said many times that I would eat dirt if that is what it would take to stay healthy or to feel good. You may not agree right now but, if you have ever had a relative that has contracted a serious disease and have seen their suffering you will start to drink this concoction every chance that you will get. Hey you can do it! Just keep trying.

Now for lunch, this is where I get to start enjoying my food a lot more. I sometimes eat two either poached or in a sandwich. If you can find eggs from range chickens, that are fertile, these are the best. In the past we used to believe that eggs raise cholesterol, but one of the most respected cardiologists in the world recommends for his heart patients to eat 2 – 6 eggs each day. Egg whites are a nearly perfect protein and yolks even though they contain cholesterol, also have a cholesterol lowering agent. I also enjoy fresh fruits and vegetables e.g. carrots, celery, cabbage and what ever I can find to toss in my lunch box. Sometimes I have a little cottage cheese or tofu with fresh fruit on it.

For dinner I really enjoy eating, as my options are much greater. I enjoy all kinds of food, fish. chicken and turkey are fine and occasionally a steak is also fun to enjoy. Now you may say no to any red meat, and I will respect you for that, but I believe a small amount of red meat is very beneficial to your health. I even allow myself to eat a piece of pie with ice cream once in a while. Try to avoid the crust if it was made with margarine. Please know that butter is a much better fat than a hydrogenated fat. A hydrogenated fat is very difficult for your body to break down because of the absence of the double bonds in the long chain molecules of the fatty acids. I always try to avoid prepared frozen meals of any sort as they are usually full of salt and have much less nutritive value than fresh foods. The same fits for most canned foods, if you can find me a healthy soup, "not full of salt" let me know. Your body recognizes very little value from quick foods.

Now, if you do screw up and go on a burger binge, here is how to get out of trouble. Go home and put 3 - 4 Tablespoons of freshly ground flax seed in a glass of water and drink it. It will tend to soak up the fat (the kind of fat that you do not want), it cleans your intestines and goes a long way to undo any further damage. So, if you are feeling a little guilty about that piece of pie or cake, remember how much you enjoyed it and go ahead and use your flax seed as it is a great aid in helping you to stabilize your sugar levels. In fact, if you indulge in two pieces of pie put the flax seed in a glass of soymilk which will raise the protein level and again you will have solved your problem. The one thing that is sometimes difficult to get out of your system is a meal high in sodium (lots of salt). If this happens, I recommend that you take some extra magnesium citrate, or a mixture of calcium and magnesium citrate. Always remember the word citrate, because some forms of calcium and magnesium are of very little value. I could give you a very long grocery list of foods to eat and not to eat, but then I would just be trying to make you a slave to a diet. Instead, I have given you a few secrets on how to get out of trouble when you over indulge, which you will, hey so do I, so please utilize that knowledge and remember that too much of anything, even a good thing isn't good for you. Everything in moderation should be your goal. Life can be fun, eating can be fun, with the possible exception of my advice on breakfast. But please don't let yourself down, not only will that breakfast drink allow you lots of freedom but, it can really improve the quality of your life.

Now as promised, here are some of the finest clinics for hormone replacement. There are others of course and you may find out about some other wonderful clinics, but these are the quality clinics that I know about.

1. Preventive Medicine Clinic of the Desert
   2825 Tahquitz Canyon
   Suite 200 Palm Springs Ca, 92262
   (706) 320-4292

2. Palm Springs Life Extension Institute
   2825 Tahquitz Canyon Bldg. #A
   Palm Springs Ca. 92262
   (619) 327-8939

3. Cenegenics Medical Institute
   8515 S. Rampart Blvd.
   Las Vegas Nevada 89145
   (702) 240-4200

Cancer

I'll bet that chapter header made you stop and put out your cigarette! This word strikes fear in the hearts of those diagnosed with this disease. Many people think that if their parents had cancer, it is inevitable that they will eventually be sentenced to the same terrible fate. My intentions here are not to tell you what to do, but to give you information that may help you to make an informed choice concerning a treatment. Again, cancer is always much easier to prevent then it is to cure. If you are free of cancer now, this information may prevent you from ever concerning yourself with this problem, even if it happens to run in your family history. I will guide you through the maze of information that is available. You will also discover some new innovations that are not even available yet. Please let me repeat one thing, many of the same things that cause heart disease also cause cancer. The research that I have done here may save your life as 80-90% of all cancers are preventable. If you have cancer, I plan to give you every tool that I know of, for you to put in your arsenal to destroy this horrible disease. This chapter will not only give you a proactive approach to cancer, but a preventable one also. If you have already contracted cancer, you will have many new treatments to consider that might just possibly give you a future to look forward to. If you follow some of these simple suggestions, you may be able to take control of your life and your fears might just turn into a feeling that you have beaten all of the odds. My primary purpose is to protect you first. However, there are several great treatments that just might facilitate the cure that you are so desperately looking for. The following suggestions will help you create a healthier lifestyle and environment that helps you prevent cancer from becoming a fact of life.

Now let's cover some of the things that you should do everyday in order to help your body prevent cancer. Soy has a very powerful anti-cancer activity. Soy contains the inhibitors and anti-oxidant activity that turns off the signals that allow cancer cells to multiply. It also guards against free radical activity, which causes the DNA to mutate and start normal cells down the road to cancer. It is also proven to inhibit angiogenesis, which prevents the growth of new blood vessels that feed tumors. Asian women have a significantly lower rate of breast cancer. It is largely believed to be caused by there large consumption of soy products. In the United States we can expect 1 in 8 women to contract breast cancer. When Asian women come to the United States and begin to embrace the American fast food lifestyle their rate of breast cancer increases to approximately the same rate as American women. I do not believe that their DNA is different from ours, but I do believe their diet is different. So let's try to make sure that you get between 25 and 50 grams of soy protein every day. Here are some of the fun ways to eat soy products. Have some tofu with some fresh fruit on it, instead of cottage cheese (4 oz. equals 10 grams of protein). Drink soy milk instead of regular milk, (8 oz. of soymilk is also worth about 10 grams of protein). When you select a soymilk product, make sure that it contains about the same number of grams of protein as carbohydrates. Lastly, use 2 Tablespoons of pure soy protein powder in a glass of juice every day (this will achieve another 10 grams of protein).

Next you need to remember your flax. I have a small coffee grinder sitting on my counter and a jar of flax seed. When I drink a glass of water I grind 2-3 tablespoons of flax seed and add it to the water. I do this several times a day. Flax seed is one of the richest sources of plant lignins. There may not be a single nutritional supplement that can offer the same level of protection against cancer and other diseases as does freshly ground flax seed and a combination of flax seed oil. Flax seed contains 100-800 times more plant lignins then its closest competitors e.g. wheat bran, rye, millet, soybeans and oats. Flax lignins are weak estrogens and they may replace the more toxic forms of estrogen that are likely to increase the woman's risk of breast cancer. The effect of flax seed may react much like the prescription drug Tamoxifen but without the serious side effects. There is a substantial amount of research that has shown that flax seed lignins are changed by the bacterium in the human intestine to compounds which are extremely protective against cancer, especially breast cancer. Again, let me reinforce the word fresh when talking about ground seed or oil because flax seed contains highly polyunsaturated oil that is extremely susceptible to damage by heat, light and oxygen. Once damaged, it may form toxic molecules of lipid peroxides which do the body no good. Fresh flax has a nut like taste, but if it is stored too long in the ground form before being used, it begins to turn rancid and lipid peroxides are formed and you will find a bitter taste. The seed, before being ground keeps the oils fresh almost indefinitely. When you grind it, consume it as quickly as possible. Here are some more benefits you will receive from the use of flax seed. It helps the eyesight, liver function, arteriosclerosis, immune system function, production of energy, rheumatoid arthritis, depression, asthma, dry skin and it also helps in the absorption of calcium. Also let me recommend that the flax seed oil that you purchase should be fresh, you will find it refrigerated in your local health food store. When you bring it home make sure that you keep it refrigerated as well. I usually buy flax seed in 25 lb. bags and keep a small jar on the counter right beside my grinder, that way I can grind it fresh several times a day. You may not like the taste of flax seed at first but believe me, the more that you learn about its benefits, the better you will like it.

Some cancers are caused by heavy metals in your blood and liver. Rather than cover the elimination of this problem again, please re-read the chapter on chelation. I try to keep the heavy metals out of my system by taking a treatment every 60 days. Chelation is very important for men as the menstruation cycle in women is of great benefit in ridding the body of heavy metals thus allowing women to make new blood every month. It also greatly benefits men to give blood. Not only will it benefit you by removing heavy metals from your system and producing new blood, but it may even save someone else's life.

There are some vegetables that are considered to be of an anticancer benefit. Broccoli, cauliflower, cabbage, and brussel sprouts should be considered a staple in your diet. Serve them regularly, raw, slightly steamed or in a stir fry with a small amount of olive oil.

Now here is a list of some anti-oxidants that are helpful in fighting cancer.

1. Coenzyme Q 10 is a key anti-oxidant. Take 200-300 mg every day. It is expensive so most vitamin companies add between 3-10 mg in their tablets and this is just about enough to make you believe that you are actually taking it.

2. Vitamin E take 1200 I .U .daily. Always remember to take some selenium with your vitamin E, as it is very poorly assimilated without selenium. Vitamin E is extremely important, as it functions in the fatty tissue. This vitamin is critical when it comes to preventing mutations and free radical damage. It prevents normal cells from becoming cancerous. It also acts as a poison to cancer cells. Vitamin E also prevents you from environmental toxins and stabilizes cell membranes. Please note, that very high doses of vitamin E could produce toxic reactions. Cancer patients often show very low levels of vitamin E, because it is used up in stopping free radicals that are produced during malignant conditions. I would like to tie selenium into this research on vitamin E. We obtain this mineral from green leafy plants. However, studies have found that areas where the soil is

poor in this nutrient people are more likely to develop cancer as well as multiple sclerosis. Selenium is synergistic with vitamin E and increases the power and development of cancer fighting cells. We only need a small amount of selenium 100-150 mcg. a day. Selenium is also important for auto-immune diseases and increases the level of sperm count. It must be noted that large doses of selenium may be very toxic, in this case the more the better does not fit! The Journal of The American Medical Association shows a substantial reduction in cancer mortality and cancer incidence in patients receiving selenium supplementation. The form of vitamin E that I use contains selenium.

3. Vitamin C (Ester form). I recommend at least 5000 mg per day. Vitamin C. protects against cancer in many ways. It increases the B-cells, T-cells and macrophages. B-cells produce antibodies that mark cancer cells for destruction and T-cells actually destroy the cancer cells. The macrophage consumes the cancer cells and digests them. It is also very effective in neutralizing free radicals and it increases the cancer fighting anti-oxidant glutathione.

4. Alpha Lipolic Acid (ALA), is the substance that ties all of the other vitamins together. ALA is extremely effective when used in conjunction with vitamin E, and vitamin C, as it can recycle them to be reused by your system. When ALA is present, vitamin C can do its job over and over

again. ALA also works in concert with vitamin E, because it acts much the same way as vitamin E. ALA is an incredible anti-oxidant even when used alone, but when used with other vitamins, it will work in a synergistic way. To understand the importance of ALA, I strongly recommend that you read as much as you can on the subject as soon as possible. ALA is so potent, that it not only destroys free radicals, but it may play an important role in neutralizing the toxic effects of radiation and chemotherapy. Researchers dealing with the Chernobyl nuclear accident in Russia, found ALA, together with vitamin E, was extremely effective against radiation poisoning and when administered, abnormal liver and kidney functions were corrected. Now, let's take a look at another function of ALA. It is a chelating agent for heavy metals. Chelation means that ALA has the ability to grab onto metallic substances, and neutralize them, thereby excreting them from the body. Excess amounts of heavy metals increase oxidative problems, and increase the levels of free radicals. There are several metals that cause serious body damage, such as excessive iron, cadmium, lead, mercury and arsenic. Mercury is possibly the most toxic of these heavy metals. There are many sources responsible for allowing mercury into your body e.g. some cosmetics, printing inks, paints, plastics, wood preservatives and the worst of these culprits are the fillings in your teeth, which may be up to 50% mercury. Farmers used to use mercury substances to treat seeds to kill the fungi; however, I believe that mercury is now entirely eliminated from seed treatments. Other sources may be fish and other meats, but if you knew about every source of mercury you probably would not eat anything, so let us try to eliminate the problem another way by taking sufficient amounts of ALA. Please do not forget about the EDTA chelation, as discussed in the chapter on the heart. The two are synergistic. However, ALA has demonstrated itself to chelate high levels of mercury in the blood stream and excretes it by way of the gall bladder. ALA also chelates arsenic, and other heavy metals found in smog, tobacco smoke, and pesticides. ALA also chelates arsenic from the blood and tissues.

Note: a diet low in sodium, fats and high in potassium along with the above mentioned vitamins are of great significance in reducing the instances of cancer of the brain, liver, and melanomas.

The development of cancer is usually a very slow process that may take many years or even decades to develop. A tumor is not cancer, but it may turn into cancer with time. There must be a mutation, (abnormal change in the genetic structure) for cancer to take hold in your body. If I could find one thing that would stop the mutation of DNA material everybody could say goodbye to cancer forever. If we could just possibly find the formula to stop any and all of the changes in genetic material, you could probably have the ability to achieve life spans that have been mentioned only during biblical times, which could be hundreds of years. The best efforts to date, are to keep up on the things that change your genetic material. Of course there are a number of factors that cause the reaction of carcinogens, most of them you can control, some of them you can't. I believe the major cause of carcinogens is the introduction of free radicals that cause mutations. That is the primary reason for using the best anti-oxidants you can, because anti-oxidants destroy free radicals before they can do their destructive damage to your body.

I would like to define cancer and look at some of the traditional treatments. My wife is a cancer survivor and this fact stimulates me to find the answers, so that she will never have another recurrence of the problem in the future. After defining what cancer is, I will show you some treatments that will help your body to destroy any malignancy that may be there. I will also answer the question of what I would do, should I ever get cancer. First, cancer is a malignant tumor of cells that have the potential of almost unlimited growth. Should it metastasize (spread) to other organs, it may become deadly. We all have cancer cells, many times over our lifetime, but we don't all get cancer. Why? The reason is that our immune system is normally set up to destroy these abnormal cells. We only get cancer when our immune system is impaired. You are usually born with a healthy immune system that has a good chance to improve quickly, especially if the mother nurses the baby and passes her immunity to the child while nursing him and giving him her colostrum (which is found in mother's first milk). When your immune system is impaired by poor diet and other previously mentioned problems, the door is opened not only to cancer, but also to a host of many other diseases. The actual disease involves an abnormal gene or genes in a cell and a deficient immune system that allows these abnormal cells to proliferate. Some things that are dangerous to your immune system are:

- Smoking, this causes your body to be more deficient in oxygen and cancer does not like oxygen.
- Highly stressed jobs or lifestyles can also depress the immune system.
- Nitrites are extremely deleterious. Nitrites turn into nitrosamines which are highly carcinogenous. Please try to show me one processed meat that does not contain nitrites. You must forget about fast foods or highly processed foods. I have spent hours looking for one processed meat (from ham to baloney) and have not found one without nitrites. Processed meats have to be a thing of the past, forever. I personally feel that our rush to fast foods is destroying our bodies from within. We really don't need terrorists as long as we have the fast food chains, they are doing a lot better job.

- Some tests have shown that a virus infection can disrupt the DNA; this is one of the few things that you may not be able to control. But a healthy immune system, which I am trying to help you develop, should stop the serious effects of a depressed immune system before they happen.
- Some toxins in the environment previously mentioned, could also start the degradation of your genetic material.
- X-rays can definitely cause the genetic material to mutate. Avoid them as much as possible. Now don't think that one x-ray will kill you, it may not even harm you, if I have a broken leg I would request an x-ray.
- Sunlight (ultraviolet rays) are not in your best interest. I try not to let the sunlight touch my skin, but don't go overboard here, just avoid sunburns and too much exposure.
- Lack of exercise can deprive your body of oxygen, thus allowing an additional opening to the problem. I usually exercise 3-4 times a week for 30 minutes.
- Please re-read the chapter on hormones, as synthetic estrogen is a total disaster when it comes to cancer-causing materials, especially to the breast and uterus.

Here are some conventional cancer treatments:
1. Surgery.
2. Radiation therapy.
3. Chemotherapy.

Let's examine all of the above treatments. I sincerely wish the conventional approach worked. In my research, I have found that there may be an 11% cure in rats. There has been no significant cut in the death rate since the 1950s. In fact, in the last 15 years, there has been a 5% increase in the death rate from cancer. Let's first look at surgery, excising the tumor with the hope of getting it all, problem? Cancer is not a localized affliction; it is a systemic disease that travels throughout the whole body. I am certainly not ruling out surgical procedures, but unless there is a major change in cancer prevention methods, in lifestyle and eating habits, then surgery may only be a short term solution.

Now let's look at a conventional helper to surgery. if surgery is not possible, radiation therapy may be used alone to try to make you well. Radiation creates increased free radicals, the very thing that you are trying to avoid. Oncologists hope that radiation therapy kills more cancer cells then normal cells and that the radiation will not start a new cancer. Progress is being made in making radiation more selective so it does not damage the surrounding organs. In my opinion radiation is far better than the next treatment to be discussed.

Following radiation, conventional doctors may inject chemotherapeutic drugs into the body. Here we again hope that chemotherapy will act more destructively only on the cancer cells than the normal cells. But what about the damage to the immune system; the very system that we are trying to save and strengthen to the point where it will destroy the cancer cells itself. What about the skin, hair and other tissues? Many times chemotherapy does more damage then good. Sometimes the bone marrow, which produces blood cells, ceases to function properly in the manufacture of red and white blood cells. The immune system often becomes so severely compromised, that the patient is now open to life threatening infections. Many feel the treatment is far worse than the cancer.

Now, this next treatment is new and may not even have FDA approval as of this date. You may be the first to even know about this great news that may make chemotherapy much more effective, without the serious side affects. On the very near horizon you will see a new formulation for existing anti-cancer chemotherapies, by utilizing a compatible immuno-beneficial drug delivery vehicle, containing polysaccharides of a certain structure for their respective sugar specific recognition. This will result in improved efficacy and decrease toxicity of the commonly used chemotherapy drugs. There are presently 3 chemotherapy drugs:
1. 5-Fluorauracil.
2. Adramycin.
3. Tuxol.

This new product not only improves the delivery system, but also improves the therapeutic value and drastically decreases the toxicity. The carbohydrate delivery molecules deliver the chemotherapy specifically to the cancer site, while isolating it to that target. Tests in animals show very dramatic results with this proprietary polysaccharide, when chemotherapy is administered at dosages exceeding the lethal dose. The mortality rate of the control group was 0 to 5, when 5 FU alone was administered, the mortality rate was 3 in 5 with severe signs of toxicity. When the drug was administered with Pro-Pharmaceuticals proprietary complex carbohydrate formula, no deaths resulted, 0 to 5. The mice not only gained weight, but also showed no signs of toxicity. When the amount of the chemotherapy drug was increased three times the lethal dose, the resulting 17 in 24 deaths for 5 FU alone, compared to 0 in 24 with the complex carbohydrate formula added. I realize that this is hard for you to believe and this may be the first time you have been introduced to anything like this, but if I have the slightest inclination to do chemotherapy, I would make sure, very sure that my oncologist went to www.pro-pharmaceuticals.com on the Internet and became very familiar with what is out there on this horizon. Just remember, you read about it here first, in the next book that I write, I will have a lot more information on this product, as I firmly believe it will have FDA approval very soon. This product is so revolutionary, that it will change the whole scenario of chemotherapy. This carbohydrate has the ability to recognize and adhere to specific binding sites on cancer cells and will make existing FDA approved cancer drugs much more effective, without the toxicity. In the next few months, you will also find out a lot of new information on the web that I cannot share with you at this time. I am so thankful that we now have something we can live with and may save many lives and still keep the lifestyle in good standing even during the treatments.

Now that you have seen some of the new technology that is out there, I would like to share with you some of the other treatments that are out there also. Please know, that the purpose of this book is not to recommend a treatment, but to educate you on the options that are available to you, so that you have the wisdom to make the correct decision.

If I had an incurable form of cancer, I would run, not walk, to a clinic in Houston TX. The clinic is run by Dr. S. R. Burzynski M.D. Ph.D. his address is
Burzynski Research Institute
12000 Richmond Ave.
Houston TX 77082
The phone number is: (281) 579-0111

Dr. Burzynski, has tested his treatment for some 20 years, with over 3,000 patients. This treatment has been proven to work consistently, sending deadly cancers into remission. The treatment he uses has virtually no side affects. He uses an anticancer drug called antineoplastin therapy. The FDA does not as of yet approve it, but in my estimation, this puts the FDA about 20 years behind.

Antineoplaston therapy, is unlike the chemotherapy agents currently in use that kill cancerous cells and healthy cells. Antineoplastons work on cancer cells to interrupt the activity of the ras oncogene, which causes the cells to divide endlessly. At the same time, antineoplastons stimulate p53 tumor suppressor genes, which tell the cells to undergo programmed cell death. Healthy cells remain unaffected under these processes.

Dr. Burzynski first discovered and named antineoplastons in the late 1960s. These drugs are safe and nontoxic, unlike traditional chemotherapeutic agents. Antineoplastons are comprised of compounds that occur naturally in the human body: amino acid derivatives and peptides from proteins and essential amino acids present in the diet of all biologic organisms. Antineoplastons are found in the blood of healthy persons and not in that of patients with cancer. Dr. Burzynski currently is using antineoplastons to treat cancer, HIV infection, and autoimmune diseases in 74 Phase II clinical trials.

The chemotherapeutic agents in common use today, cannot manage cancer for two reasons. First, they destroy healthy cells; therefore, these drugs cannot be taken over long periods, as can antineoplastons. Second, no one chemotherapeutic drug can kill all the cancer cells. Just as there are antibiotic-resistant strains of bacteria, cancer cell types exist that are resistant to specific chemotherapeutic agents. When a chemotherapeutic agent leaves 10% of cancer cells remaining, there may be billions of cells that survive, say, 100 billion. A different chemotherapeutic agent may kill 90% of those cells, leaving behind 10 billion cells. Still another agent may destroy 90 percent of those cells, leaving one billion cells. Of course, all the while, these cells are multiplying.

Because they reprogram cancer cells instead of killing them, antineoplastons do not stop working as do traditional chemotherapy agents. Therefore, antineoplastons are making cancer a manageable disease.

There are two genes that regulate cellular growth. Oncogenes cause cells to divide and grow and tumor suppressor genes stop cells from dividing when they should not. Antineoplastons reverse the deadly trend. The cancer stops growing and begins shrinking until it is finally gone, it works at the genetic level to normalize cell growth. It eliminates the cause of cancer. It is a sad day, when the medical profession convinces the FDA to fight a treatment like this, that costs much less than conventional treatments and has a 700% higher survival rate than surgery, radiation and chemotherapy. If you want to read a fascinating story of Dr. Burzynski's fight for survival in an effort to defend his cure, please go to his website and you will see some things that will seem almost unbelievable. This man has risked almost everything in order to offer his cure to everyone that could save millions of lives. The testimonials of some of his patients can be found at his website also. Some of his cases seemed completely hopeless. His priority is often with children, such as two your old Dustin, who had no chance of survival. Six months after he began treatment, his MRI was clear and he is a happy normal six year old now. I could fill this book with testimonials. If you think that, your case is impossible, please read all you can about this exceptional doctor and his treatment. This is truly one of the greatest medical breakthroughs of this century.

I would be remiss if I did not mention other treatments, e.g. there is a cancer treatment center that uses some of the best technology available, along with alternative treatments, that may augment the success of standard treatments. It is the Cancer Treatment Centers and you can call for further information at 1-800-675-3055. These cancer centers are unique, as they are on the cutting edge of traditional treatments e.g. surgical procedures, chemotherapy and radiation, as well as newer biological therapies and immunotherapy's. They treat the whole body, using dietary programs and vitamin and mineral supplements to help stimulate the immune system. Also available to the patient, is spiritual support if desired, as they believe in treating the mind, body and spirit together. You may ask if you can be treated with just naturopathic medicine, the answer is no, their program is designed to complement other medical treatments and not a mainline treatment for cancer. Their naturopathic physicians are well trained and all instructors are ND's, Ph.D.'s and M.D.s. These people are trained in clinical diagnosis, laboratory diagnosis, diagnostic imaging, botanical medicine, pharmacology, nutrition, physical medicine, homeopathy, surgical counseling an emergency training. You can find out additional information from the American Association of Naturopathic Physicians, 60001 Valley streets #105, Seattle, WA 98109. These people have made a tremendous contribution to the advancement of cancer treatments. Their goal is to treat the underlying cause of the disease and assist you in correcting the cause so you can completely recover. If you take the traditional treatments and just continued to do the same things that got you there, what advantage is there to just prolonging your life a short time so that you can go through it all over again. If symptoms only tell you that the body is in trouble, to heal the symptoms does not get at the cause. Causes occur at many levels and this treatment center uses therapeutic treatments that are synergistic with the healing process and minimize the risk of harmful effects. The patient is taught to take responsibility for his health. The physician is only the catalyst to inspire hope as well as understanding on how to stay healthy and free from cancer forever. The ultimate goal of naturopathic medicine is to prevent the disease. The real emphasis is on building health rather than fighting the disease. In treating the whole person (not just the disease) naturopathic practice includes, but is not limited to:

- Clinical nutrition.
- Botanical medicine.
- Physical medicine.

- Oriental medicine (do not be afraid of this concept, there is great value here).
- Psychological medicine including stress management and biofeedback.
- Homeopathic medicine.

Cancer Treatment Centers of America are located in Seattle WA, Tulsa OK, Zion IL and Goshen IN. The clinic based in Seattle, is an outpatient clinic. All patients work with a naturopathic physician and a medical oncologist. The state of WA is one of the few states where naturopathic medicine may be covered by insurance. However, the insurance may need to be a WA based company. If it is not WA based, you need to verify with your company, or you may be paying your expenses out of pocket. The clinic located in Tulsa OK, is a stand alone health care consulting firm, not associated with the hospital. The patient may consult with a naturopathic physician and have naturopathic medicine incorporated with their treatment. Classes are given at the hospital. The clinic based in Zion IL is a naturopathic program and is fully integrated into the medical program. I would like to recommend that you call the 1-800 number for information on each facility or go to www.CancerCenter.com I have tried to cover this option for you as best as I can in the smallest amount of space possible this treatment as well as the other treatments deserve at least another 20 pages.

The next treatment for you to consider involves Laetrile and the City of Hope clinic. Dr. Ernestro Contreras Sr. has treated more than 80,000

American patients since 1963. The cure rate at the Oasis of Hope is in the 17% range. You may not think that 17% is very good until you understand that some of the largest cancer centers in the world only have a cure rate of about 11%. I recall reading in a highly rated journal of medicine wherein doctors admitted their cure rate with conventional treatments was no better than Laetrile, the treatment of choice by Dr. Contreras. This doctor is extremely accomplished and qualified in not only his scientific background but also his spirit of care and love may be the most powerful medicine available at the Oasis of Hope.

The man that is now guiding the medical team at the Oasis of Hope is Dr. Francisco Contreras, a surgical oncologist. Along with his many medical degree's you will also find an atmosphere of caring and integrity.

Dr. Contreras calls his cancer therapy metabolic, because it enhances normal functions of organs while provoking an adverse environment for malignant cells. This is accomplished through a treatment program that provides detoxification, natural anti-tumor agents' e.g. Laetrile, whole foods and juices, emotional and spiritual support, and immune system stimulation from vitamins, minerals, phytochemicals and enzymes. An interesting note is that in 1981, 95% of his patients arrived at his clinic with stage IV cancers after conventional therapy had failed. In other words, doctors and conventional methods failed and they were sent home to die. Seeing this as their last hope, they arrived at the clinic and were treated by Dr. Contreras and his staff. After treatment, their overall five-year survival rate for all types of cancer was 30%. Malignancies in the lung, breast, colon and prostate were the most prevalent. Statistics for the clinic when compared to conventional statistics are dramatically better. The patients at the Oasis of Hope clinic have already had surgery, radiation, or chemotherapy. They had endured the hair loss, nausea, burns and devastation of energy and immune system functions. The next table has some interesting statistics:

Type Of Cancer	Number Of Patients	5 yr. Survival Rate	
		Oasis	Conventional
Lung Cancer	200	30%	2%
Breast Cancer	130	39%	21%
Colon Cancer	150	30%	8%
Prostate Cancer	600	86%	33%

The conventional group received no previous treatment to damage their general condition, they had a fresh start. The resulting a cure rate of lung cancer is very dramatic. I realize we all look for a 100% cure rate, but if that is not possible, we had better look for the next best option. The statement that I believe best fits this clinic is, "medicine is much more than just science, it is a healing art".

The good news is that now new U.S. laws will allow you to re-enter the country with your medications as long as you have a prescription. The Oasis of Hope offers a four-day treatment with a five-year follow-up program. There are three points that are highly recommended, should you choose the home treatment after your first four-day treatment:

- Adhere to the therapy.
- Communicate with the Oasis Hospital. There are some 21 phone calls over the five-year treatment to monitor your progress.
- Plan to visit the Oasis Hospital should modifications in your medications be necessary. These visits will be two days each and every six months during the five-year period, the visits are at no charge.

You can order the vitamin supplements, as you need them. Here is a list of what can be shipped:

- Preven-Ca.
- Vitamin A+E emulsion.
- Esther C.
- Shark cartilage.
- Enzymes.

They can be ordered by phoning 1-888-500-HOPE. Again, I would like you to know that this may be a controversial treatment, but many of the most effective cancer treatments are controversial. The conventional treatments have changed very little and still have the same side effects. They may not be controversial to the FDA, but may be very controversial to your body and future health. The Oasis of Hope does not limit its patients to either alternative or orthodox therapies but to the most effective and least harmful options. It is certainly worth a call from you to continue your education on the beneficial options.

MGN-3

MGN-3 might possibly be one of the most powerful immune system boosters available. This new product is used extensively in Japan. It is produced from extracts of mushrooms e.g. shiitake, kawaratake and suehirotake. Then it is integrated with the outer shells of rice bran. This substance increases the natural killer cells ability to recognize and destroy the cancer cells. MGN-3 can be used as a preventative as well as a possible cure for cancer. Natural killer cells provide protection for most other diseases as it increases interferon levels. Interferon by itself when administered is expensive but may be effective in many viral infections e.g. hepatitis. It also increases the activity of T cells and B cells. Another factor is that it is non-toxic in all cases that I have studied. It seems to work well for all types of cancer, as would a non-compromised immune system. In one such experiment, three grams of MGN-3 per day increased the natural cell activity by a factor of eight in just one week. In two months, it increased the killing activity of cancer cells by a factor of 20.

I recommend that anyone who has had cancer or has a family proclivity towards cancer to consider using

MGN-3 as a preventative. My wife has been taking MGN-3 as she has already had a bout with cancer. It seems to be very effective with breast cancer, cervical cancer, prostate cancer, leukemia and one of the most difficult cancers, myeloma. The reason my wife takes this product for prevention is because I personally believe it to be synergistic with the other recommended treatments I have suggested. Its value with prostate cancer is very significant as in one experiment 66% experienced complete remission. It is similar in its curative effects with ovarian cancer. If you have contracted cancer, take three grams of MGN-3 per day, and if you are taking it for prevention 1 g per day will suffice.

MGN-3 is fairly expensive, but is usually available at your local health food store, or they can order it for you. It may also be helpful for patients with HIV. This is the newest research available on this product at the time of this writing. However, breakthroughs are being discovered almost daily, and that is why you should go to the Internet, library, or your local health food store and ask them for the most recent publications on this subject. This is an extremely powerful stimulant to the immune system and is definitely worthy of your consideration. What we do know as of this writing is that MGN-3 is a potential biological response modifier, as it highly increases killer cell activity within two weeks. It represents a new immune therapeutic approach in the treatment of cancer. The killer cells each contain small granules. When the killer cell recognizes a cancer cell it attaches itself to the cells outer membrane and injects the granules directly into the interior of the cell where it explodes, destroying the cancer cells within five minutes. The killer cell then moves on to other cancer cells and repeats the process. There are also some additional advantages as an immune system booster:

- It increases the formation of tumor necrosis factors.
- It increases the level of interferon, a substance that inhibits the replication of viruses.
- It increases the activity of T-cells and B-cells.

One last consideration involves multiple myeloma (one of the deadliest forms of cancer). Here is a patient who underwent several months of chemotherapy, and his blood still showed markers for multiple myeloma, eight months after the chemotherapy. He began taking MGN-3 and in less than six months, his lab work showed no indication of cancer. Eight years later, he is one of very few ever to survive multiple myeloma. I could give you many similar examples where MGN-3 has appeared to save lives. I submit this information for your consideration, as how to best use this substance in your treatment or for the prevention of cancer. Remember, it is also synergistic with most of the conventional as well as other treatments listed in this book.

ALZHEIMER'S

When we began writing this book, we asked several people what health problems seemed to be plaguing our society today. In every questionnaire that we gave out, the one disease that was listed every time was Alzheimer's. if there were but one disease, and only one, that I could cure it would be Alzheimer's. The problem lies in the fact that no one knows for sure what causes this disease, that is what makes the cure so elusive. Over 100,000 Americans die annually from Alzheimer's. 10 percent of Americans over 65 have this disease. That number increases to 50 percent in those over 85 years of age. However, it can strike people even in their early 40s. If you have read this entire book, you have most of the tools needed and the knowledge to possibly prevent this disease. Again, maybe we know more about prevention then cure. The following list will give you some interesting factors that people with Alzheimer's almost always have:

- possible immune system malfunction. Prevention for this is covered throughout the book.

- Low levels of B-12, zinc, folic acid, vitamin A (including beta-carotene), vitamin C and E.

- High concentrations of aluminum and possibly mercury.

- Low estrogen levels (in women).

- Diets high in hydrogenated fats, low fiber diets.

As you reach middle-age, the onset of high cholesterol and high blood pressure seem to produce a 50 percent greater chance to develop Alzheimer's as you age. Researchers have discovered that when you have a cholesterol-managing gene called (the e4 version) you have a 50 percent chance of contracting Alzheimer's before the age of age 50. If you have that particular gene and consume a high-fat diet, your chances of getting Alzheimer's increases by 30 percent.

Methods Of Prevention

Eat a well-balanced diet, paying close attention foods containing:

- Vitamin A: green, yellow and orange fruits and vegetables; fish liver and fish liver oils, and garlic

- Vitamin B-12: brewer's yeast, clams, eggs, herring, kidney, liver, mackerel, milk and dairy products, seafood, and soybeans

- Vitamin C: berries, citrus fruits, green vegetables, cantaloupe, onions, persimmons, radishes, and tomatoes

- Vitamin E: leafy vegetables, oils (soybean, safflower, and corn), seeds and nuts, legumes, whole grains, and wheat germ

- Carotenoids: from Vitamin A foods

- Zinc: brewer's yeast, egg yolks, fish, lamb, legumes and beans, sunflower and other seeds, and whole grains

- Fiber: whole-grain foods, bran (try oats, flax or rice), and raw foods

Lower your fat intake to less than 30 percent of your diet.

Decrease your exposure to aluminum and mercury. Whether these mineral levels are high because of Alzheimer's disease or their being high as a factor of the disease is still being debated. Still, it couldn't hurt to avoid them if possible. Some products contain aluminum, others don't. If you want to minimize your exposure to aluminum, you'll have to read the labels on the following:

- Cookware

- Antacids

- Anti-diarrhea medicines

- Buffered aspirin

- Cans (acidic fruit juices, beer, and soft drinks); opt for bottles.

- Deodorants

- Douches

- Food additives (from cake mixes to pickling salts to cheese on your burger)

- Shampoos

- Baking Powder

- Aluminum Foil and foods packaged in aluminum

Coenzyme Q10

The use of CO Q10 has a fascinating list of biological wonders. It is a naturally occurring antioxidant in the body that is necessary for normal cellular reactions. When CO Q10 is boosted, so is your immune system potential. It was found at the New England Institute, that the life span of mice were increased by 50 percent with a supplement of CO Q10. It can also be said that the quality of their life also increased proportionately with their increased longevity. It is well known that adenosine triphosphate (the energy molecule to ATP) can not function properly without CO Q10. As we age, the body loses its ability to supply this much needed component. Before use you should consult a physician, however, I have been taking 100 milligrams a day for about 15 years now. It works very effectively as an antioxidant and protects the cells against free radicals. Dr. Carl Fulkers calculated that when the level of CO Q10 falls to a level of 25 percent, death is usually close at hand. When it falls lower than 75 percent of the normal overall average, diseases began to take hold of the body. This substance plays such a gigantic role in immunocompentence. It is also an important factor in preventing heart disease.

Human Growth Hormone (HGH)

Almost nothing escapes enhancement by the use of HGH. It increases the size of most organs, grows bones in young children, reverses bone deterioration in adults and can regenerate damaged brain tissues. Cass Terry from the Medical College of Wisconsin believes that HGH may have the same beneficial effect on the brain that it does on the heart. It is believed to reverse the decline in cerebral blood flow, which is a major cause of brain deterioration. Louis Aguillar and Jose Contu from the Institute for Research of Cell Regeneration in Guadalajara Mexico, reports that HGH helps motor activity by stimulating the growth of the myelin sheath on nerve cells. In Alzheimer's disease there is a loss in the number of neurotransmitters e.g. acetylcholine which stimulates growth hormones. Unbelievably by the time we are reaching the age of 90, our brain shrinks to the size it was when we were only three years old. With Alzheimer's, you also get a shrinking of the brain and hormone replacement therapy might help to restore the normal metabolism of the brain by adding water to the tissues and removing the fats. While trying to find the cure for this horrible disease, we cannot leave one stone unturned. And this stone

HGH, might just play a greater role then previously thought.

Ginkgo biloba

Ginkgo biloba is a plant extract that has several compounds that might have positive results on cells within the brain and the body. Ginkgo biloba assists the brain by increasing its supply of blood and oxygen. Nerve transmissions are improved and the ability of the brain to transmit impulses are improved thereby increasing short-term memory. Some 100,000 physicians worldwide prescribed ginkgo biloba as a regular part of their practice. Studies of ginkgo biloba in Alzheimer's looks promising, if not exciting. It may not only delay, but reverse some of the symptoms of Alzheimer's in the early stages. Ginkgo biloba is not a fast acting cure all; it may take several months to see a change. However, it is a powerful natural product and is extremely safe. No significant adverse actions are known. However, because it could interact with blood thinners, you should consult your physician before and during use. Ginkgo biloba is thought to have both antioxidant and anti-inflammatory properties, to protect cell membranes, and to regulate neurotransmitter function. Ginkgo has been used for centuries in traditional Chinese medicine and currently is being used in Europe to alleviate cognitive symptoms associated with a number of neurological conditions.

In a study published in the Journal of the American Medical Association (October 22/29, 1997), Pierre L. Le Bars, MD, PhD, of the New York Institute for

Medical Research, and his colleagues observed in some participants a modest improvement in cognition, activities of daily living (such as eating and dressing), and social behavior. The researchers found no measurable difference in overall impairment.

Results from this study show that ginkgo might help some people with Alzheimer's disease, but a lot more research is needed to find the exact reasons why Ginkgo works in the body. These are just preliminary results because there is such a low number of participants, only about 200 people.

Huperzine A

Huperzine A is an extract from a type of moss that is used in traditional Chinese medicine and has been for centuries. It has properties that match several FDA-approved Alzheimer medications, and being a natural extract, it is a good alternative treatment for Alzheimer's disease, as it has considerably less side affects. Also most treatments that occur in nature almost always work better then drugs synthesized by science.

Phosphatidylserine

Phosphatidylserine (pronounced FOS-fuh-TIE-dil-sair-een), PS, is a naturally occurring phospholipid nutrient. It is essential to the function of all cells, but is most concentrated in the brain. Clinical studies suggest that PS can support brain functions that tend to decline with age. Until very recently, PS was only available from animal sources, but now a plant source for PS has been developed. This is a dynamic substance and is definitely worth your consideration. Cognitive functions are greatly benefited, as are age related memory decline. There are some 64 human studies on PS, with some being double blind studies, which will greatly increase our studies on the benefits of PS. Mental functions in geriatric patients show, that dietary supplementation with PS at the rate of 200-400 milligrams per day benefited on tests that measured short term memory and concentration. The statistical significance of the trials that I have studied are overwhelming. Brain performance may be globally enhanced with PS. Acetylcholine activity in the brain is also enhanced. The activity of the pituitary, hypothalamus and adrenal glands appear to be enhanced also. This may result in an increase in human growth hormones. PS is a treatment that strengthens the cell membranes and protects the brain cells from degenerating. I am unable to list any beneficial foods containing PS, as it is somewhat limited in our diets, but when taken by mouth, it quickly reaches the brain and is readily absorbed across the brain barrier. Animal studies also support the human research. The memory center appears to be protected by PS. This natural occurring nutrient seems to have an excellent record of safety with little or no side affects. It appears that it can be taken with other medications without adverse interactions. The long-term use seems to also be safe; with benefits lasting long after use is terminated. This may be the best means currently available to preserve intellect. Your further study of this effective dietary supplement is sincerely warranted. PS has so many potential advantages, that it could not only save you from imminent danger from Alzheimer's, but could reverse years off of the progression of the disease.

Vacha

Vacha is a renowned herb in the classical Ayurvedic text. It has been in use for thousands of years for rejuvenating the mind and nervous system which it purifies and revitalizes. Vacha clears the subtle channels of toxins, promotes cerebral circulation, increases sensitivity, sharpens memory and enhances awareness. Vacha is also used for Alzheimer's disease, epilepsy, shock, coma, loss of memory, hysteria, neuralgia, insanity, high blood pressure, heart diseases and strokes.

Zink

Zinc plays a key role in nutrient-brain relationships. After death, analysis of the brains of Alzheimer's patients shows a marked decrease in zinc levels. Zinc has been suggested as a key contributor to the progression of Alzheimer's. Zinc is also one of the most common nutrient deficiencies of the elderly. It was found in one study that eight out of ten Alzheimer's patients improved with zinc supplements. The form of zinc that is best absorbed by the body is zinc picolinate, which is a simulated much better then zinc aspartate. All cellular functions are decreased with a zinc deficiency. It is difficult to relate to zinc research, because, it seems that its importance does not demand the funding that it deserves. Hopefully, we will be learning more about case studies in the future.

Vitamin E

Published in the Journal of the American Medical Association (JAMA), are studies that show Alzheimer's patients who consumed the highest levels of the antioxidant vitamin E, reduced their risk of Alzheimer's by about 70 percent. Another study in the Netherlands showed about a 40 percent reduction. Eating foods rich in vitamin E Is definitely worth serious consideration. Remember selenium is an important mineral to be used in conjunction with vitamin E. There are ongoing studies concerning the role of supplemental vitamin E. Those studies are supported by the National Institute on Aging. Along with eating foods high in vitamin E, I also take supplemental vitamin E (at least 400 I.U. daily) along with selenium.

B 12 and Folic Acid

Further studies have concluded that a majority of geriatric patients were found to be deficient in folic acid. Folic acid deficiency is one of the most common deficiencies in the United States. Strangely enough this is a very inexpensive vitamin with which to supplement your diet. Folic acid is synergistic with vitamin B-12. A deficiency of B-12 is found to be significant in Alzheimer's patients, supplementation has resulted in almost complete reversal of symptoms in the early stages in some cases, though not the majority.

Traditional Medicines Position

At this time there is no cure for Alzheimer's disease, and no way to slow its progression. For some people in the early or middle stages of Alzheimer's disease, medication like tacrine (Cognex) may relieve some cognitive symptoms. Donepezil (Aricept), rivastigmine (Exelon), and galantamine (Reminyl) may slow the debilitation of some symptoms for a limited time. Another drug, memantine (Namenda), was recently approved for use in the United States. Combining memantine with other Alzheimer's based drugs might be more effective than other drugs used singularly. One controlled clinical trial found that patients receiving donepezil plus memantine had better cognitive functions than patients receiving donepezil alone. Also, other medications may help control behavioral symptoms such as sleeplessness, agitation, wandering, anxiety, and depression.

Memantine (Namenda)

For Alzheimer's disease Namenda is a new medication, recently approved by the FDA for treating moderate-to-severe Alzheimer's disease. Namenda is an inhibitor of glutamine transmission and helps preserve neural transmission. It works by a different mechanism than current treatments like donepezil (Aricept), a cholinesterase inhibitor approved for mild-to-moderate Alzheimer's disease.

In Conclusion

We have tried to present a fair evaluation of treatments, both preventative and things that could possibly lead to improvement. I believe that in the next few years you could possibly see dramatic improvements in the treatments for Alzheimer's patients. Better yet, when we find the cause of the disease, a cure will not be far behind. Until then, let's do everything that we can to prevent and slow the progression of this debilitating disease.

PARKINSON'S DISEASE

Parkinson's disease is one of the fastest growing diseases in the adult population today. It can happen in your early 40s but more often than not it occurs in the latter years, and it becomes more rampant. I have a very close friend who asked me for help. I tried to point him to all of the things that I knew at the time, e.g. antioxidants, flax seed etc.. I could only hope to slow this debilitating disease. Parkinson's disease is caused by a decrease of a neurotransmitter called dopamine. So why not just administer dopamine and cure the problem? The reason is, dopamine will not cross the brain barrier. So, drugs such as L-dopa or Sinemet are given which supply some of the raw materials for the production of dopamine with the hope that your body can begin to produce it again. You can supply the raw materials for human growth hormone too, but if your body isn't producing HGH, the raw materials are worthless. When there is no medical answer for a disease, one of the worst complications becomes depression. However, with no hope in sight for a cure, who wouldn't become depressed when you see your friends or family members unable to eat and drink from a glass of water and realizing the certainty that they are heading for the wheelchair and worse, it's hard to find a rainbow.

I have been studying the use of procaine for over 20 years as I knew of its value in cellular regeneration-especially in nerve cells. Some 15 years ago I tried procaine therapy on my son who had serious back pain due to an accident. It had some short term benefit. But the half-life of procaine is very short-some 36 seconds at most. Half-life means that one-half of the procaine is metabolized in 36 seconds or less and then it's gone. Somehow, someone had to find a better delivery system.

In the 1950s Dr. Aslin began to improve upon basic procaine hydrochloride. She buffered and stabilized the product until, she was able to protect some 15 percent of the procaine so it should be used by the body. Even this small amount was able to rejuvenate cell so that it could repair its cellular malfunctions while rebuilding its membranes, thus revitalizing the cellular function. They were even then beginning to see improvements in Parkinson's disease, multiple sclerosis, diabetes, arthritis, depression etc. Now for the exciting part, Dr. Koch a biochemist from Salt Lake City Utah, developed a process of complexing the procaine with B vitamins, vitamin C, amino acids and other compounds and protected 100 percent of the procaine. Procaine now becomes at least six times more potent in its revitalizing benefits to the cell. Now the no hope theory becomes some 83 percent destroyed. I have studied many case histories, called patients with Parkinson's and the users of this revolutionary product developed by Dr. Koch called, GH 7. Finding all of this new information caused us to say stop the presses! We always wanted to say that anyway. Had I not studied procaine for some 20 years, I would have missed this drastically improved patented product.

To this day, I am still thankful for the person who told me about this product. You will probably never see it on TV, or hear about it on the radio, even though thousands of Americans have gone to Romania to be treated by Dr. Aslin. You may recognize a few of these names, the Gabor sisters, Marlena Dietrich, Charlie Chaplin, Lillian Gish, John F. Kennedy, Lena Horne, Dick Clark and many others. You can be thankful that you have the opportunity to experience the rejuvenating effects of an even better product then the above famous people had to travel for.

It is always important for me to test a product before recommending it. I am 68 years old now and have absolutely no pain or debilitating disease to truly test it on, however, the first day I noticed a dramatic increase in my energy levels. Instead of a running one mile I ran two, with greater ease than the first mile the day before. Before I give you a description of the chemistry, let me a share a testimonial from a dynamic lady by the name of Dorothy Draper. Dorothy had the tenacity and intelligence to try anything to help her husband who contracted Parkinson's disease 11 years ago. She didn't quit until she found something called GH 3 at the time. Her husband now takes two tablets of GH 3 and one tablet of GH 7 in the morning and two of the GH 7 and one GH 8 in the afternoon on an empty stomach one hour before eating, or two hours after eating. He is still working 11 years later, has no leg cramps and said the turn around all started when he began using procaine HCL. He states that he doesn't know where he would be today without it. He gives all the credit to his wife who faithfully searched until she found a better answer. It also appears that procaine is synergistic with most of the drugs commonly used by the medical profession for Parkinson's disease e.g. Sinemet, which he also uses. Dorothy also uses GH 7 and GH 8.She started after a surgery she had for pain from scar tissue and she began taking the procaine HCL. After which, she said the scar tissue lump and pain was gone in about two weeks. As a byproduct, she says her husband's blood sugar also went down from 340 to 90-105, shortly after beginning the use of procaine HCL. This is a pretty nice side effect. The most important statement he made was that he feels a better now then he did years ago.

Chemically, procaine when taken orally in a complex form, acts as a vitamin. It is the PABA (Para amino-benzoate acid) ester of amino cell called DEAE (2-diethylamino-ethel). PABA is a B vitamin and DEAE is a biologically active precursor of the B vitamin Choline see figure below:

Fig. 1

$$O$$
$$\parallel$$
$$C\text{-}OH$$

$$+ \; HO\text{-}CH_2CH_2\text{-}N \begin{array}{l} C_2H_5 \\ C_2H_5 \end{array}$$

$$O$$
$$\parallel$$
$$C\text{-}O\text{-}CH_2\text{-}CH_2\text{-}N \begin{array}{l} C_2H_5 \\ C_2H_5 \end{array} \text{-HCl}$$

NH_2 NH_2

PABA   **DEAE**   **PROCAINE-HCl**

(p-amino benzoic acid)   (n.n diethylaminoethanol)

Procaine when taken orally, is absorbed through the
villi in the small intestine. Most of the procaine HCL
enters the bloodstream molecularly intact and is
eventually removed by the liver, chemically changed
and excreted by the urine. The complex procaine
compounds developed by Dr. Koch (GH 7 and GH 8)
are protected from the action of the enzymes in the
blood and tissue, thus giving procaine enough time
to be transferred into the cells of the body, where it
helps the cells to rebuild, repair and detoxify. This
action of the procaine complex is responsible for the
remarkable improvements in health, that result from
this product. Dr. Koch believes that people should
grow old because they are old, not because they are
sick. GH 7 and GH 8 are not sold as a cure for
anything, however it gives the cells a fighting chance
for survival. I use the product because I know what
it does, not because I am sick. It opens the door for
better cellular function. If you are interested, you
can order the product (GH 7 and GH 8) from

Nutritional Engineering Limited
        1-800-225-6799
        Ask for James and if you mention
        this book physical justice, the
        shipping will be free and they will
        also supply additional information
        about their products.

Hepatitis

Hepatitis is an inflammation of the liver. There are three kinds of hepatitis viruses that attack the liver:

- Hepatitis A is transmitted by fecal contamination. Contaminated food is the usual cause. It is not likely that you will die from this virus and you may have a mild case without any symptoms. It has an incubation period of two to six weeks.
- Hepatitis B is usually transmitted by blood or sexual secretions. A high percentage of this disease occurs in homosexuals or intravenous drug users. This carries a potential fatality rate of about five times that of hepatitis A.
- Hepatitis C is usually transmitted by blood transfusions, and causes chronic liver disease and has a death rate as high as 10 to 12%. As many as 10 to 15% of those receiving blood transfusions may get this disease. I highly recommend that if you are contemplating some form of surgery, and have the time to do it, have some of your own blood saved ahead of time, your life and health could depend on this.

Almost all cases of hepatitis are preventable, for hepatitis A you may be able to closely watch your food, where you eat, and practice simple rules of hygiene e.g. wash your hands after using the bathroom especially before cooking or eating. For hepatitis B never use illegal drugs or practice unsafe sex. Homosexuals are especially at high risk for hepatitis B because of the extremely high possibility of blood transfer. Hepatitis C is the most deadly, but is much less common as it is contracted primarily through blood transfusions. However, this may be impossible for you to control should you be involved in a severe accident or should a surgery go astray.

The symptoms may be flu like, and accompanied by tenderness in your liver and possibly some yellowing of the skin. A blood test will help you diagnose the disease as certain enzymes become elevated.

If you are planning to travel in any foreign countries you can find several good sterilants to use on your hands without water. Your greatest risk of contracting hepatitis may be in the water, so be very careful when it comes to consuming uncooked fruits and vegetables. Another little mistake that is made all the time is to order a canned or bottled beverage thinking that it will be safe, then putting ice in it to cool it off; oops you just drank the water. Try to use the ice on the outside of the can or bottle and make sure that none of the melting ice enters the contents.

Years ago when I was in Mexico, building a church and eating with the native Indians (who were wonderful to us and gave us the best they had), I did not have any sterilants with me, so I rubbed salt on my hands before eating, ate only cooked foods, and did not use the freshly washed silverware, thankfully there was no problem. They had a very relaxed lifestyle there and there were times that the chickens would jump up on the tables and help themselves, but the experience was worth it and I would do it again the first chance I have.

Now for the potential remedies of all forms of hepatitis. Listed below are several successful treatments for hepatitis e.g.

- The first line of defense and maybe the least expensive is extremely high doses of vitamin C (Ester form). By high doses I mean take it to bowel tolerance or intravenously if necessary. By bowel tolerance I mean take enough to cause you to experience either gas and or diarrhea. Take the vitamin C three times per day and when you experience the above symptoms, gradually reduce the amount until the symptoms disappear. Only you can determine this amount, it might be from 1000 mg to 15 to 20,000 mg. In severe cases you may need to take intravenous vitamin C. Vitamin C is very safe and leads to the production of larger amounts of interferon in your body. When I was in Japan, they were treating hepatitis with interferon. Interferon is very expensive when compared to of the expense of vitamin C. I also recommend that you use Alpha Lipolic Acid which arguments the ability of vitamin C to do its work as it recycles the vitamin C back into your bloodstream.

- My first experience with silymarin was when the heart medication I was using caused abnormal liver function. I began using silymarin (milk thistle) and L Systein and my liver function soon returned to normal. Silymarin has the important benefit of regenerating liver function. Take at least 200 mg. 3 times per day. If you ever contract hepatitis, look for the value of a product, not the price. A company called Enzymatic Therapy produces the best quality product that I know of. I have never known of any company to be more consistent in its quality.

- Another extremely valuable treatment consists of Thymus extract. I personally use the brand called Pro Boost, thymic protein A. It contains purified calf thymus protein and can be purchased from Med Quest, the number is 1-888-222-2956. You can also purchase another product called ThymuPlex from Enzymatic Therapy. This treatment alone has shown to be so successful that it may rid your blood of the virus entirely in both the acute or chronic phase of the disease.

I sincerely believe that you now have all of the tools necessary to conquer this disease. Here are some other things that you should avoid while trying to treat this disease:

- Sugar or any product containing sugar
- Alcoholic beverages
- Fats, especially hydrogenated

Also, please remember to take a quality multivitamin (including sub lingual B12), fresh ground flax seed, and 100% soy powder. One thing you can be thankful for is that a damaged liver can rejuvenate itself.

Diabetes

Here is an instance where this disease should be renamed to diet-beats-us. We Americans, like no other culture on the planet are being lured into this disease by eating ourselves into oblivion with the wrong foods. Go into any fast food restaurant, watch the youth of our country, and count the ratio of those who are overweight with those of normal weight. In a very short time, the overweight youth will become obese. Now go to a buffet or a restaurant and take a count of the 30-40 year olds who are obese. We consume more sugar and fat than any country on earth. Our prepared and processed foods are a much greater threat to our health then any other disease that I can think of. The only good part of this story is that 90% of the diabetics have a disease that is almost completely controllable. Now, if you have the funds and time to travel, I recommend that you head for Newport Beach, California as fast as you can, if you can do this, you can quit reading this chapter right now. You need to contact:
Whitaker Wellness Institute
4321 Birch Street, Suite 100

Newport Beach, California
(714) 851-1550

If you decide to spend some time there, I predict that most of you with Type II diabetes will be free of the medications you are now using. I also predict that insulin dependent Type I diabetics will be able to cut the amount of insulin that you use drastically. If you are unable to do this, then please read this chapter as you and you alone control your own destiny. If you follow the information in this chapter, you will be on your way to good health, allowing you to avoid most of the devastating effects of this dreaded disease. Some of the catastrophic side effects of diabetes include:

- Arteriosclerosis-heart disease is greatly increased.
- Diabetic retinopathy.
- Foot and leg ulcers.
- Macular degeneration that can lead to blindness.
- Excessive thirst.
- Fatigue.
- Dry skin.
- Numbness and tingling of the extremities.
- Severe nerve damage.
- Severe kidney damage.
- High blood pressure.
- It is the leading cause of blindness in the US.
- Leading the eyes of foot and leg amputations.
- Triples your risk of stroke.

Now if your physician tells you that diabetes can only be managed by taking insulin or by taking prescription drugs like Glucophage or Precose, find another physician who has done more extensive research on the disease. Always remember, if you have contracted a disease, you need to do some extensive research for yourself, as managing any disease should be done in harmony between you and your physician. Always find a physician that is open to new suggestions, and will answer any questions that you propose to him.

Let me explain the differences between Type I and Type II diabetes:
Type I Diabetes:

- May be genetic in origin and usually begins in your youth you might possibly even be born with it.
- Might be autoimmune in origin where your body destroys the ability of the pancreas to function.
- Represents less than 10% of diabetics.
- Type I diabetics may not be overweight as normal weight is also common.
- Always requires treatment with insulin.
- The beta cells of the pancreas may be completely destroyed by your own white blood cells. Without beta cells no insulin can be manufactured.

Type II Diabetes:

- Usually manifests itself at the age of 40-45 years of age.
- Represents greater than 90% of all diabetic cases.
- May take a considerable amount of time to develop noticeable symptoms.
- Obesity usually accompanies Type II diabetes.
- Your body might be producing insulin in abundance.
- The cells are unable to utilize the sugars because of insulin resistance.
- Insulin injections are usually not required.
- Insulin may be present, but the cells of the body become resistant and blood sugar is unable to cross the cellular walls. That is why you may have elevated levels of both insulin and sugar.

If you have any suspicions about having diabetes, the sooner your physician diagnoses you the greater your chance of managing this disease without medications that have a devastating effect on your body. Always check the PDR (Physicians Desk Reference) before taking any medications. If you feel uncomfortable with the side effects of the drugs prescribed by your physician, see if there is another treatment possible. Your normal fasting blood glucose level should be between 70-105 milligrams per deciliter. If your fasting lead glucose level is greater than 140 milligrams per deciliter, you might have diabetes.

There is astounding new research being done in the field of diabetes, but for now I will not be easy on you because you can prevent or stop diabetes in its tracks for over 90% of the cases of Type II diabetes. Over two thirds of Type II diabetics are overweight. This can be controlled through diet and exercise. When I eat at an all you can eat buffet, I can usually predict those people who have or will eventually get diabetes by their shape and by the foods that they eat to get that way. If your weight is largely in the upper portion of your body, you are more prone to diabetes then if your body is pear shaped. If you have diabetes and your doctor is not dealing with your diet and weight find another physician. The good news is that if you are overweight, you have the ability to control it or possibly cure your diabetes.

Now for the hard part of controlling diabetes, losing weight. The solution is simple but the road to success is sometimes difficult. You have to control your diet and exercise. Forget the fact that you ever saw a fast food restaurant. Stay away from processed foods; they are usually full of sugars and fats. You must find the ability to convince yourself that you will not become a statistic and that you will normalize your weight. If you find that you cannot do this alone, you may need to join a weight loss program. Sometimes getting advice from someone that has achieved your goal before you can be a fantastic incentive. You might even try some of those exercise machines that are sold on television, they might help. If they do, please write to me, so I can pass the word on to others. Just think you might be the one to write the next chapter, imagine how you will feel if you have helped someone else control this dreaded disease.

Now for just one small testimonial, I had an overweight woman call and ask me for help and I gave her one simple suggestion. One week later, she called me back and was ecstatic, she was not hungry during the daytime and felt much better. The simple solution to her over eating problem was fresh ground flax seed. I suggested that she purchase some fresh flax seed and a small coffee grinder. Then I suggested that she grind 3 tbsp. of the fresh flax seed and put it in a glass of water and drink it twice a day. After trying this simple solution, she found that she was not getting hungry during the day. The key to stabilizing your blood sugar is fiber, fiber, and more fiber. The best carbohydrates are raw vegetables e.g. broccoli, cauliflower, cabbage and there are several more of them that you can choose from the chart on the following pages. Another wonderful fiber is psyllium (without sugar) and Knox Nutra-Joint, a product that you can purchase at your local grocery store. Some other fine foods are beans, as they are very high in fiber. Peas and green beans provide few calories to your diet. Fiber rich foods slow food absorption and prevent sharp swings in your blood sugar levels. Burning sugar is easier when the diet is low in fat. Both soluble and insoluble fibers show benefits to diabetics even though they do not affect the blood the same way. Soluble fibers found in fruits, vegetables, beans, oats etc. have a great effect on blood sugar. Keeping your weight down also

inhibits the clumping of blood platelets, which leads
to possible strokes.

We will get back to the diet later. Now it is time for
you to go to work. Exercise is of little value unless
you can control your diet. You can't possibly exercise
enough to overcome deep fried foods, sugary
desserts, high-fat (especially hydrogenated fats),
processed foods, etc. if you don't believe me, just
check the fat content of a coated chicken fried steak
or a baked chicken breast. Those fast foods taste so
good as they take you down the road to an early
grave. If I sound like I have gotten back up on my
soap box again you are right, as redundant as this
sounds I will keep telling you this over and over
again because I want you to be healthy. If I don't
help you, I have failed and I don't like to fail.
Success is a lot more fun for both of us. You can't
imagine how satisfying it is to hear from someone
who has tried one of my suggestions and they have
called back to say it worked and I am healthy again.
It is not so important as to what works as it is that
something worked and changed your life for the
better. Now, regular exercise can help prevent
diabetes also, if you already have diabetes, exercise
can enable you to manage it without drugs. Inactive
people, are much more likely to develop diabetes
than those who get regular exercise, why?
- It helps the body to metabolize sugar.
- It increases the cells sensitivity to insulin
  making it much more efficient.
- It helps to keep your weight down.

- It inhibits the clumping of platelets, thus decreasing the possibility of strokes.
- It increases the resistance to diseases.
- It decreases circulatory disorders.
- After exercise, you may feel a high and get addicted to it. I hope so.

When you exercise, it should be a vigorous aerobic type of exercise for 20 minutes or more three times a week. What exercises are best?
- Brisk walking is good. Use your arms to make it more vigorous. I like to slowly jog (Slowly) for mile after mile. It will bring on a sense of well being that might last you through the whole day.
- Swimming is probably the best, as it is gentle on all of your joints, you can run in the water, lift your knees high and keep it up for 20 minutes. Swimming laps is also good if you can keep it up for 20 minutes without stopping.
- Bicycling is also a wonderful form of exercise. Whether on a stationary bike or riding in the great outdoors, cycling can have great benefits to your health. It is also a type of exercise that you can do with your whole family. Just think of all the fun that you can have by having a picnic at the end of your journey. Not only will you be spending quality time with your family but the health benefits will be great also. Men, make sure that you purchase a comfortable seat because it can slow the blood flow to your genital area and could do permanent damage.

Go to your local bicycle shop and ask them for an appropriate seat.

- Sit-ups are also a great form of exercise. It not only makes your abdominal muscles look good but it strengthens your lower back.

- If you have back problems and find that you cannot do sit-ups, you can do leg raises. Lay flat on your back keeping your legs together, raise both legs six inches above the floor and hold them there for as long as you can. Repeat this 10 to 15 times and try to increase the amount of time that you hold your legs off the floor as you progress.

- Jumping rope is also a great form of aerobic exercise. Go to a sporting goods store and purchase yourself a quality jump rope. Fifteen minutes of constant jumping should suffice. As you progress, you might want to purchase some lightweight wrist and ankle weights to increase the difficulty of the exercise.

- Lifting weights is probably not the best exercise, as it does not burn calories as well as aerobic exercise and might possibly raise your blood pressure. However, you might want to consider purchasing some light weights that you can hold in your hand while you are doing aerobic exercises or stair stepping to increase the difficulty.

When you decide to begin, any of these forms of exercise, always be sure to consult your physician, as there may be other considerations involving your particular health situation.

Now for some supplements that you can add to your diet in your quest to control diabetes:

- Use all of the antioxidants previously mentioned e.g. beta-carotene vitamin C (Esther form) and vitamin E with selenium.
- Pay particular attention to Niacinamide. There have been many studies done and even though conclusions appear mixed, it is worth your consideration. Take 500 milligrams daily as a preventative. If you catch the problem early enough, the Niacinamide seems to cause a greater affect. In fact, some studies show Niacinamide can help restore the activity of insulin manufacturing beta cells. I am watching some of the new research coming out of Europe and it appears there may be a major breakthrough concerning Niacinamide. In the meantime, don't wait for the FDA to recommend this, as you may not live long enough to see it happen. Even some Type I diabetics have shown remarkable results. It may not build you a new pancreas, but it certainly seems to slow down the progression of the disease.
- There are two supplements that seem to work in a synergistic manner, chromium picolinate and vanadium sulfate. These two supplements should always be used under the supervision of your physician, as they might just be too effective, your insulin levels may change so drastically that it could be very dangerous.

Chromium works with insulin in facilitating the transportation of glucose across the cellular walls. We know that chromium is important to blood sugar metabolism. We also know that chromium deficiency will block insulin action. As you understand the action of chromium, you will be better able to make a decision about its use. Again, with either of these substances, take them only with the careful guidance of your physician. Vanadium sulfate may also have a powerful effect on blood sugar. If you are taking insulin, you will have to watch the results very closely. Of the studies I have seen and been involved in, there has been some amazing results with vanadium sulfate, up to and including the cessation of the use of insulin and the return of normal blood sugar levels.

- Magnesium levels have shown to be very low in persons with diabetes. Magnesium is also a very beneficial mineral for your heart. If you choose to use magnesium you should always use magnesium citrate, I personally recommend that everyone should use magnesium as my research has concluded that most of the people living in the United States are deficient in this mineral, especially diabetics.

- Vitamin B-6 is also found to be deficient in most diabetics. This may be beneficial should nerve abnormalities appear.

- There is fairly new research on an herb that shows exciting results and may even play a role in regenerating cells in the diabetic pancreas.

This herb is Gymnema Sylvestre and it has been used for many years in India and has been found to decrease blood sugar levels, normalize blood lipids (cholesterol and triglycerides), lower insulin levels and it enhances production of insulin by the pancreatic cells. This herb has even been known to regenerate the insulin producing cells of the pancreas. Anything that claims to regenerate beta cells gets my attention immediately. Some interesting facts about this herb is that when administered to non-diabetics nothing happens, no lowering of blood sugar. When administered to diabetics, many find that it is able to maintain normal sugar levels with the extract alone, very interesting when you consider that there are no known side effects. If you decide to use this herb, the normal dosage of this extract should be 400 milligrams per day. I would like to recommend a manufacturing company called Enzymatic Therapy. I have found all of their products to be the highest quality available. When you compare the side effects of this herb to the side effects of the insulin control drugs favored by Western doctors, it gives you a little appreciation for the people who have tried to control diabetes prior to the advent of these drugs. I only hope that our medical community will be open-minded enough to try and recommend Gymnema Sylvestre to their patients. Again, never try something new by yourself, because you may not need insulin after taking this herb or you may require a highly reduced amount.

- Something that few researchers have considered as a possible deterrent to diabetes and its complications is Alpha Lipolic Acid (ALA). The obvious first chronic complication is high blood sugar, but possibly the most destructive part is the production of abnormal glucose metabolism (free radicals), which cause neurological, vascular, kidney, and visual problems. You need to understand the action of a disease in order to be able to try to fix it.

- Diabetic neuropathy does damage to the arteries that supply the nerves with blood. This may result in a "pins and needles" feeling that may progress to a burning feeling in the feet. As the free radicals continue their damage, it may eventually affect the eyes and kidneys. Retinopathy (eye damage) may grow worse with age and ultimately cause blurring of vision that could lead to blindness. Diabetes is probably the main cause of kidney dysfunction in the United States. The filtering units of the kidney (glomeruli) become damaged. I covered coronary heart disease briefly but heart attacks are the leading cause of death in Type II diabetics. If the coronary arteries to the brain become occluded, a stroke just might occur. Peripheral vascular disease may shut down the blood supply to the feet and legs leading to gangrene and amputation. I am not telling you this to try to scare you, however, if you have diabetes you need to do something to prevent these problems from happening. If I could prevent these problems for you with one simple fix, I would. You determine your own destiny and can live a good life without the complications mentioned if you act on the knowledge presented in this book along with the vast amount of knowledge you can glean from diabetic organizations or through research on the internet.

- For further consideration, you may be wise to restrict milk from your diet if you suspect diabetes. Both types of diabetes are found to be much lower in countries that have low milk consumption. Reason, cows milk may have similar proteins to the pancreas causing the body to develop antibodies against the pancreatic cells. I have avoided cow's milk for years, not only for this reason, but for other reasons as well. Homogenized milk makes a fat that is very destructive to your arteries.

- ALA is a very valuable substance for diabetics. ALA is already a prescription drug in Europe and is currently showing an increase of activity to bring it on the market as an intravenous prescription drug. It can now be purchased at health food stores and I personally recommend that you take 100 milligrams three times a day. The more you read about the biological functions of your body, the better you can prepare your cells to live a healthier life. You cannot expect your physician to know every possibility involving your health care; you need to do research to possibly help him with your specific needs. Only then can you become an informed patient to help your physician to select the best possible therapy available. I strongly recommend that you acquire a book listed in my bibliography called Alpha Lipolic Breakthrough by Bert Berkson, M.D. Ph.D. it is an excellent book that you can read in just a few hours and it opens the door to exciting and dramatic results in the treatment of many diseases. I spend a massive amount of time studying every research document and book along with my own research in order to bring you the most conclusive answers to your physical needs. My co-author is a master at the art of Internet research and is a valuable contributor to your knowledge of each subject covered. Now back to the subject, ALA can be a valuable treatment for diabetics. Not only is ALA a powerful antioxidant, it rounds up and destroys free radicals. Another great asset of ALA is its ability to chelate heavy metals. In other words, it grabs on to the heavy metals in your blood stream, neutralizes them and makes it possible for your body to excrete them. Two metals that cause serious damage your system is mercury and arsenic. Mercury is found in dental fillings (sometimes your fillings may contain 50% Mercury), paints, cosmetics, wood preservatives, and many other products that you commonly use. Until recently, I remember farmers treating seeds with mercury products to kill fungi. ALA chelates Mercury and excretes it from the body by way of the gall bladder without side effects. There are optional treatments to the use of ALA but you will not like them. Arsenic is a toxic metal found in tobacco smoke, pesticides and other industrial chemicals. ALA has been found to be of significant value in chelating arsenic in removing it from the blood and tissues. ALA can also chelate copper and excess iron and lead. It is a very therapeutic agent for heavy metal poisoning. Go back and read the chapter about the heart where I described the good and bad cholesterol. The bad cholesterol (LDL) proves to be very destructive to the blood vessels when it is oxidize. ALA being an ideal antioxidant plays a role in preventing the oxidation of (LDL) that is helping to prevent the development of arteriosclerotic vessel disease. Diabetics usually have higher levels of the bad cholesterol in their system. To help you understand this further, copper levels are often higher in diabetics. In addition, it is common for excess copper to cause vascular disease. Remember in the previous page, I described how ALA eliminates excess copper from your system. ALA is also essential for sugar metabolism in the mitochondria. This along with the ability of ALA to improve glucose transport across the cellular wall tends to lower blood sugar. Now it is important to recognize that ALA is both fat-soluble and water-soluble, it has a very beneficial effect on the eyes as well. German physicians regularly prescribed ALA for the treatment of diabetes. Diabetes is a very complex disease and you should not try to treat it by yourself. Find a nutritionally minded doctor who is open minded enough to do the research necessary to meet your needs. You can go to the National Library of Medicine web site and do a search on Alpha Lipolic Acid, as there is soon to be a massive amount of material coming on this amazing substance. Remember that the leading researchers in the medical field are not only scientists but also dealers in hope. This is what this book is for, to show you the best research available and to allow you a small window into this world of science and hope. Our hope is that we can convince you to continue your studies so that you can provide a healthier happier lifestyle for you and your family.

- Coenzyme Q10 is also very important to proper sugar metabolism. People who began taking coenzyme Q10 usually begin to show lower blood sugar levels right after they start taking it. I recommend at least 200 milligrams per day. It also has an added benefit to your heart muscle. Coenzyme Q10 may take some time for you to notice a marked improvement. It can also affect weight loss, as it is very essential for energy production. Coenzyme Q10 taken in conjunction with flax seed or flax seed oil increases its absorption rate and there are no adverse side effects reported. Over 50% of obese people are deficient in coenzyme Q10.

This is an expensive supplement and most of you will consider taking only a small amount. However, do not be fooled, you need at least 100 to 200 milligrams per day to create the necessary response in your system. Coenzyme Q10 also promotes the lowering of your need for large caloric intake and this enables you to accelerate weight loss. Even though a United State's scientist isolated coenzyme Q10 in the mid 1950s, it remained unnoticed for some 30 years, but Japan began research on it and some 10% of the population now uses it regularly. It has demonstrated to boost heart performance even when heart disease is serious. It does its work even without exercise. It not only lowers blood pressure but boosts the immune system as well. There is wonderful research that shows that coenzyme Q10 extends a person's life, as the older we get, the greater its response.

Before concluding this chapter on diabetes, I would like you to consider some of the foods that you may want to avoid and some of the foods that you may want to use in abundance. Remember, if you screw up, fiber (normally fresh ground flax seed) covers up many mistakes. It is not my intention to make you become a captive to your diet, however, I want your diet to be an additive to your health and happiness. Because of the complexity of nutritional issues, I recommend that you expand your knowledge of food far beyond the following information. You may want to consider working with a registered dietitian.

Effective management of nutrition must be on an individual approach and be appropriate to your lifestyle. You may want to consider calling the American Association of Diabetes Educators at 1-800-832-6874 and they will give you the names of several diabetes educators in your zip code area.

I would like to give you a list of sugar content of some selected popular foods, these sugars are categorized as monosaccharides, (galactose, glucose, and fructose), disaccharides (lactose, sucrose and maltose). The USDA recommends that the average non-diabetic person eat no more than 10 teaspoons of sugar per day. In order to convert these charts below, always remember that one teaspoon equals five grams of sugar. The sugar data in the table below appear as the sums of all of the forms of sugar and represent the total sugar content of that food item.

Food Items:	Common Measures:	Total Sugar Grams:
Baked Products:		
White Bread	1 Slice	1.0
Breakfast Bar	1 Bar	17.8
Fruit Cake	1 Piece	48.7
Chocolate Chip Cookies	10 Small Cookies	11.0
Rye Crackers	1 Cracker	.2
Cake Doughnut	1 Doughnut	8.5
Fruit Pie	1 Slice	46.1
Beverages:		
Beer	1 12 oz. Bottle	25.3
Cola	1 12 oz. Can	39.2
Diet Cola	1 12 oz. Can	0.0
Root Beer	1 12 oz. Can	44.0
Coffee	12 oz. Cup	0.0
Frozen Citrus	8 oz.	26.3
Orange Juice	8 oz.	24.9
Wine Rose¯	8 oz.	2.6
Wine Cooler	12 oz.	35.5
Dairy Products:		
Chedder Cheese	1 oz.	.5
Cottage Cheese	1 Cup	1.4
American Cheese	1 oz.	2.7
Ice Cream	1 Cup	28.7
Whole Milk	1 Cup	12.2
Skim Milk	1 Cup	10.8
Milk Shake	10 oz.	51.2
Yogurt Plain	8 oz.	11.6
Yogurt Strawberry	8 oz.	34.7
Fruit:		
Apple	1 Small	18.4
Pears	1 Small	17.4
Pineapple	1 Cup	18.4
Pineapple Juice Unsweetened	8 oz.	31.2
Rasberries	1 Cup	11.7
Strawberries	1 Cup	8.6
Watermellon	1/16 mellon	43.4
Grains & Cereals:		
Farina Cooked	1 Cup	1.1
Oatmeal	1 Cup	1.1
Whole Wheat	1 Cup	1.0

Food Items:	Common Measures:	Total Sugar Grams:
Corn Flakes	1 1/8Cup	1.9
Sugar Coated Corn Flakes	3/4Cup	11.9
Rice Crispy's	1Cup	2.5
Puffed Rice	1Cup	0.0
Puffed Wheat	1Cup	0.2
Sugar Coated Puffed Wheat	3/4Cup	16.3
Oat Bran	1Cup	0.9
Pasta Cooked	1Cup	1.8
Popcorn Air Popped	1Cup	0.0
Legumes:		
Beans Cooked	1/2Cup	1.9
Lenties Cooked	1/2Cup	1.8
Mung Beans	1/2Cup	1.9
Peanuts	1oz.	1.2
Peas Cooked	1/2Cup	2.8
Soybeans Cooked	1/2Cup	2.6
Tofu	1/4Block	.05
Beef	3oz.	0.6
Ham	2Slices	0.8
Luncheon Meat	2Slices	1.9
Turkey	2Slices	0.1
Nuts:		
Almonds	1oz.	1.6
Cashews	1oz.	1.8
Coconut Raw	1Piece	1.6
Sweetened Coconut	1Piece	32.0
Sesame Seeds	1Tablespoon	0.1
Sunflower Seeds	1oz.	0.9
Deserts:		
Chocolate	1oz.	13.7
Milk Chocolate	1oz.	14.6
Coconut Bar	1oz.	12.3
Hard Candy	1oz.	18.9

Food Items:	Common Measures:	Total Sugar Grams:
Honey	1 Tablespoon	18.9
Sugar Brown	1 Cup	197.8
Sugar Granulated	1 Cup	193.6
Vegetables:		
Asparagus	1/2 Cup	1.4
Beans Snapped	1/2 Cup	1.2
Broccoli	1 Spear	3.0
Cabbage	1 Cup	0.4
Carrots Raw	1 Carrot	4.8
Cauliflower Raw	1/2 Cup	1.2
Celery	1 Stalk	0.4
Chard	1/2 Cup	0.2
Cooked Corn	1/2 Cup	2.1
Garlic	1 Clove	0.0
Lettuce	1/2 Cup	0.6
Mushrooms	1/2 Cup	0.7
Cooked Peas	1/2 Cup	4.7
Potatoes Baked	1 Potato	3.2
Tomatoes Raw	1 Tomato	3.4
Yams Cooked	1/2 Cup	0.3
Popular Foods:		
Snickers Bar	2.1oz.	29.0
Tasty Cake Honey Bun	31.4oz.	43.0
Lowfat Fruit-Flavored Yogurt	8oz.	35.0
Burger King Cini Minis	4.7oz.	48.0
Pepsi	12oz.	51.0
McDonalds McFlurry W/Butterfingers	13 3/4oz.	69.0
Sunkist Orange Soda	12oz.	65.0
Dairy Queen Mr. Misty Slush	32oz.	140.0

These charts are just a partial list, however, complete lists are easily obtained. Try to choose a diet that is moderate in sugars and low in fat with plenty of grains and vegetables. Always use caution when consuming salt and alcohol. Fiber modifies the speed that sugars enter the blood stream. Even with normal blood sugar levels, you should never eat anything sweet without using several teaspoons of fresh ground flax seed afterwards. Your protein intake should be normal, as there is limited scientific data for protein recommendations for diabetics. Always avoid saturated fat in any form. Nonnutritive sweeteners e.g. saccharin, aspartame and sucralose require further study and should be used in small amounts, until we know more about their long-term usage. It is almost impossible to cover all of the beneficial foods or the foods that you should try to avoid as each individual has different dietetic needs. The charts listed above are of minimal help and are primarily for comparison. If you are into experimentation, get a good diabetic cookbook and enjoy. Generally speaking, a diabetic cookbook would be good for the general population as well. You should probably try to eat that way as much as possible even if you are not a diabetic. Remember to consult the internet, local diabetic foundations, or a nutritional expert that deals with and educates diabetics.

Arthritis

As with many diseases, this disease is much easier to prevent than it is to cure. My only hope is that the information in this chapter gets to you before you have a problem. I am 68 years of age and have run all of my life, and still jog several miles a week and have thankfully never experienced any joint pain in my body. My hands and other joints feel and work as well as they did when I was in college. Therefore, I do not have a background of personal problems that I can work from. However, I have been able to help a considerable number of people who fight this painful disease on a daily basis. Arthritis is an autoimmune disease that has no quick fix, but it is not only possible, but probable that you can become almost entirely free of pain and function on a fairly normal basis. In this chapter, the door will be opened to several curative natural methods that have little or no destructive side effects. The first thing for us to do is to try to shut the door on the so called "quick fixes" that could eventually cost you your life. Some of the quick fixes involve:

- Aspirin or aspirin like drugs. Even though they may suppress the pain and act as an anti-inflammatory, they do not get at the cause. The net effect may be highly negative when compared to other NSAIDs (nonsteroidal anti-inflammatory drugs) e.g. phenylbutazone (Azolid), ibuprofen (Advil) and naproxen (Naprosyn). Although these drugs may provide a quick fix, their long-term use may only aggravate the situation and make the disease worse. Not only can they cause ulcers, but also you might end up in the hospital and some people will die because of NSAID therapies. For some, NSAIDs do not prove at all effective in controlling symptoms. The key here is finding something that will not only relieve symptoms, but also cause a healing process that does you no harm. NSAIDs do not fit those criteria.

- Now let us go to the next form of treatment that only continues to aggravate your physical well-being. This treatment involves corticosteroids. Corticosteroids are a very strong anti-inflammatory hormone. Their long-term adverse side affects may be far worse than the disease. They tend to decrease the normal function of the immune system and increase the susceptibility of a variety of diseases. Some of the long-term side effects might include:

1. Weight gain.
2. Skin made thin and weakened.
3. Ulcers may develop.
4. Blood pressure may rise.
5. Diabetes may develop.
6. Osteoporosis may develop.
7. Blood clot formation may increase.
8. Depression may be a factor.
9. May cause addiction over time.
10. Weakens adrenal glands.
11. Moon faced appearance.
12. May affect pre-existing retinal problems.
13. May affect pre-existing cataracts.
14. Tends to slow absorption of protein.
15. Curtails the production of male and female hormones.

As you can see, the short time feel good, may be worse than the long- term effects. I personally believe that an occasional shot of steroids (may be every three months) will not produce many of the above-mentioned symptoms. However, as a regular treatment, it would be better to think twice and try to find an alternative treatment that will not do as much damage to your health.

Good health seldom comes from the use of drugs. Rheumatoid arthritis usually requires long-term treatments, so let us consider some things that you may be able to use over the long-term without serious side effects. Some of the other autoimmune diseases are lupus, ulcerative colitis, Crohn's disease and possibly multiple sclerosis. If you can change your lifestyle, add a good regimen of vitamins, and add some of the things that I have mentioned earlier in the book you will be making a start in the right direction.

People with the most common form of arthritis, osteoarthritis, frequently turn to complementary or alternative therapies in the hopes of getting better without experiencing the side effects associated with prescription drugs. In 1997, a national survey reported that 26 percent of people with self-reported arthritis had used a complementary or alternative therapy within the previous 12 months. The same year, another survey reported that nearly two-thirds of rheumatology patients used complementary or alternative therapies, with osteoarthritis patients constituting the most frequent users. The most common complementary and alternative remedies are discussed below.

Colostrum

The first substance I recommend you try is colostrum. I could give you testimonial after testimonial concerning this product. The feedback I get from this product is truly nothing short of miraculous. The scientific data shows that this substance (mother's first milk) is a very good source of regulating and enhancing the immune system. I suggest that you use the liquid form made by the Cuprem company. You can contact them at 1-800-228-4253. You may also get results from the tablet form but most of the tablets are made in Australia and do not seem to produce the same results of the unprocessed liquid. In addition, I personally believe that the liquid form has gone through more rigorous testing and it is considerably more potent. The best way to use this product is to take 1/4 cup twice daily for one week then decrease the amount to 2 tablespoons per day. Always take it on an empty stomach as it contains large molecules and should stay in your digestive tract as long as possible for maximum absorption. Remember to keep this product refrigerated after opening. If you decide to choose the tablet form, remember that 20 tablets are less than 1/4 cup of the liquid when it comes to results. However, do not give up on the idea of using the tablets if that is your choice. The best way to ingest the tablet form is to pulverize the tablets, mix them up in some juice, and add some honey so you can get it down. After rigorous testing this product has never shown any serious side effects. I have seen this product work in a very short period and you should begin to see results within the first week. Not only is it highly anti-inflammatory but it may work with all of the other autoimmune diseases mentioned above. You can use this for the rest of your life without problems. I have used it for years as a booster to my immune system. However, the benefit has been that I have never had any sore joints or swollen fingers. I was possibly one of the first people to do research on colostrum in the United States and I have a long history of recommending its use.

Glucosamine

Glucosamine has been used for many years in Germany and other parts of Europe, glucosamine has recently gained popularity in the United States. A study of more than 200 patients with osteoarthritis, published in the British journal Lancet in January 2001, appears to support these claims. People treated with glucosamine reported fewer symptoms and exhibited less progressive damage on X-rays than did people treated with placebo.

Although glucosamine's effect on joint damage is still debated, most medical experts believe this supplement reduces pain and is safe. Because glucosamine may affect glucose metabolism, people with diabetes should avoid this supplement until its effects on blood glucose levels are better understood. The usual dose is 500 milligrams three times a day. Twice this amount may be recommended for the first few weeks. It may take four to eight weeks to get significant benefit, and like most remedies, glucosamine does not work for everyone. Because this supplement is relatively expensive, consider stopping after eight to 10 weeks if you do not experience any improvement.

Chondroitin And Sam-e

Two other supplements on the market, chondroitin and sam-e adenosylmethionine (SAM-e), are not as well studied or accepted in the United States as glucosamine. However, at least one large study of SAM-e found similar benefit to naproxen (a drug prescribed to relieve pain and inflammation) but with fewer side effects.

Enzymatic Therapy

The Company Enzymatic Therapy makes a product called curazyme. This product has the potential to benefit the treatment of rheumatoid arthritis. There are no known side affects, and it may very well decrease joint swelling and other inflammatory conditions.

Shark Cartilage

Shark cartilage inhibits angiogenesis (the generation of new blood vessels). Rheumatoid arthritis depends on the generation of new blood vessels, therefore this may provide some therapeutic effect. There are many kinds of shark cartilage on the market but I recommend a brand called Cartilade. You will find it

at your local health food store and you can expect
fair to excellent results.

DMSO

DMSO is a very potent painkiller. The only side
affects that I have found is that it might cause a slight
metallic taste in your mouth, but its benefits may far
outweigh any temporary discomfort it may cause you.
Do not use DMSO in conjunction with cayenne pepper.
This product should be always used by itself. Your
hands and back should be clean as it absorbs through
your skin almost immediately. You can purchase
DMSO in a cream or liquid form. Either is
satisfactory and certainly worth a try. If you would
like some additional information about DMSO, I
recommend that you order a comprehensive study of
this substance written by Dr. David Williams. The
title of the book is DMSO The Complete Up To Date
Guidebook. If you cannot find the book in your
bookstore, you can call (210) 367-4492 and ask for
the book, it is well worth the cost.

It is very possible that DMSO could be as effective as
morphine for pain without the drastic side affects. In
fact, the side effects may be very beneficial. I realize
that DMSO has had a rather stormy background but I
try to keep some around should I need it. The book
that I asked you to purchase contains both
precautions as well as the current research. This is
one solvent that moves very quickly through the skin.
If I covered all the research that I have done on DMSO

it would take an entire book so I am trying to guide you to the best information available.

Super Blue Stuff

The name sounds kinda hoakey doesn't it? Well aside from that, just about everything about this "stuff" is nothing short of miraculous. This product is tremendous when you add it to your arsenal for pain. One of my close friends was in an almost fatal accident causing injuries that will last for the rest of his life. The pain was almost intolerable in his back and shoulders. However, after topically applying Blue Stuff to the affected areas, his pain subsided an estimated 90%. My wife also testifies to its quick response in alleviating pain. If you have a computer and an internet connection, you can find out more information about this product by going to www.bluestuff.com . It is made from natural ingredients consisting of, MSM, Aloe Vera, other herbal concentrates and Emu oil. It acts incredibly fast, in most instances just a few minutes. Not only is it extremely effective for the pain caused from nerve damage, but is fantastic for all types of arthritis, including Fibromyalgia. If you are interested in buying this product, you can order it by calling 1-888-222-3919. I know that most of you have seen this product offered on T.V. infomercials and for the most part, like the rest of you, I shy away from those types of products. However, this is one offering that is definitely worth a try.

Herbal Remedies

Many herbs, including evening primrose, ginger, stinging nettle and curcumin, are said to have beneficial effects on arthritis. However, definitive studies have yet to be published.

If you pursue herbal therapies, take your time. If you decide to try herbal remedies, keep in mind that achieving results may take several weeks or more. Always discuss the use of herbs or other supplements with your doctor to check for interactions and side effects. Take herbs one at a time, under the guidance of your doctor and a knowledgeable herbal therapy practitioner.

If seeking an herbal therapy practitioner, first ask your doctor for the name of a local practitioner whom he or she trusts. Another source of information is the National Center for Complementary and Alternative Medicine. Search their Web site to find research centers at universities and medical schools throughout the United States that are conducting studies on complementary and alternative therapies. Try to find the name of a researcher near you who is conducting an herbal study; find out if that person provides guidance to patients as well.

Homeopathy

Homeopathy is a method of treatment based on administering tiny, often undetectable amounts of a substance that in higher doses might cause symptoms or disease in healthy persons, but could cure ill persons. Homeopathic approaches to the treatment of osteoarthritis are advocated by some, but compelling scientific evidence of benefit is lacking. A recent review in a British homeopathic journal identified only four methodologically sound studies and concluded that the available studies "do not allow a firm conclusion as to the effectiveness of homeopathic remedies in the treatment of patients with osteoarthritis."

Vitamins And Fish Oil

The antioxidant vitamins A, C, D and E are commonly recommended for arthritis. According to some studies, people with rheumatoid arthritis taking EPA fish oil capsules (containing omega-3 fatty acids) experience modest benefits involving decreased inflammation. Based on these studies, some practitioners and patients recommend including fish such as salmon, mackerel, herring or sardines in your diet several times a week. It is not clear; however, if increasing your fish intake has the same benefit as taking moderate to high doses of omega-3 fatty acid supplements. In order for this supplement to work you, need to take three capsules three times per day. You can reduce the amount over time as you begin to see results. It is also unclear if this treatment will help people with other, more common forms of arthritis, such as osteoarthritis. One final note on fish oil, it can stop your blood from clotting. It may not be wise to mix fish oil with aspirin, which is also an anti-clotting drug. You may want to check with your health practitioner if you consider mixing the two.

Alkaline State

This may seem to be an old folk remedy, but it has significant scientific data to back it up. As we age, our body naturally becomes more alkaline. When your system is too alkaline, it does not deal well with calcium absorption. It causes the calcium to deposit itself in the joints and cause bursitis and other painful symptoms. To help create an acid condition you should use:

- Some vinegar twice daily.

- Hydrochloride acid tablets.

- Grains.

- Nuts.

- Cheese, natural not processed.

- Lentils.

- Animal protein from (fish, Turkey or chicken).

Acupuncture And Acupressure

Acupuncture is an ancient Chinese treatment for many conditions, including arthritis. By inserting hair-fine needles into the skin along defined tracts called meridians, practitioners believe they can stimulate the flow of "qi," or vital life energy.

Acupressure and shiatsu, a Japanese form of acupressure, use no needles but involve pressure applied to certain points on the body. You can be taught to perform these techniques on yourself by a qualified practitioner.

Although medical experts do not understand how acupuncture and acupressure work, many people with arthritis have found these techniques helpful.

Magnet Therapy

Magnet therapy has become popular for alleviating symptoms of arthritis and for improving sports performance and general well-being. However, scientific evidence of its benefit is lacking. Therapeutic magnets of various strengths can be purchased in many products, from jewelry to mattress pads. If you decide to try this therapy, just remember to keep them away from your computer!

Diet Therapy

Efforts to find food allergies that cause arthritis have not yielded definitive results. The usual approach is to eliminate vegetables from the nightshade family: white potatoes, tomatoes, peppers and eggplant. Tobacco also belongs to this family. (Of course, there are more compelling reasons to avoid tobacco than its effect on arthritis.) Some people with arthritis also feel that dairy products aggravate their symptoms.

If you suspect food allergies may be affecting your arthritis (for example, if your symptoms become worse after you eat certain foods), keep a record of what you eat for several weeks, along with notes about your arthritis symptoms. Eliminate from your diet foods that seem to cause trouble; after a period of time, gradually reintroduce these foods one at a time, noting any change in symptoms. Please let me know about your results because all of the data that you can provide might just help others in their fight against this disease.

Exercise And Weight Control

Exercise and weight control are among the most effective self-help measures for alleviating the symptoms of osteoarthritis (and perhaps other types of arthritis). The objective is to improve or maintain cardiovascular fitness, range of motion and muscle tone while avoiding excessive stress or injury to joints. Walking, biking, cross-country skiing and swimming are the best choices. Water offers support and gentle resistance; if possible, water temperature should be 83 to 88 F or warmer.

In one study, 33 adults with arthritis reported being better able to manage their disease symptoms and enjoyed better health after a three-month tai chi program, another study found improved balance and abdominal muscle strength. Other studies of moderate, low-impact exercise have suggested a benefit in arthritis symptoms. Guidelines for appropriate exercise may be obtained from the Arthritis Foundation (1-800-283-7800). If you have arthritis, consider setting up an exercise program with the advice of a physician or physical therapist.

He or she can also suggest effective weight control measures if needed.

Self-Help Measures

Many arthritis sufferers find that warm showers and baths -- particularly whirlpool baths -- are often helpful in reducing pain and stiffness, especially first thing in the morning. For arthritis in the hands, the simple act of squeezing a sponge in a basin or sink full of warm water provides gentle exercise and relief of stiffness. Warm, wet compresses, especially castor oil compresses (available where specialty health products are sold), may provide comfort for sore joints.

Helpful suggestions abound in books and magazines and on the Internet about joint-sparing techniques for ordinary activities. For example:

- Pick up a coffee cup with both hands instead of thumb and finger.

- Open doors with the side of your arm and body.

- Open a car door with both hands.

Your doctor may refer you to an occupational therapist who can teach these and many more helpful techniques.

Massage

Massage by an expert in therapeutic massage can contribute to an overall feeling of relaxation and well-being. There are many types of massage, including Western, Swedish, Deep-Tissue and Neuromuscular. Each type uses a slightly different approach, but all have similar emotional and physical benefits. A massage therapist can teach you some do-it-yourself techniques.

Massage therapists are required to be licensed in at least 28 states and the District of Columbia. You can find a qualified practitioner by asking your physician or by contacting a professional massage therapy association.

Other types of bodywork, as established by The National Certification Board for Therapeutic Massage and Bodywork or The America Massage Therapy Association, include Feldenkrais, a system of gentle body movements that offers improvement in strength and flexibility, and the Alexander Technique. Classes and individual instruction can be found in many locations.

A Positive Outlook

Like any person with a chronic disease, a person with osteoarthritis may be more prone to depression. You may worry about becoming increasingly unable to perform activities of daily living or doing things you enjoy. The capacity to adapt, cope and continue full function varies greatly among patients. Some patients feel disabled by their symptoms, but only a very small percentage will ever become severely disabled. A positive outlook, focusing on what you are able to do rather than what you are unable to do, can be immensely helpful. Some people find that meditation and other stress-reduction techniques help them to relax and better adjust the pace of their lives to the limitations imposed by their arthritis.

Back Pain

Low back pain is a common musculoskeletal symptom that may be either acute or chronic. It may be caused by a variety of diseases and disorders that affect the lumbar spine. Low back pain is often accompanied by sciatica, which is pain that involves the sciatic nerve and is felt in the lower back, the buttocks, and the backs of the thighs.

Low back pain is a symptom that affects 80% of the general United States population at some point in life with sufficient severity to cause absence from work. It is the second most common reason for visits to primary care doctors, and is estimated to cost the American economy $75 billion every year.

Low back pain may be experienced in several different ways:

- In localized pain, the patient will feel soreness or discomfort when the doctor palpates, or presses on a specific surface area of the lower back.

- Diffuse pain is spread over a larger area and comes from deep tissue layers.

- Radicular. The pain is caused by irritation of a nerve root. Sciatica is an example of radicular pain.

- Referred. The pain is perceived in the lower back but is caused by inflammation elsewhere-- often in the kidneys or lower abdomen.

Acute pain in the lower back that does not extend to the leg is most commonly caused by a sprain or muscle tear, usually occurring within 24 hours of heavy lifting or overuse of the back muscles. The pain is usually localized, and there may be muscle spasms or soreness when the doctor touches the area. The patient usually feels better when resting.

Chronic pain

- Chronic low back pain has several different possible causes:
  Chronic strain on the muscles of the lower back may be caused by obesity ; pregnancy ; or job-related stooping, bending, or other stressful postures.
- Low back pain at night that is not relieved by lying down may be caused by a tumor in the cauda equina (the roots of the spinal nerves controlling sensation in and movement of the legs), or a cancer that has spread to the spine from the prostate, breasts, or lungs. The risk factors for the spread of cancer to the lower back include a history of smoking, sudden weight loss, and age over 50.
- Ankylosing spondylitis is a form of arthritis that causes chronic pain in the lower back. The pain is made worse by sitting or lying down and improves when the patient gets up. It is most commonly seen in males between 16 and 35.

Ankylosing spondylitis is often confused with mechanical back pain in its early stages.

- Disk herniation is a disorder in which a spinal disk begins to bulge outward between the vertebrae. Herniated or ruptured disks are a common cause of chronic low back pain in adults.

- Back pain that is out of proportion to a minor injury, or that is unusually prolonged, may be associated with a somatoform disorder or other psychiatric disturbance.

- Low back pain that radiates down the leg usually indicates involvement of the sciatic nerve. The nerve can be pinched or irritated by herniated disks , tumors of the cauda equina, abscesses in the space between the spinal cord and its covering, spinal stenosis , and compression fractures . Some patients experience numbness or weakness of the legs as well as pain.

All forms of treatment of low back pain are aimed either at symptom relief or to prevent interference with the processes of healing. None of these methods appear to speed up healing. Acute back pain is usually treated with nonsteroidal anti-inflammatory drugs (NSAIDs), such as ibuprofen, muscle relaxants , or aspirin . Applications of heat or cold compresses are also helpful to most patients. If the patient has not experienced some improvement after several weeks of treatment, the doctor will reinvestigate the cause of the pain.

Patients with chronic back pain are treated with a combination of medications, physical therapy, and occupational or lifestyle modification. The medications given are usually NSAIDs, although patients with hypertension , kidney problems, or stomach ulcers should not take these drugs. Patients who take NSAIDs for longer than six weeks should be monitored periodically for complications.

Physical therapy for chronic low back pain usually includes regular exercise for fitness and flexibility, and massage or application of heat if necessary. Lifestyle modifications include:

- Giving up smoking.
- Weight reduction (if necessary).
- Evaluation of the patient's occupation or other customary activities.
- Patients with herniated disks are treated surgically if the pain does not respond to medication.
- Patients with chronic low back pain sometimes benefit from pain management techniques, including biofeedback , acupuncture , and chiropractic manipulation of the spine.
- Psychotherapy is recommended for patients whose back pain is associated with a somatoform, anxiety , or depressive disorder.

Treatment of sciatica and other disorders that involve the legs may include NSAIDs. Patients with long-standing sciatica or spinal stenosis that do not respond to NSAIDs are treated surgically. Although some doctors use cortisone injections to relieve the pain, this form of treatment is still debated.

Chiropractic

Chiropractic treats patients by manipulating or adjusting sections of the spine. It is one of the most popular forms of alternative treatment in the United States for relief of back pain caused by straining or lifting injuries. Some osteopathic physicians, physical therapists, and naturopathic physicians also use spinal manipulation to treat patients with low back pain.

Traditional Chinese medicine

Practitioners of traditional Chinese medicine treat low back pain with acupuncture, tui na (push-and-rub) massage, and the application of herbal poultices.

Herbal medicine

Herbal medicine can utilize a variety of antispasmodic herbs in combination to help relieve low back pain due to spasm. Lobelia (Lobelia inflata) and myrrh (Commiphora molmol) are two examples of antispasmodic herbs.

Homeopathy

Homeopathic treatment for acute back pain consists of applications of Arnica oil to the sore area or oral doses of Arnica or Rhus toxicodendron. Bellis perennis is recommended for deep muscle injuries. Other remedies may be recommended based on the symptoms presented by the patient.

Super Blue Stuff

I know that if you just read the chapter on arthritis, you just read about this product. However, I am listing this again here as it works for back pain as well. The name sounds kinda hoakey doesn't it? Well aside from that, just about everything about this "stuff" is nothing short of miraculous. This product is tremendous when you add it to your arsenal for pain. One of my close friends was in an almost fatal accident causing injuries that will last for the rest of his life. The pain was almost intolerable in his back and shoulders. However, after topically applying Blue stuff to the affected areas, his pain subsided an estimated 90%. My wife also testifies to its quick response in alleviating pain. If you have a computer and an internet connection, you can find out more information about this product by going to www.bluestuff.com . It is made from natural ingredients consisting of, MSM, Aloe Vera, other herbal concentrates and Emu oil. It acts incredibly fast in most instances just a few minutes. Not only is it extremely effective for the pain caused from nerve damage, but is fantastic for all types of arthritis, including fibromyalgia. If you are interested in buying this product, you can order it by calling 1-888-222-3919. I know that most of you have seen this product offered on T.V. infomercials and for the most part like the rest of you, I shy away from those types of products. However, this is one offering that is definitely worth a try.

DMSO

DMSO is a very potent painkiller. The only side affects that I have found it is that it might cause a slight metallic taste in your mouth but its benefits may far outweigh any temporary discomfort it may cause you. Do not use DMSO in conjunction with cayenne pepper. This product should be always used by itself in your hands and back should be clean as it absorbs through your skin almost immediately. You can purchase DMSO in a cream or liquid form. Either is satisfactory and certainly worth of try. If you would like some additional information about DMSO, I recommend that you order a comprehensive study of this substance written by Dr. David Williams. The title of the book is DMSO The Complete Up To Date Guidebook. If you cannot find the book in your bookstore, you can call (210) 367-4492 and ask for the book it is well worth the cost.

It is very possible that DMSO could be as effective as morphine for pain without the drastic side affects. In fact, the side effects may be very beneficial. I realize that DMSO has had a rather stormy background but I try to keep some around should I need it. The book that I ask you to purchase contains both precautions as well as current research, this is one solvent that moves very quickly through the skin. If I covered all the research that I have done on DMSO it would take an entire book so I am trying to guide you to the best information available.

Vitamins Minerals Herbs and Other Supplements

I would like to start this section off by reminding you that I do not sell anything, receive no kickbacks from any product or publications, so I strive to be totally objective about all of my recommendations. My pay consists of helping you to succeed in your quest for good health.

A – Natures safest source is beta-carotene as your body uses this to produce vitamin A with little fear of overdose. A vital antioxidant, it is synergistic with other antioxidants.

Acidophilus – Excellent for increasing favorable intestinal flora. Should always be used after taking an antibiotic or with a yeast infection.

Alphalfa – Good source of vitamin A, beneficial for arthritis, it may also thicken the blood.

Alpha Lipolic Acid – Extremely important as an antioxidant. It recycles vitamin C and E back into the bloodstream. Also helps rid the body of mercury.

Aloe – May be beneficial for burns and dry skin, also as a liquid form may have beneficial effects on the stomach lining and aids in regulating bowel movements.

B – Vitamins are a complex of 11 vitamin factors. They are water-soluble and aid in the metabolism of fats, carbohydrates and proteins. Extremely important in the function of the nervous system. B vitamins are all synergistic and should be taken together. The B vitamins should include B-1 (thiamine hydrochloride), B-2 (riboflavin), B-6 (pyrodoxine hydrochloride), B-12 (cyanocobalamin), biotin, choline, inositol, niacin (B -3), PABA (para-aminobenzoic acid), pantethine (B-5) and folic acid.

Bee Pollen – This substance contains all 22 elements in the human body enzymes, hormones, vitamins and amino acids.

Bilberry – Increases night vision and strengthens muscles and the nerves of the eyes. Along with zinc, it can prevent and even reverse eye damage caused by blood vessel deterioration.

Birch Bark – May relieve urinary problems and play a role in expelling intestinal parasites.

Black Cohosh – Has similar effects to that of synthetic estrogen without the possible side affects of cancer.

Bromelain – Works similar to a blood thinner without the side effects. Helps to prevent clotting and may help rid the body of excess fluids.

Calcium – The body cannot produce calcium therefore, it must be ingested in food or supplement form. It plays a significant role in optimal bone health as well as the fact that if your body is deficient in calcium, it will steal it from the bones making them brittle thin and porous.

Capsicum (Cayenne) – This herb is very important for heart and stomach problems. Also helps the circulatory system and causes veins, arteries and capillaries to maintain their elasticity.

Cascara – A gentle remedy for chronic constipation. It is synergistic with flax oil, flax seed, and psyllium.

Chamomile – A gentle relaxant. As a tea, may give you a good nights sleep. Best when used with magnesium citrate and valerian root.

Chromium – Is a key component of the glucose tolerance factor. It supports the body's ability to metabolize proteins and fats. It is very beneficial to most diabetics and may help in weight loss.

Coenzyme Q10 – This is a powerful antioxidant that fights damaging free radicals. It plays a gigantic role in oxidative stress. It is a key factor in producing ATP (the energy component) and is a key factor in recycling vitamins C and E. And sufficient amounts (200 or more mg per day) will play a key role in oxygenating the heart muscle.

Colloidal Silver – Colloidal silver is a natural antibiotic that is supposedly deadly to all single celled organisms. The way colloidal silver kills invading microbes is by dissolving (via an electrochemical reaction) an enzyme that metabolizes oxygen for these primitive organisms. Thus, the cell suffocates and dies. However, the verdict is still out on this one.

Copper – The body needs copper for normal growth and health. For patients who are unable to get enough copper in their regular diet or who have a need for more copper, copper supplements may be necessary. Generally, they are taken by mouth but some patients may need to receive them by injection. Copper is needed to help your body use iron. It is also important for nerve function, bone growth, and to help your body use sugar. Lack of copper may lead to anemia and osteoporosis (weak bones). Some conditions may increase your need for copper. These include burns, diarrhea, intestine disease, kidney disease and pancreas disease.

Creatine – Creatine is produced naturally in the kidney, liver, and pancreas of humans. Creatine is also supplied in meat and fish. Most creatine in the body is stored in the muscles, in the form of phosphocreatine. Creatine is a quickly available source of energy for muscle contraction. Creatine is also involved in muscle growth.

Damiana – May help with sexual impotence in both males and females. Damiana is also sometimes said to be helpful for treating asthma and other respiratory diseases, depression, digestive problems, menstrual disorders, and various forms of sexual dysfunction for example impotence in men and the inability to achieve orgasm in women.

Deglycyrrhizinated Licorice – This is an extremely important substance for both ulcers and acid reflux. It promotes the stomach lining allowing healing to occur.

DHEA (Dehydroepiandrosterone) – A hormone produced by the adrenal glands, it is the most abundant hormone in the steroid family found in your bloodstream. The adrenal gland begins producing less DHEA by the age of 20 and by age 60, our bodies produce 5 to 15% as much as when we were 20. DHEA helps with lupus, adrenal failure and possibly osteoporosis, slowing aging, improving general well-being, depression, impotence, Alzheimer's disease, chronic fatigue syndrome and sports performance.

Dong Quai – Dong Quai is used as a treatment for menstrual cramps, irregular menstruation, dysmenorrhea, PMS, as well as hot flashes and other menopausal symptoms.

E – Vitamin E is an antioxidant that fights damaging natural substances known as free radicals. It works in lipids (fats and oils), which makes it synergistic with vitamin C which also helps to fight free radicals. Important note: vitamin E must be taken in conjunction with Selenium or it will not be absorbed by your system.

Echinacea – Excellent treatment for recurring infections of the upper respiratory system and lower urinary tract. It is also a popular treatment for colds and flues as well. Thought to be a fantastic short-term immune system booster.

EPA (Eicosapentaenoic Acid) – A great source of omega-3 fatty acids (essential fatty acids) special fats that the body needs as much as vitamins. Helpful in the prevention of heart disease, fish oil lowers triglyceride levels, raises the HDL good cholesterol, slows down arteriosclerosis and helps to treat arteriosclerosis. Also effective in lowering ocular pressure in the eyes.

Eye Bright – As you would expect, this herb is excellent for eyesight and tends to decrease several vision problems, (natures eye drops).

Fever Few – Aids significantly in the prevention of chronic recurring migraine headaches. However, it is not believed to be effective for cluster or tension headaches.

Folic Acid – This is an extremely important antioxidant formula. Primarily used in the prevention of birth defects of the brain and spinal cord, heart disease and cancer prevention.

Garlic – This is a valuable herb for your heart health. It will help to maintain normal cholesterol levels; it is also a very important antiviral substance. In Europe, garlic is seen as an all-around treatment for preventing arteriosclerosis, one of the major causes of heart disease and strokes.

Ginger – This herb makes a wonderful tasting Tea. Also, helps relieve nausea (motion sickness, morning sickness in pregnancy, post surgical nausea). In addition, it is suggested to aid in arteriosclerosis, migraine headaches and rheumatoid arthritis.

Ginkgo Biloba – This herb is primarily used for Alzheimer's disease, non-Alzheimer's dementia, and normal age related memory loss. It is also said to alleviate problems with impaired circulation in the legs, PMS symptoms, altitude sickness, sexual dysfunction due to antidepressant drugs, macular degeneration, assisting antipsychotic medications, tinnitus, depression, complications of diabetes and Ray nod's phenomenon.

Ginseng – This herb is reported to strengthen immunity against colds, flu's, and other infections, stimulating the mind, helping to control diabetes, and improving physical performance capacity. It is also reported to help prevent cancer, fight chemical dependency, and improve sexual performance.

Glucosamine – This product is often combined with chondroitin sulfate and has very favorable results with many arthritic conditions. It provides the building blocks for rebuilding cartilage. It is especially good for anyone seeking joint and tissue support.

Golden Seal – Is commonly used for poorly healing sores, fungal infections, inflamed mucous membranes, minor digestive problems, sore throat and urinary tract infections. Please note: masking positive findings on drug screens is a fallacy, so if you plan to purchase it for that reason, remember a word to the wise...it doesn't work!

Gotu Kola – Renders a good nerve tonic and is used for the relief of pain associated with varicose veins. It is also used for hemorrhoids, keloid scars, burn and wound healing, liver cirrhosis, scleroderma and the improvement of mental function.

Grape Seed Extract – Grape seed extract is one of nature's richest sources of flavinoids, which have a potent free radical scavenging activity. It contains extracts that show the same similar beneficial results as red wine without any side effects.

Green Barley Grass – Barley grass contains eighteen amino acids, including the eight essential ones–that is, the amino acids that we must get from our diet. The body cannot produce them itself. Amino acids are the building blocks of proteins, which are the major contents of every cell and body fluid (except urine and bile) and are necessary for continuous cell-building, cell regeneration, and energy production needed for life. An added benefit of the green barley leaf proteins is that they are polypeptides–smaller proteins that can be directly absorbed into the bloodstream, where they enhance cell metabolism.

Hawthorn – This herb is used to treat congestive heart failure in its early stages along with benign heart palpitations, hypertension, angina and atherosclerosis.

Iron – The element iron is essential to human life. However, it shouldn't be taken by men unless they suffer from iron deficient anemia. Women also use it for menorrhagia (Heavy Menstruation).

Kava Kava – Can be used for the reduction of anxiety, insomnia, tension headaches and alcohol withdrawal. While prescription drugs used for anxiety are much stronger, kava does not impair mental function.

Kelp – Excellent source of iodine, which is the key to proper thyroid function. Kelp has other beneficial properties among them are calcium, potassium and magnesium.

L-Carnatine – This is important as it strengthens the muscles of the heart. The L form is the natural form and is best utilized by the body.

L-Cysteine – This may play a role in helping normalize liver enzymes. It works especially well when used in conjunction with milk thistle. Certain drugs tend to denormalize liver enzymes and these two substances are synergistic. Remember, the L form as this is important in the utilization of the product.

Lecithin – Provides a natural source of choline, insitol and linolic acid, which are vital components of the cell, walls and play an important function in cellular growth. May also help lower cholesterol.

Lycopene – Is a powerful antioxidant found in tomatoes, watermelon, guava and pink grapefruit. Like beta- carotene, lycopene belongs to a family of chemicals known as carotenoids. In addition, as an anti-oxidant it is about twice as powerful as beta-carotene. There is also a direct correlation between Lycopene and the absence of prostate disease. Along with pygeum and saw palmetto, it is synergistic to prostate health.

Magnesium – Is an essential nutrient mineral, meaning your body needs it for healthy functioning. It is found in large quantities all over the body and is utilized by the system for numerous purposes. Among them are, muscle relaxation, blood clotting and it is one of the building blocks for ATP (adenosine triphosphate, the bodies' main energy molecule). It is sometimes referred to as nature's calcium channel-blocker. This is why magnesium affects migraine headaches and high blood pressure. It is also the key to the proper rhythm of the heart muscles.

Ma Huang – Ephedra (also called ma huang) is living proof that even herbs if abused can be hazardous. The plant is the natural source of ephedrine, a stimulant found in many prescription and nonprescription drugs including decongestants, bronchodilators, and allergy medications. Ma huang was traditionally used by Chinese herbalists during the early stages of respiratory infections and for the short-term treatment of certain kinds of asthma, eczema, hay fever, narcolepsy, and edema. However, ma huang was never supposed to be taken for an extended period of time, and people in poor health were warned to use only low doses or avoid ma huang altogether.

Manganese – Is a trace mineral necessary to facilitate skeletal development. It provides needed protein and carbohydrate production and is necessary to nutrify the nerves.

Melatonin – Is a natural hormone that regulates sleep. Melatonin helps with jet lag or other sleep disturbances. It also seems to help people suffering from insomnia. Can be used to help people who have been using sleeping pills and want to quit.

MGN-3 – Is highly supportive to the immune system. It has been used successfully increase the killer cells, and there has been positive effects in the treatment of cancer and other viral diseases.

Milk Thistle – Is used as a treatment for alcoholic, alcoholic fatty liver, liver cirrhosis, liver poisoning, viral hepatitis and from the effects of liver-toxic medications.

MSM – Is an excellent source of organic sulphur, which is one of the key structural components in cartilage. It is possible that it could help to alleviate arthritic pain, and can play a synergistic role with glucosamine.

Oregano – Oil of Oregano is a potent antiseptic, meaning it kills germs. Research proves that it is highly effective for killing a wide range of fungi, yeast, and bacteria as well as parasites and viruses. It may be used topically and taken internally.

PABA (para-aminobenzoic acid) – This is a B vitamin that helps in the synthesis of folic acid.

Peppermint – This herb makes a wonderful substitute for coffee. It is also used as a digestive aid, and for the treatment of coughs and colds, gallstones and candida yeast infections. Peppermint oil is also used for congestion e.g. Vicks VapoRub, Solarcaine and Ben-Gay.

Pregnenolone – This hormone is a precursor to DHEA and is produced by the adrenal glands. It also enhances DHEA's activity in your system.

Psyllium – A soluble fiber that acts as a gentle laxative. It is valuable to your colon as it adds valuable fiber to your system.

Pygeum – This is very valuable in the support of the prostate gland. Note as previously stated, pygeum is synergistic with lycopene and saw palmetto.

Red Clover – Helps to purify the blood. It has also been used in the treatment of cancer. Other uses are skin problems e.g. acne, eczema and psoriasis.

Red Raspberry – Raspberry leaf tea is used during pregnancy to prevent complications and make delivery easier. It also helps to control excessive menstruation and diarrhea.

Rose Hips – As their name implies, they come from the rose plant, they are what remains after the petals fall off. Rose hips have been used as a source of Nutrition for centuries. They are a highly recognized source of vitamin C, and they contain vitamins E and K, and the B vitamins riboflavin and folate.

Saw Palmetto – The beneficial properties of saw palmetto make it the leading herb for men's prostate health. It contains phytochemicals that inhibit the transformation of testosterone into dihydrotestosterone, which is damaging to the prostate gland.

Soy Protein Powder – Soy protein supplies important nutrients and essential amino acids, it is very low in fats and free of carbohydrates.

St. Johns Wort – Produces a calming effect and could be used to replace anti-depressants as it has much fewer side effects. Note do not take St. Johns Wort with other medications as it may have serious side effects.

Sublingual B-12 – This B vitamin is being mentioned separately here as it has little value if it is swallowed. The sublingual tablet dissolves under the tongue and is absorbed directly into your system through the mucus-membranes.

Valerian Root – Excellent when used as a relaxant or for minor anxiety, it has a very calming effect. May be used in capsule form or as a tea (never boil) prior to retiring. If you suffer from insomnia or anxiety, it might take several weeks for this herb to accumulate and produce its full effect.

Vanadyl Sulfate – This is the biologically active form of vanadium and may be extremely effective for diabetics. It plays a role in desensitizing the cells to insulin. It is synergistic with chromium picolinate. If you use these products and have diabetes, do so with a doctor's supervision, as your insulin levels might change drastically.

Vitamin K – This vitamin is necessary for the production of prothrombin, which is required for blood clotting. However, it may thicken your blood, so you should use extreme caution if you are taking a blood thinner.

Yohimbe – This herb has gained recent popularity in its possible role as an aphrodisiac. It is extremely important that you do not overdose on this product, as it can be toxic.

Zink – This is an essential mineral in human nutrition as it is found in every cell of the body. It is involved in the synthesis of protein and many enzymatic reactions.

I would like to conclude this chapter with some ideas about where to find some of the supplements listed above.

- Your local health food store is usually the first place to start. Most owners are very knowledgeable about the products that they sell. If you cannot find something, they will usually order it for you.
- Ask your health care provider for information about where you can purchase quality products.
- If you or someone that you know has an internet connection, you can find many first

rate supplements. When selecting a company try to find out if their products are rated as standardized. Standardized supplements have been tested for quality and potency. Most companies will send you a free catalog just for the asking.

JUST FOR FUN

The following pages are a collection of drugs, treatments and herbal treatments of the late 1800's. Some of them still have considerable value and have become the basis for modern medicine. Others have thankfully fallen by the wayside by either being of no efficacious value, or by just being deadly. Whatever their classification, they were the best treatments that medicine of that time had to offer. The authors want you to be sure to understand that we in no way recommend any of these treatments. In fact, we strongly suggest that you never try any of these treatments. However, you might just want to read them for the fun of it. Some of the ingredients listed in these remedies will sound like a witch's cauldron. So have fun with them, get a shock or a laugh, we always do. All credit goes to the original author the doctors, scientists and researchers without whom medicine would not be the same today.

LEE'S

Priceless Recipes
A VALUABLE COLLECTION OF

TRIED FORMULAS AND SIMPLE METHODS
•FOR

Farmers, Housekeepers, Mechanics, Manufacturers, Druggists, Chemists, Perfumers, Barbers, Chiropodists, Renovators, Dyers, Bakers, Confectioners, Woodworkers, Decorators, Painters, Paper-hangers, Metal-workers, Hunters, Trappers, Tanners, Taxidermists, Stockmen, Etc., and all People in Every Department of Human Endeavor.

ALPHABETICALLY INDEXED

COMPILED BY

DR. N. T. OLIVER

CHICAGO

LAIRD & LEE, Publishers
_____ 1897.

LEE'S PONY REFREFERENCE LIBRARY.

Entered according to Act of Congress In the year eighteen
hundred and ninety-five by

WILLIAM H. LEE,

In the office of the Librarian of Congress at Washington.
APPARATUS.

The following are of great assistance In the making up of medical preparations. and although other articles can be used, it is by far the best plan to procure the tools of the trade if satisfactory results are expected:

Mortars.–These are among the articles of most frequent use in pharmaceutical processes. They are made of glass, wood, porcelain, iron, composition, marble and other substances, and vary in size from one ounce up. They are used for mixing ointments. cerates and soft pulverized substances; also for pulverizing barks, spices, etc.

The Pestle is the necessary assistant of the mortar, and is
usually made in two pieces. This necessary piece of apparatus
can be purchased of any drug supply house.

Scales are an absolute necessity, as the proper

proportions of the materials cannot be ascertained without them. Two pairs should be used—one known as the prescription scale for weighing 1 drachm and under, and a larger pair for weighing over 2 drachms.

Graduates or graduating glasses are glass vessels marked
with a scale, and are necessary for measuring liquids. They can
be obtained in. several sizes.

Spatulas are made of glass, Ivory and steel, are a flat, flexible bladed knife, used for mixing. The steel spatula or palette is the best for ordinary purposes. They come in several sizes. A common case knife answers the purpose.

Percolator is a vessel made of tin, glass or wood, and is used for extracting the soluble principles from vegetable substances. (See Percolation.) Sometimes they are made of porcelain or earthenware. The tin is the most generally used. It is in the form of a tube about 8 inches long and 334 Inches in diameter, terminating at one end in a funnel, and contains easily removable loosely, fitting perforated plates. The instrument acts somewhat on the principle of a strainer. See Processes, article on Percolation.

DEPARTMENT I.
Funnels, or tunnels, are made of glass, porcelain, hard rubber, tin or other metals. They are used in transferring liquids, and several sizes are necessary.

Retorts are made of glass or iron and are in several sizes. With them are needed stands or frames to support them, and funnels, filtering and displacement apparatus are necessary. Retorts are used in all processes of distillation. See Distillation.

Filter Rack.—A funnel-shaped framework of wire used to
hold the filtering paper. See Filtration.

Lamps used in the process of distillation. The alcohol lamp is the best for the purpose and should be provided with a frame or rack in which to place it. A cap is required to place over the wick of the alcohol lamp after using to prevent evaporation.

Baths are used for securing a more uniform and fixed degree of heat than are obtained from the open flame or an ordinary heating apparatus. They are of various kinds, but those most generally used are the Sand Bath, made of an iron or copper vessel containing ordinary clean sand, in which the vessel containing the material to he heated is so imbedded and surrounded as to prevent the two vessels coming in contact, and the Water Bath, which consists of one vessel within another, as an ordinary double glue pot, so arranged that they cannot come in contact at any point to which the heat is applied.

Sieves come in several sizes; are fitted with silt or brass wire gauze for fine purposes, or horse-hair cloth or wire netting for coarser ones. Drum sieves are such as are furnished with covers, rendering loss and dust impossible. Sieves are used in preparing powders, mixing vegetable pulverizations, etc.

NOTE.–The above are the articles in most general use, and are the most needed in large laboratories. Test tubes, crucibles, Drug mills, tincture presses and a host of others are made use of. but for all ordinary purposes the list as here given is all that will be required We will now pass on to the various ways of compounding medicines

PROCESSES.

Decocting.–A method for extracting the active or useful principle from animal or vegetable substances, where the same cannot be injured by heat. It consists of boiling for a certain length of time; where the proportions are not given, use one ounce of raw, material to one pint of water.

Distillation.–The vaporization of a liquid in one vessel and conducting it In this condition to another, where it is condensed and collected. It is used for separating liquids from the solids with which they are mixed; for separating more volatile liquids, as ether, alcohol, etc., from Others less so with which they are mixed, and for impregnating liquids with the volatile principles of plants, etc., as In the preparation of the aromatic spirits, cologne water etc. It is performed with a retort and receiver. Apply the heat with a spirit or alcohol lamp under the bulb of the retort, and, produce condensation by wrapping

301

cloths, wet with cold water around the retort. When the principle desired will be effected.

Filtration.–A process for separating Insoluble matters, precipitates, etc., by means of porous medic, or the medium of slow pouring or dripping, which allows the passage of the liquids only, and employed for rendering liquids, tinctures, etc., clear and transparent and separating valuable precipitates. Tincture and dilute spirits are usually filtered through a specially prepared paper called filtering paper, and which can be procured of any druggist. It is cut in a peculiar manner, made into the shape of a funnel and placed in a rack or funnel, where it cleanly separates the articles to be run through. The process of making the paper filter is as follows: cut a circular disc of filtering paper in two through the line of its diameter; take either half and fold it across the line of the radius, bringing the edges close together; then turn down the double edge of the cut side and fold it several times: finally, run a smooth hard surface along the seam thus produced, to compress it, and spread the finished filter into an appropriate rack or funnel, first moistening it with water before the liquid to be filtered is poured in.

A Cheap Filter is made by taking an ordinary, large-sized flower pot; plug the hole with a piece of sponge; then put a layer of powdered charcoal about 1 inch thick, the same of silver sand: then a layer of small stones and gravel about 2 inches thick. This makes an excellent filter for impure water.

Another method of purifying water is by placing in a tank of impure water a vessel so arranged that a sponge, which it contains, shall lap over the edge and dip into the water of the tank. The sponge gradually sucks up, purifies the water in the reservoir, and allows it to drop into a smaller vessel or receiver, from which it can be drawn off by a tube. By placing a few lumps of charcoal in the receiver, filtration of the most perfect kind is effected. Any Vessel open at both ends (one smaller at one end than the other is preferable) can he used as filter by setting it in an upright position and puffing straw, sand or charcoal in the bottom, and passing the liquid to be filtered through it. Magnesia in small quantities placed in the paper filter
greatly assists in clarifying tinctures. etc.

Clarification. The removal of impurities from liquids by the admixture of some substances, usually albumen in some form, as milk, the white of an egg, or a solution of gelatin, which, by 'being coagulated, entangles and precipitates the contained impurities, rendering the liquids clear. Vegetable acids will clarify the expressed juices of plants. The following composition is said to bleach all colored liquids: Albumen, 300 parts; neutral tartrate of Potash, 2; alum. 5; sal ammoniac, 700. The albumen must of course not be coagulated. The ingredients are first dissolved in a little water and then added to the liquid to be clarified. Expression is required to separate the last portions of tinctures, Infusion, etc.; also the juices of fresh plants. fruits, etc., after they are properly crushed. A screw press Is generally used, but strong bags or cloths can be made use of.

Infusion.—When the principles to be extracted from any substance are soluble in water, and at the same time but slightly volatile, pour boiling water on It. cover the vessel carefully and allow the Whole to remain untouched for several minutes or even hours, according to the greater or less penetrability of the substance. Tea is properly made by Infusion. When the proportions are not given, it is to be generally understood that 1 ounce is to be used to 1 pint of boiling water.

Percolation. This is the most rapid process for extracting the Soluble principles from vegetable substances. First, reduce the material to a powder, then mix together by means of the sieve or mortar and pestle, according to the recipe for preparation. Moisten the mass thoroughly with alcohol, allow it to stand or macerate for 12 hours In a close covered vessel, then place in the percolator, pouring in more alcohol and water, If in the recipe, and permitting it to run through the percolator. if the liquor, which first passes through, is thick and turbid, introduce again into the instrument. Be very careful not to have the powder too coarse or loosely pressed or it will permit the liquid to run through too rapidly; on the other hand not too fine or it will offer an undesired resistance. A simple percolator can be made by using a large funnel with a plug of carded cotton in the neck, or a fine sponge will answer the purpose; then fill the funnel with hay or straw, a piece of cotton cloth allowed to bang loosely over the edge, forming a sort of bag in the interior, completes the apparatus.

MEDICAL PREPARATIONS.

CORRECT CLASSIFICATIONS.

Antacids are remedies for acidity of the stomach. Their action is purely chemical and are simply palliatives. or a relief for the time being. Dyspepsia and diarrhea are the principle affections for which they are employed. The alkalies are the principles antacids. Ammonia, carbonate of lime, washing soda and magnesia come under this head.

Antiseptics are medicines used for preventing putrefaction.
Among them are boracic acid, carbolic acid, powdered charcoal,
creosote, nitric acid and chloride of lime,

Anthelmintics are medicines, which destroy or expel worms from the stomach and intestines. Among them are calomel, kousso. male fern. oil of turpentine, pink root, pumpkin seeds, santonin and wormseed.

Astringents.–These are substances, which contract and strengthen the animal fibres. Alder, alum, birch, blackberry root, sumach, tannic acid and wintergreen are valuable for this purpose.

Absorbents stimulate those vessels and glands, which concur in the exercise of absorption. They carry off poisonous or irritant substances are used in diarrhea, vomiting, and are chiefly included in antacids and cathartics.

Alternatives.–Medicines which change the morbid or unhealthy action of the system. This class is largely included in emetics and tonics.

Anodynes.–Preparations used for the relief of pain, included tinder the head of cerebro-spinants.

Antiarthritics.–Medicines which subdue an influence in the blood which gives rise to rheumatism, gout, or diseases of the joints. They are classified under the head of antacids, cathartics and tonics.

Anticonvulsives correct convulsive disorders dependent upon blood deterioration and nervous debility. Embraced in tonics and cerebro-spinants.

Antiemetics.–Medicines which prevent vomiting. They will be found among stimulants and cerebro-spinants.

Antiperiodics have an influence over diseases, which have a periodic tendency, such as malarial fevers. This class is largely included in tonics.

Antiphlogistics counteract all Inflammatory processes; are used in inflammatory fevers, etc. Many medicines of this class will be found under the head of emetics, cathartics, diapboretics, diuretics and refrigerants.

Antiscorbutics.—Medicines, which counteract blood deteriorations caused by scurvy. These are embraced in tonics.

Antispasmodics antagonize spasms and allay nervous irritation. Included in emetics and cerebro-spinants.

Cathartics are medicines, which exercise a strong action upon the bowels. They are divided into two kinds: the excessive and the moderator, or the purgative and the drastic. Among others are aloes, blue flag. calomel. castor oil, prunes, rhubarb, rochelle salts, senna sulphur and may apple or mandrakes.

Cerebro-Spinants are of that class which affect the brain and spinal cord. They are either paralysers, stupefaciants or intoxicants, and care should be exercised in their use. Among them are to be found, aconite, alcohol, belladonna, bromide of potash, camphor, chioral. hydrate. chloroform, cocaine,, hops, morphia, opium, strychnia, sulphuric ether, tobacco, valerian, etc.

Carminatives.—Medicines having a spicy smell, an agreeable odor and a soothing effect upon the bowels used with pur*gatives,* they prevent griping. They are mentioned among stimulants.

Chologogues stimulate the action of the liver and increase
the flow of bile. They belong to the class entitled cathartics.

Deliriants.–Substances having a sedative effect over the
heart and circulation. They are mentioned among the cerebro-spinants.

Demulcents are a class of soothing medicines, used in cold or obstinate coughs, to shield the passages from the cold air, or to protect the coating of the stomach from the action of corrosive or irritating acids. poisons, etc. They are also used to save the mucous membrane of the urinary organs from the arid action of the water in certain affections of the kidneys and bladder; are used either by the mouth or in the form of an injection. Among them are included arrowroot, gum arabic or gum acacia, gum tragacanth, Iceland moss, Irish moss, licorice, marshmallow and slippery elm.

Diaphoretics.–These are medicines, which exercise almost
exclusive action on the skin, producing perspiration. The use of diaphoretics is indicated In nearly all diseases accompanied by fever and a dry skin, particularly in febrile and pectoral affections. Catnip, citrate of potash, sage, sassafras and sweet spirits of nitre are reliable medicines of this class.

Diluents.–These are preparations employed to quench thirst. dilute and make thin the thickened blood and cool the fevered system. Tea, barley water, water gruel and similar articles are the most common diluents after pure water. The copious use of diluents is recommended in all acute inflammatory diseases not of a congestive character.

Diuretics act upon the kidneys and produce an increased flow of urine from the bladder. There are few diseases where medicines of this class are not of great benefit and in dropsy, they become paramount. Uva ursi, carrots, balsam of copaiba, cream of tartar, dandelion, juniper berries, onions, parsley, acetate of potassa, tar and the infusion of watermelon seeds are peculiarly adapted for diuretics.

Emetics are of that class of drugs, which produce vomiting and are of vast benefit in cases of poisons. They should never be given to persons disposed to apoplexy or a tendency to rush of blood to the head: women in pregnancy should refrain from the use of them. Warm or tepid water is a reliable emetic; ipecac, lobelia, mustard and tartar emetic are others.

Emmenagogues will promote the menstrual discharge when either restrained or suspended, and are few in number, ergot and madder being the only drugs, which exercise a direct Influence on the uterus. There are a number, however, which act upon the general system, producing the effect by constitutional treatment, Cotton root, iron, mather root, saffron, pennyroyal and savine are among the articles in common use.

Emollients are medicines, which soften the skin when applied externally. They diminish the pain of inflamed parts and aid the suppuration process. They owe their virtue to the moisture they contain. The mode of applying emollients is by poultice, oftenest made from flaxseed or meal most of the demulcents are emollients when applied externally, slippery elm being an instance of this character,

Epispastics are substances, which produce blistering or irritating action on the skin. Principally used are cantharides, mustard and cayenne.

Escharotics._These are caustic medicines used to eat off, as
it Is popularly called, fungoid growths or excessive granula
tions, or what is known as proud flesh. Burut, alum, iodine,
lunar caustic, mercurial caustic nitric acid caustic and zinc
caustic are among the reliable escharotics.

Expectorants Increase the secretion of the tracheal and bronchial mucous. Vapors are the only agents that can act directly upon the organs affected, those that are taken into the stomach acting only in all indirect manner. The inhaling of the vapor of warm water simply mixed with vinegar is very
useful in this way. Ammonia, balsam of tolu, garlic and syrup of squills are used as expectorants,

Febrifuges have the power of checking fever. They are found principally among diaphoretics and diuretics; also to some extent among cathartics, emetics and refrigerants.

Hemostatics when taken internally, contract the blood vessels and check hemorrhage. They are included in astringents,

Hypnotics are medicines, which produce sleep. They are included under cerebro-spinants,

Laxatives are similar to cathartics, but their action is milder.

Narcotics._poisonous substances acting principally upon the brain either as a sedative or a stimulant. See cerébro spinants.

Nervines._.Medicines, which act upon the nerves, quieting nervous excitement. Embraced in cerebro-spinants.

Nutritives. Medicines, which possess the quality of nourishing. They are largely included in tonics and stimulants,

Refrigerants. These are named from the cooling effects on the surface or the body produced by their use. They are employed in cases of high vascular action, as In fevers unaccompanied with typhoid symptoms. Although sedative in their general impression, some of them, as antimony, produce a local stimulant effect upon some of the organs, Acetic acid, vegetable acids, antimonial wine, borax, citric acid, muriatic acid and orange are all refrigerants.

Rubifacients.–These are medicines, which produce inflammation of the skin when applied externally. The indications for their use and general application are much the same as in epispastics. The latter are preferred where a slow stimulant effect is to be produced. the former where the effect is to be quick and transitory. Cayenne, mustard and croton oil are well-known rubifacients

Stalagogues are a class of medicines, which produce a quick flow of saliva, principal among which is the extract of jaborandi.

Sedatives have a calming effect on the nervous system. Embraced in cerebro spinants.

Stomaehies.–Medicines which improve the stomach and appetite. They are included in stimulants and tonics.

Sudorifics produce a moist condition of the skin. Included In diaphoretics.

Stimulants.–These are agents which produce a quickly diffused and transient increase of vital energy and force of action in the heart and arterial system. Sesqui carbonate of ammonia, aniseed, benzoic acid. cayenne pepper, cod liver oil, coriander, corrosive sublimate, ginger, myrrh, pancreatin, valerian and Virginia snake root come under the head of stimulants.

Tonics.–These are a class of medicines, which gradually and permanently increase the tonicity, and general tone of the system; strengthening and invigorating it when weakened and debilitated. increasing the appetite, assisting the digestion and thus building up the entire system. Angelica, arsenic, black cahosh boneset, burdock, chamomile. cinchona or Peruvian bark, golden seal, elecampane. iron, pepsin, quinine, sarsaparilla and wild cherry are all in the class of tonics.

HOW TO PREPARE DECOCTIONS AND INFUSIONS.

When the disease for which the preparations are intended is
not mentioned refer to "Classification of Medical Preparations,"
where will be stated the class or character of the remedy.

Alder, Decoction–of. Bark of common alder 1 ounce, water 20 ounces; boil to 16 ounces. Dose, *2* ounces to be taken every 4 hours.

Alkaline Infusion.–Hickory ashes 1 pound, wood soot 1/4 pound boiling water '4 gallon. Let them stand 24 hours, then filter through a cotton cloth. Dose, wine glass full 3 times daily. A good remedy for dyspepsia with acidity. An antacid.

Arnica, Decoction of. Flowers of arnica montana 1 ounce. water 3 pints; boil to 1 quart, filter and add of syrup of ginger 3 ounces. Dose, 1 to 2 fluid ounces every 2 or 3 hours, in aphonla, paralysis of the voluntary muscles, rheumatism, ague, etc.

Barley, Decoction of. Pearl barley (washed clean) 1 ounce; boil for 20 minutes in 15 ounces of water, and strain. This is used as a demulcent In fevers, consumption, etc. it is slightly laxative. If this is objectionable, add a few drops of laudanum.

Blood Root, Infusion of. Blood root 1/2 ounce, boiling water 1 pint. Is used as a stimulant an emetic. Dose for stimulant or alterative, 1 teaspoonful 3 times daily; as an emetic 1 or 2 tablespoonfuls every hour until vomiting Is produced.

Blue Flag, Infusion of. Pulverize root of blue flag ounce. boiling water 1 pint; steep hours and filter. Dose, teaspoonful with 10 drops of tincture of capsicum or cayenne once in 2 hours until Its laxative or diuretic effects are experienced by the bowels or kidneys.

Boneset or Thoroughwort, Infusion of. Boneset and sage of each 1/2 ounce, cascarilla 1 dram, boiling water 1 1/2 pints, infuse until cold, then strain. In hectic fever a wineglass of this efficient remedy administered every hour until nausea and per- spiration are indicated has - been highly recommended in influenza.

Buchu, Infusion of. Buchu 1 ounce, boiling water 1 pint; let stand for two hours In a tightly closed vessel. then strain. Used in affections of the kidneys and bladder. A superior diuretic. Dose, 1 to 2 ounces twice daily.

Bran, Decoction of. 1. Bran 1/4 pound. water 1 1/4 pints; boil to 1 pint. In diabetes; and sweetened with sugar as a demulcent and laxative drink for cough and sore throat. 2. Bran I quart. water 1½ gallons; boil *5* minutes, and add cold water enough to bring to proper temperature. Use as an emollient footbath.

Capsicum or Cayenne Pepper. Infusion of. Powdered capsicum 1/2 ounce, boiling water 1 pint. Dose, 1/2 fluid ounce.

Cascarlila, Infusion of. Cascarilla in coarse powder 1 ounce boiling water (distilled) 10 ounces; infuse for 1 hour in a closed vessel, then strain. Dose, 1 to 2 ounces, usually combined with carbonate of soda and tincture of cascarilla 3 times daily. An excellent remedy for dyspepsia. debility and diarrhea.

Chamomile, infusion of. Chamomile flowers ounce. boiling water 10 ounces, infuse for 15 minutes and strain. This is tonic, bitter, stomachic and emetic; drink cold. It is an emetic when warm. Dose as stomachic, 1 to 3 ounces; as an emetic,5 to 10 ounces.

Coffee, Decoction of. Ten drams of raw coffee berries boiled in 8 ounces of water down to 5 ounces. Give 3 doses during the Intermission of intermittent fever.

Cotton Root, Decoction of. Inner part of the root of

the cotton plant 4 ounces. water 1 quart; boil to 1 pint. Dose, 1 wine glass full occasionally as an emmenagogue. or every 30 or 40 minutes to produce uterine contraction, for Which purpose it is said to be as effectual as ergot of rye.

Dandelion, Infusion of. Bruised root of dandelion *2* ounces, boiling water 1 pint; steep two hours and strain. Dose, a wine glass full 3 times a day. It is a tonic, resolvent and stimulant.

Elecampane, Decoction of. Elecampane root *1/2* ounce, water 1 pint; boil a few minutes and strain. Tonic and expectorant, and in some cases diuretic and diaphoretic. Dose, 1 wine glass full every hour or two.

Elm Bark, Infusion of Steep 1 ounce of slippery elm bark bruised and sliced in 1 pint of boiling water for two hours in a closed vessel, then strain. Use freely as a drink in coughs and kidney affections, and in inflammatory diseases of the bowels.

Ergot, Decoction of. Ergot of rye 1 dram, water 6 fluid ounces; boil 10 minutes and strain. Dose, 1/3 every half hour until the whole is taken, as a parturifacient.

Fern Root, Decoction of. Dried fern root 1 ounce, water 1 pint; boil to 16 fluid ounces and strain. Dose, wine glass full, fasting until It excites slight nausea. As a vermifuge, more particularly for tapeworm.

Figs. Decoction of. Figs chopped 1 ounce, water 1-pint boil and strain. Demulcent and pectoral taken freely as a drink.

Flaxseed, Infusion of. Flaxseed 1 ounce, boiling water 1 pint; let it stand for 2 hours and then strain. Useful In inflammatory diseases of the lungs and affections of the kidneys. The addition of a tablespoonful of cream of tartar, sufficient lemon peel or of lemon juice, with sugar to sweeten to taste, improves this remedy, and increases its action upon the kidneys.

Hoarhound Infusion of. The leaves 1 ounce, boiling water 1 pint steep 2 hours then strain. Given in wine glass full doses. Demulcent, pectoral, a popular remedy in coughs, colds, hoarseness. etc.; taken freely.

Hops infusion of. Hops 6 drams, boiling distilled water 1 pint. steep 4 hours In a covered vessel, then strain and press. Tonic and anodyne. Dose. 2 fluid ounces 3 times a day.

Iceland Moss, Decoction of. Iceland moss 1 ounce, water 1 1/2 pints boil for 10 minutes in a covered vessel and strain. Nutritious demulcent. pectoral and tonic. Dose, 1 to 4 fluid ounces every 3 or 4 hours, in chronic affections of the chest and stomach, especially pulmonary consumption, dyspepsia, old coughs, dysentery and chronic diarrhea.

Irish moss Decoction of. Carrageen or Irish moss 1

ounce. steep in 1 pint of lukewarm water for 10 minutes, then take it out, drain and boil in water or milk 3 pints for 15 minutes. and strain through linen. If twice the above weight of moss is employed It forms a mucilage which, if. sweetened. Makes an excellent article of spoon diet. It is taken in the same cases as Iceland moss, and is often used for giving solidity in cooking blanc mange, etc.

Indian Sarsaparilla, Decoction of. Root of Indian sarsaparilla 2 ounces, water 1 1/2 pints; boil to 1 pint. Diuretic, alterative and tonic. Indian Sarsaparilla, Infusion of Indian or scented sarsaparilla 2 ounces, boiling water 1 pint. steep 2 hours; uses same as decoction. Dose, tablespoonful 3 times daily, which is the same to be used for the decoction.

Juniper, Infusion of. 1. From the berries alone. As a stimulant-diuretic in dropsy. Juniper berries 2 1/2 ounces. boiling water 1 pint. 2. To this add when cold 10 fluid drams compound spirit of juniper, bitartrate of potassa 1 dram.

Kino, Infusion of. Kino 5 drams, boiling water 1 pint. In diarrhea also, diluted in 5 times its bulk in water, as an injection for chronic gonorrhea. Dose, 1 dessertspoonful.

Kousso, Infusion of. Kousso powdered fine 1/2 ounce. boiling distilled water 8 fluid ounces, steep in a covered vessel for 15

minutes, must not be strained. Dose, from 1 wine glass full to 1
tumbler full, for tapeworm,

Licorice, Decoction of. Sliced licorice root 1 1/2 ounces, water 10 fluid ounces; boil 10 minutes and strain. A mild demulcent dose, wine glass full taken freely.

Marshmallow, Decoction of. Dried root and herb of marshmallow 4 ounces. stoned raisins 2 ounces, water 7 pints: boil. down to 5 pints. strain, allow the sediment to settle and runoff the clear liquid. Demulcent. Dose, a cupful at pleasure, in coughs, colds, calculus affections and diseases of the urinary organs.

Oak Bark, Decoction of. 1. Bruised oak bark '10 drams, water 1 quart; boil down to 1 pint and strain. 2. Oak bark 1 1/2 ounces, water 1 1/2 pints; boil 10 minutes and strain. It is an astringent, used as a gargle in ulcerated sore throat, relaxation of the uvala, etc.; as a wash and as an injection in piles, leucorrhea hemorrhages, prolapsusani, etc. 3. Bruised oak bark 1 1/2 ounces. distilled water 1 pint;- boil for 10 minutes and strain.

Orange Peel, Infusion of. Dried bitter orange peel cut small 1 ounce, boiling water 20 ounces; infuse for 15 minutes, then strain. Bitter and stomachic; an excellent, effective remedy.

Parsley Root, Infusion of. Made from the root of the

garden parsley, bruised. 2 ounces, boiling water 1 pint; steep 2 hours in a covered vessel, then strain. Dose. 2 fluid ounces. Aromatic, diuretic and slightly aperient. Recommended for dropsy.

Pennyroyal, Infusion of. Pennyroyal 1 ounce, boiling water 1 pint: steep 15 minutes and strain. A remedy for nausea, flatulence, colds, whooping cough, hysteria, obstructed menstruations, etc. Should not be taken during pregnancy. Dose, tablespoonful 3 times daily.

Peppermint, Infusion of. Peppermint 3 drams, boiling water pint; steep 15 minutes and strain in flatulence, colic, griping and as a vehicle for other medicines.

Peruvian Bark, Decoction of. Yellow cinchona or calisaya bark, bruised, 1 1/4 ounces, distilled water 1 pint; boil for 10 minutes in a tightly closed vessel, and when cold strain and pour on the bark sufficient water to make 1 pint. Dose, 1 to 2 fluid ounces 3 or 4 times daily. As a tonic, stomachic and febrifuge

Pink Root, Infusion of. Made from Indian pink root. Is a vermifuge, and a good one. Pink root 1 ounce, boiling water 1 pint; steep 20 minutes, strain and give, combined with or followed by a purge, in 1 or 2 tablespoonful doses to a child 3 to 5 years of age.

Pomegranate Root, Decoction of. A wonderful remedy for tapeworm. Bark of the root 2 ounces, water 1 pint; boil to 1/2 pint. This is the form used in India. Take a wine glass full half-hourly until the whole is taken; a light diet and a dose of castor oil having been taken the day previously. It usually expels the worm In 5 or 6 hours. Look for the head, and if it does not appear, repeat the dose in a day or so.

Sage, Infusion of. Made from the leaves of the common garden sage; 1/2 ounce of the leaves steeped in 1/2 pint boiling water for 1/2 hour, then strained, proves a fine remedy for hectic fever, in tablespoonful doses. Carminative and stomachic, for flatulence and dyspepsia; drank in water, it lessens night sweats.

Sarsaparilla, Decoction of. Sarsaparilla sliced and bruised 6 ounces, bark of sassafras root sliced, gualacum wood rasped, licorice root bruised, of each 1 ounce, megereon sliced 3 drams; steep for 12 hours in 4 pints of water, then boil for 15 minutes and strain. Used in certain scrofulous and depraved conditions of the system. In syphilis, chronic rheumatism and a number of skin diseases. Use freely in wine glass full doses. The addition of one-fifth alcohol to this recipe makes it a valuable medicine.

Savine or Savin, Infusion of. Fresh leaves or herb 1 dram, boiling water 1 fluid ounce; infuse in a covered vessel. Stimulant. emmenagogue and vermifuge in chiorosis and suppressed menstruation, depending on torpid action of the uterine vessels; in chronic rheumatism, worms, etc. Dose, 1 to 2 tablespoons full, cautiously administered. Should not be taken during pregnancy.

Senna, Infusion of. 1. Senna 1 ounce, ginger sliced 30 grains, boiled distilled water 10 ounces; infuse 1 hour and strain. Dose, 1 to 2 ounces. 2. Senna 15 drams, bruised ginger 4 scruples, boiling water 1 pint; steep for 1 hour in a covered vessel and strain. 3. Senna 1 1/2 ounce, ginger 1/2 dram, boiling water 1 pint. 4. Senna 1/2 ounce. ginger 1/2 dram, boiling water 1/2 pint. Purgative. It is usually given in doses of 1 to 1 1/2 fluid ounces, combined with 3 to 6 drams of epsom salts or other saline purgative under the name of 'black draught." Add 1 grain of nitrate of potassa to each ounce to prevent spoiling in warm weather.

Slippery Elm, Infusion of. Inner bark of slippery elm 1 ounce. boiling water 16 fluid ounces; infuse for 2 hours, then strain. Demulcent.

Squill, Decoction of. squill 3 drams, juniper berries 4 ounces, snake root 3 ounces, water 4 pounds; boil to one-half. strain and add of sweet spirits of nitre 4 fluid ounces. In chronic coughs and other chest affections, unaccompanied with active inflammatory symptoms. Dose, 1 to 3 fluid ounces 2 or 3 times daily.

Sweet Flag, Infusion of. Sweet flag 1 ounce, boiling water 1 pint; steep 2 hours in a covered vessel and strain. Dose, 1 wine glass full an aromatic, stimulant, tonic and stomachic.

Tansy, Infusion of. From the dried herb, or the green

herb twice the quantity. Pansy dried and bruised 1 ounce, boiling water 1 pint: steep 2 hours in a covered vessel and strain. Dose. 2 teaspoons full every 4 hours. Aromatic, bitter, tonic and vermifuge.

Tar. Infusion of. Wood tar 1 quart, cold water 1 gallon; stir with a stick for 15 minutes, then let the tar subside, strain and keep in well-corked jars. Taken to the extent of 1 pint daily in chronic catarrhal and nephritic affections, also used as a lotion in chronic cutaneous diseases, especially those of the scalp in children.

Tobacco, Infusion of. Tobacco leaves 1 dram. boiling water 16 fluid ounces; steep for 1 hour. Used for enemas in strangulated hernia or rupture, obstinate colic, etc., observing not to administer more than 1/2 at a time.

Wild Cherry Bark, Infusion of. Dry wild cherry bark bruised 1/2 ounce (If green a small handful). cold water 1. pint; let it stand covered closely 24 hours and strain. Useful in nervous irritability with increased action of the heart, in debilitated conditions of the stomach. and in general debility following inflammatory diseases. Dose, 1 tablespoon full 3 times a day.

Wintergreen, Decoction of. Chimaphila (dried herb) 1 ounce, water 1 1/2 pints; boil to 1 pint and then strain. Tonic stomachic alterative and diuretic. Dose, 1 to 2 fluid ounces in dropsy, scrofula, debility, loss of appetite, etc.. and in those affections of the urinary organs in which uva ursi is commonly given.

Waterdock, Decoction of. Root of common waterdock 1-ounce water 1 pint; boil for 10 minutes and, strain. Dose. 2 fluid ounces. This decoction is astringent and used as a remedy for scurvy and some other cutaneous diseases. It is the only remedy, which proves efficacious for that disease when the ulcers are healed and the patient is attacked with asthma.

NOTE.–The decoctions and infusions herein mentioned form a cheap and reliable system of treatment for all diseases, can be easily prepared. and are always effectual. Look through them carefully. They will save you doctor's bills.

LINIMENTS, OINTMENTS, SALVES, CERATES, ETC.
Of these external remedies liniments are thicker than water, but more liquid than salves or ointments. Cerates have a greater consistency than salves, but are not so pasty or as thick as poultices. Among those here given are many preparations well known to the public; patent medicines that have been on sale for years. All of these formulas are of great value, having been tested and found effectual.

Aconite Ointment.–Alcoholic extract of aconite 1 dram, lard 2 **drams;** rub together carefully and thoroughly. For neuralgia.

Alum Ointment.–Alum, in very fine powder, 1 dram, lard 1 1/2 ounces; mix thoroughly. For piles.

Belladonna Liniment.—Extract of belladonna 1 dram, Olive oil 1 ounce; stir together. Useful in rheumatism, neuralgia, etc.

Benzoin Ointment.—Tincture of benzoin 2 ounces. lard 16 ounces: melt the lard, add the tincture. stirring well. For itch and skin diseases.

Black Liniment.—Sulphuric acid 1 dram, olive oil 1 ounce, turpentine ounce; mix the acid with the oil slowly. When cold add the turpentine. A fine counter irritant. Effectual in swelling of the joints. Apply twice a day on lint.

Calomel Cerate.—Calomel 1 dram. spermaceti cerate 7 drams. In herpes and other skin diseases.

Camphor Liniment.—Camphor 1 ounce, olive oil. 2 fluid ounce: dissolve the camphor in the oil. For rheumatism and neuralgia.

Carbolic Acid Ointment.—Camphor 1 ounce, carbolic acid in crystals 1 ounce. simple cerate 14 ounces; mix. Antiseptic, stimulant and detergent.

Centaur Linament.—Oil spike 1 ounce, oil wormwood 1 ounce, oil sassafras 1 ounce, oil organum 1 ounce, oil cinnamon 1 ounce. oil cloves 1 dram, oil cedar 1 dram. sulphuric ether 1 ounce. aqua ammonia 1 ounce, tincture opium 1 ounce. Alcohol 1 gallon: mix. This is an excellent liniment, and good whenever a liniment is needed.

Cucumber Ointment.—Oil of sweet almonds 7 fluid ounces, spermaceti 18 drams, white wax 5 drams, glycerin 1 fluid ounce, green cucumbers 4 pounds; cut the cucumbers in small pieces, mash in a mortar (wooden). let them stand in their own liquor for 12 hours, press and strain; melt the almond oil, spermaceti and wax together, add to it the strained liquor of the cucumbers, stirring constantly so as to incorporate the whole together; set aside in a cool place until it becomes hard, then beat with a wooden spoon, so as to separate the watery portions of the cucumbers from the ointment; pour off the liquor thus obtained and mix the glycerin with the ointment without the aid of heat, by working it with the hands until all are thoroughly mixed: put up in 4-ounce jars, cover with a layer of rose water and set aside in a cool place. This ointment is one of the finest preparations for the skin known to medical science, and thus prepared will keep for 12 months.

Davis' Pain Killer,—Proof alcohol 1 quart, chloroform 1 dram. oil sassafras 1 ounce, gum camphor 1 ounce, spirits of ammonia 1 dram. oil cayenne 2 drams; mix well, and let stand 24 hours before using.

Downers' Salve.—Beeswax 4 ounces, opium ounce. sugar of lead 1 ounce; melt the beeswax and rub the lead up in the wax, then the opium, then add 1 gill of sweet oil: mix all thoroughly together and spread lightly on cloth. Good for burns, piles, etc.

Emollient Liniment.—Camphor 1 dram, peruvian

balsam 1/2 dram, oil of almonds 1 fluid ounce; dissolve by heat, add of glycerin 1/2 fluid ounce. agitate well, and when cold further add of oil of nutmeg 15 drops. Good for chapped hands, lips, nipples, etc.

Eye Ointments (the best in use).—1. Nitric oxide of mercury. carbonate of zinc, acetate of lead and dried alum, of each 1 dram. corrosive sublimate 10 grains, rose ointment 1 ounce. Used in chronic aphthalmia, profuse discharges, etc., usually diluted. 2. Nitrate of silver 10 grains, zinc ointment 2 drams. balsam of peru 1/2 dram. Used in ulceration of the cornea and in acute, purulent and chronic aphthalmia: great caution should be employed in its use. 3. Spermaceti ointment 1 dram, solution of diacetate of lead 15 drams, nitrate of silver 2 to 10 grains. Use as the last and in cases where direct caustic action is desired; the stronger ointment often occasions intense pain. 4. Black oxide of mercury 2 grains, spermaceti cerate and walnut oil, of each 1 dram. Used in chronic affections of the eye and eyelids, particularly in those of a syphilitic character. 5 (Petit's). White wax 4 ounces, spermaceti 12 ounces, olive oil 2 pounds, white precipitate *3* ounces. oxide of zinc 4 ounces, benzoic acid 2 drams. sulphate of morphia 48 grains, oil of rosemary 20 drops; melt the spermaceti. wax and olive oil together, rub the precipitate, zinc and benzoic acid in a portion of the warm mixture, add: together, lastly add the rosemary, stir till cool. This is the finest preparation of its kind known.

Flagg's Instant Relief.—Oil of cloves 1 fluid dram, oil of sassafras 2 fluid drams, spirit of camphor 1 *1/2* fluid ounces; mix well.

Green Mountain Salve.—Powdered verdigris 1 ounce, oil of wormwood 1/2 ounce, venice turpentine 1/2 ounce. oil of red cedar, organum, hemlock and balsam of fir, each 1 ounce, mutton tallow, beeswax and burgundy pitch, each 4 ounces, resin 5 pounds; melt the resin, pitch, beeswax, tallow and balsam together, add the oils with the verdigris and other ingredients; mix well, Used for all sores, excoriations, chilblains, etc.; very fine.

Good Samaritan Liniment.—Take 98 per cent alcohol 2 quarts, and add to it the following articles: Oils of sassafras, hemlock, spirits of turpentine, tincture of cayenne, catechu, guaic (guac) and laudanum, of each 1 ounce, tincture of myrrh 4 ounces, oil of organum 2 ounces. oil of wintergreen 1/2 ounce, gum camphor 2 ounces, chloroform 1 1/2 ounces. This is one of the best applications for internal pains.

Hamlin's Wizard Oil.—Oil of sassafras 2 ounces, oil of cedar 1 ounce, gum camphor 1 ounce, sulphuric ether 2 ounces, chloroform 2 ounces, tincture of capsicum 1 ounce, aqua ammonia 2 ounces, oil of turpentine 1 ounce, tincture of quassia, 3 ounces, alcohol 1/2 gallon; mix, and you have a fine liniment.

Hops Ointment.— Hops 2 ounces, lard 10 ounces, Useful In painful piles and cancerine sores.

Indian Oil (Healy & Bigelow's).–Oil of sassafras 2 ounces, oil of cloves 1 1/2 ounces, gum camphor 4 ounces, tincture of myrrh 4 ounces, tincture opium (laudanum) 4 ounces, tincture capsicum 4 ounces, spirits of ether *4* ounces, alcohol 2 gallons, water 1 2/3 gallons; mix. The above will fill 240 2-ounce vials. The addition of 1/2 ounce of menthol to every gallon greatly improves this excellent remedy.

Iodide of Mercury Ointment,–I. White wax 2 ounces, lard 6 ounces; melt them together, add of iodide of mercury 1 ounce and rub them well together. 2. Green iodide of mercury 23 grains, lard 1 1/2 ounces. Useful in tubercular skin diseases, as a friction in scrofulous swellings and indolent granular tumors, and as a dressing for ill-conditioned ulcers, especially those of scrofulous character.

Iodoform Ointment,–Iodoform 1 dram, vaseline 1 ounce; reduce the Iodoform to a powder and add to the vaseline, heat until dissolved. Antiseptic; healing for all sores.

Itch Ointment,–l. Unsalted butter 1 pound, burgundy pitch 2 ounces, spirits of turpentine 2 ounces, red precipitate, pulverized, 1 ¼ ounces; melt the pitch and add the butter, stirring well together. then remove from the fire and when a little cool add the spirits of turpentine and lastly the precipitate; stir until cold. 2. Alum, nitre and sulphate of zinc, of each in very fine powder 1 1/4 ounces, vermillion 1/2 ounce; mix, add gradually of sweet oil 3/4 pint;

triturate, or mix together until well mixed, then add of lard 1 pound, with oils of anise, lavender and organum quantity sufficient to perfume. 3. Chloride of lime 1 dram. rectified spirits 2 fluid drams sweet oil 1/2 fluid ounce, common salt and sulphur of each 1 ounce soft soap 2 ounces, oil of lemon 20 drops. Cheap, effectual and inoffensive.

King of Pain.–Alcohol 1 pint, tincture of capsicum 1 dram, spirits of turpentine 1 dram. gum camphor 1 ounce, sulphuric ether 1 ounce; mix.

Kickupoo Buffalo Salve.–Vaseline 1 pound, tallow 1 pound. white wax 3 ounces, oxide of zinc 1 3/4 ounces. red precipitate 1 1/2 ounces, oil of cedar 3/4 ounce; melt and stir together until cold, then box.

Magnetic Ointment.–Elder bark 1 pound, spikenard root 1 pound, yellow dock root 1 pound; boil in 2 gallons of water down to 1, then press the strength out of the bark and roots and boil the liquid down to 1/2 gallon; add best resin 8 pounds, beeswax 1 pound and tallow enough to soften. Apply to the sores, etc., by spreading on linen cloth.

Magic Oil–Sweet oil 1 gallon. oil of hemlock 2 ounces, oil of organum 2 ounces, chloroform 2 ounces, spirits of ammonia 4 ounces; mix, let it stand 24 hours and it is ready for use. Dose, Internally, 1 teaspoonful for adults. Bathe the affected parts well. This is a great remedy for aches and pains, rheumatism, neuralgia. and all nervous and inflammatory diseases.

Magnetic Toothache Drops.—Take equal parts of camphor. sulphuric ether, ammonia, laudanum, tincture of cayenne and 1/8 part oil of cloves; mix well together. Saturate with the liquid a small piece of cotton and apply to the cavity of the diseased tooth, and the pain will cease immediately.

My Own Liniment.—Take oil of cajuput 2: ounces, oil of spike 1 ounce, oil of sassafras 1 ounce, oil of cloves 1 ounce. oil of organum 1 ounce, oil of mustard 1/2 :ounce, tincture of capsicum 1 ounce, gum camphor 2 ounces, alcohol 1/2 gallon. Use as other liniments for any ache or pain. For sore throat or hoarseness. saturate a towel with the liniment, place it over the mouth, let it remain so for 4 or 5 hours and you will be cured. For croup. bathe throat and chest with the liniment. Give 1/4 -teaspoonful of liniment in one teaspoonful of warm water every 5 to 10 minutes until relieved.

Mustang Liniment.—Linseed oil 14 ounces. aqua ammonia 2 ounces, tincture of capsicum 14 ounce, oil of organum 1/4 ounce, turpentine 1 ounce. oil of mustard 1/4 ounce; mix.

Mustard Ointment.—1, Flour of mustard 3/4 ounce, water I fluid ounce; mix, and add of resin cerate 2 ounces, oil of turpentine 1/2 ounce. Rubifacient and stimulant, as a friction in rheumatism, etc. 2. Flour of mustard 3 ounces. oil of almonds 1/2 fluid ounce, lemon juice quantity sufficient. Used in freckles, sunburn etc. a fine preparation.

Pile Ointment.—1. Burnt alum and oxide of zinc, of each 1/2 dram, lard 7 drams. 2. Morphia 8 grains, melted spermaceti ointment 1 ounce: mix together until complete, then add of finely powdered galls 1/2 dram, essential oil of almonds 12 to 15 drops and stir until the mass becomes hard. This is useful in painful piles, prolapsus, etc.; it does not soil the linen as most other liniments.

Radways Ready Relief, or R. R. R.—Alcohol 2 pints, oil of sassafras 2 ounces, oil of organum 2 ounces, spirits of camphor 1/2 ounce, tincture of opium 1 ounce. chloroform, 1 ounce; mix.

St. Jacob's Oil.—Gum camphor 1 ounce, chloral hydrate 1 ounce, chloroform 1 ounce. sulphate of ether 1 ounce, tincture of opium (non-aqueous) 1/2 ounce, oil of organum 1/2 ounce, oil of sassafras 1/2 ounce, alcohol 1/2 gallon: dissolve gum camphor with alcohol and then add the oil, then, the other ingredients.

Tar Ointments.—1. Tar and suet, of each 1 pound; melt them together and press the mixture through a linen cloth. 2. Tar 5 ounces. beeswax 2 ounces., melt together and stir the mixture briskly until it concretes. 3. Tar 1/2 pint, yellow wax 4 ounces. A detergent application In ringworm, scald heads. scabby eruptions foul ulcers. etc.; at first dilute with one-half its weight of lard or sweet oil.

LOZENGES, TROCHES, TABLETS, COUGH DROPS, WORN WAFERS, ETC.

Are made of finely-powdered ingredients, mixed with gum or
something of like character to make them firm. Great care must be taken to have the ingredients finely powdered and carefully mixed. They can be rolled out the same as bread or pastry dough and cut into shape with a thimble having the small end open. This is the simplest method.

Brown's Bronchial Troches.–Take 1/2 pound of pulverized extract of licorice. 34 pound of pulverized sugar, 2 ounces each of pulverized cubebs and gum arabic, and 1/2 ounce of pulverized extract of conium.

Caffeine Lozenges.–Each lozenge contains 1/4 grain of caffeine and 1/2 grain of citric acid. Useful in hemicrania, hypochondriasis, etc.

Calomel Lozenges.–Each lozenge contains 1 grain of calomel. Alterative. etc.; they afford a simple way of introducing mercury into the system during their use, salt food and acid liquors should be avoided. When given for worms, they should be followed in a few hours by a purge.

Carbolic Acid Lozenges–Carbolic acid 350 grains, gum arabic 220 grains, refined sugar 12 1/2 ounces.

mucilage 1 ounce. distilled water sufficient quantity to make 1 pound; divide into 350 lozenges, and finish as with benzoic acid lozenges.

Catechu Lozenges.–1.Extract of catechu 4 ounces, sugar 16 ounces, mucilage of *gum* tragacanth sufficient quantity; make into 10-grain lozenges. 2. Magnesia 2 ounces powdered catechu 1 ounce, sugar 13 ounces, mucilage of gain tragacanth (made with cinnamon water) sufficient quantity to mix. These *are* taken in diarrhea, in relaxation of the uvula, in irritation of the larynx and to disguise a fetid breath; the one containing magnesia is also sucked In dyspepsia, acidity and heartburn.

Charcoal Lozenges._Prepared charcoal 4 ounces, white sugar 12 ounces, mucilage sufficient quantity to mix. Used In diarrhea, cholera. dyspepsia,, etc.

Ching's Yellow Worm Lozenges.–Fine sugar 28 pounds, calomel, washed with spirits of wine, 1 pound, saffron 4 drams; dissolve gum tragacanth sufficient to make a paste, make decoction of the saffron in 1 pint of water. strain and mix with it. Each lozenge should contain 1 grain of mercury.

Chlorate of Potassa Lozenges.–1. Each lozenge contains 1 1/2 grains of chlorate of potassa. Used in phthisis, sore throat. etc. Dose, 6 to 12 a day. 2. Chlorate of potassa, in powder 3,600 grains 8 1/4 ounces). refined sugar, in powder, 25 ounces. gum acacia, in powder, 1 ounce, mucilage 2 ounces, distilled Water 1 ounce, or a sufficiency; mix the powders, and aid the mucilage and water to form a proper mass; divide Into 720 lozenges.

Chloride of Gold Lozenges.__Each lozenge contains 1-40 grain of neutral chloride of gold. Dose, 2 to 4 daily, in scrofula, Cancer, etc.

Clove Lozenges.–Cloves, powdered along with sugar, 2 ounces, or essential oil 1 fluid dram to each pound of sugar. Carminative and stomachic, also used as a restorative after fatigue: added to chocolate to improve its flavor anti sucked to sweeten the breath.

Cough Lozenges.-_Dissolve licorice in water to the consistency of thin molasses, add to the dough, made of gum water and sugar. and work it well; also work in at the same time 2 ounces of ipecacuanha. 1-dram acetate of morphia (morphine). 1 ounce oil of aniseed, 1 ounce powdered tartaric acid: mix thoroughly, roll out and cut.

Croton Oil Lozenges.–Croton oil 5 drops, powdered starch 40 grains, white sugar 1 drain, chocolate 2 drams; divide into :30 lozenges: 5 or 6 generally prove cathartic.

Cubebs Lozenges.–.Cubebs 2 drams, balsam of tulu. grains; mix, and add extract of licorice 1 ounce, syrup of tulu 1 dram, powdered gum sufficient quantity; divide into 10-grain lozenges. One of these allowed to melt gradually in the mouth, is said to alleviate the obstruction in the nose in coryza.

Ginger Lozenges.—Best unbleached jamaica ginger and gum arabic, of each, in very fine powder 1 1/2 ounces double refined lump sugar 1 pound, rose water, tinged with saffron, sufficient quantity. A still finer quality may be made by using an equivalent proportion of essence of ginger instead of the powder; inferior qualities are prepared with coarser sugar, to which some starch is often added. Ginger lozenges are carminative and stomachic, and are useful in flatulency, loss of appetite, etc.

Hemlock Confection.—Fresh hemlock leaves beaten up with an equal weight of sugar. Dose, 10 to 20 grains, as a pill, 2 or 3 times daily, where the use of hemlock is Indicated. The confection of other narcotic plants may be made in the same way.

Iceland Moss Chocolate.—Simple chocolate 32 parts, sugar 29 parts, dried jelly of Iceland moss 11 parts; mix.

Indian Worm Killer (Healy & Bigelow's).—Kousso flowers 3/4 pound. scammony 4 ounces, santonin 4 ounces, pulverized jalap 4 ounces, pulverized sugar 12 pounds, oil of anise 2 ounces, cornstarch 4 pounds. Gum tragacanth 8 ounces: dissolve the gum in water of sufficient quantity to make thick mucilage, make an Infusion of the kousso flowers, then mix the other ingredients with the gum. adding the kousso infusion, making a stiff mass: mix with the cornstarch and knead thoroughly; when well mixed roll out into sheets and cut with a round die or thimble about the size of 1-cent coin: the sheets should be quite thin. Dose, 1/2 to 1 lozenge twice daily.

Opium Lozenges.–1. Opium 2 drams, tincture of tulu 1/2 ounce; triturate together add of powdered sugar 6 ounces, extract licorice and powdered gum acacia of each 5 ounces: mix and divide into 10-grain lozenges. Each lozenge contains 1–6 to 1-7 opium. Used to allay tickling cough and irritation of the fauces, and as an anodyne and hypnotic. 2. Opium In fine powder 2 drams. extract of. licorice, gum arabic and sugar. of each 5 ounces, oil of aniseed. fluid dram, water sufficient quantity: divide into 6-grain lozenges.

Pomegranate Electuary.–l. From the root bark 1 dram, asafetida 1/2 dram. croton oil 6 drops, consene of roses 1 ounce. Dose, 1 teaspoonful night and morning. 2. Extract of the root bark 6 drams, lemon juice 2 fluid drams. linden water 3 fluid drams. gum tragacanth. sufficient quantity to make an electuary. Take 1/2 at once; the remainder In an hour. Both are given in tapeworm.

Squill Honey.–1. Thick clarified honey 3 pounds. tincture of squill 2 pounds: mix. 2-Dried squill 1 ounce. boiling water pint: infuse 2 hours, strain and add of honey 12 minces, and evaporate to a proper consistence.

Tannic Acid Lozenges.–Tannic acid 300 grains: tincture of tulu. 1/2 ounce, refined sugar 25 ounces. gum acacia 1 ounce. mucilage 2 ounces. distilled water 1 ounce: dissolve the tannic acid in the water; add first the tincture of tulu, previously mixed with the mucilage, then the gum and the sugar, also previously well mixed: form the whole into a proper mass and divide into 720 lozenges, and dry them in a hot-air chamber with a moderate heat. Dose, 1 to 6 lozenges.

Tulu Lozenges.—1. Sugar 4 pounds, balsam of tulu 3 drams. or the tincture of the balsam 1 fluid ounce, cream of tartar 6 ounces. or tartaric acid 1 dram; dissolve gum sufficient to make a paste. These may also be flavored by adding 1/4 ounce of vanilla and 60 drops of the essence of amber. The articles must be reduced to a fine powder with the sugar; they are pectoral and balsamic. 2. Balsam of tulu and rectified spirit of each 1 ounce; dissolve and add of water 2 fluid ounces. heat the mixture in a water-bath and filter. Make a mucilage with the filtered liquor and gum tragacanth 80 grains, add of sugar 16 ounces; make a mass and cut it into lozenges.

Vermifuge Lozenges.—Santonin, 60 grains, pulverized sugar 5 ounces, mucilage of gum tragacanth sufficient to make into thick paste, worked carefully together, that the santonin shall be evenly mixed throughout the whole mass: then, if not in too great a hurry, cover up the mortar in which you have rubbed them, and let them stand from 12 to 24 hours to temper, at which time they will roll out better than if done Immediately: divide into 120 lozenges. Dose, for a child 1 year old, 1 lozenge night and morning; of 2 years, 2 lozenges; of 4 years, 3 lozenges; of 8 years,

4 lozenges; 'of 10 years or more. 5 to 7 lozenges. In all cases to be taken twice daily, and continuing until the worms are discharged.

Wistar's Cough Lozenges.—Gum arabic, extract of licorice and sugar, of each 2 1/2 ounces, powdered opium 1 dram. oil of aniseed 40 drops; for 60 lozenges. Dose, 1 three or four times a day.

Worm Lozenges.—Most of the advertised nostrums under this name have a basis of calomel, and require to be followed by a purge a few hours afterwards. I. Ethereal extract of worm seed 1 dram, jalap, starch and sugar, of each 3 drams. mucilage of gum tragacanth sufficient quantity; divide in 60 lozenges. 2. Wormseed 1 ounce, ethiops mineral and jalap. of each 3 drams, cinnamon 2 drams, sugar 7 ounces, rose water sufficient quantity. _____

PLASTERS AND POULTICES

Alum Poultice.—Powdered alum 1 dram, whites of two eggs; shake them together until they form a coagulum. Applied between the folds of soft linen for chilblains, sore nipples, inflamed eyes, etc.

Antiseptic Poultice.—Barley flour 6 ounces, powdered peruvian bark 1 ounce, water sufficient quantity; boil and when cool add powdered camphor 1 dram.

Boynton's Adhesive Plaster.—Yellow resin 1 ounce, lead plaster 1 pound: melted together. Recommended for bad legs and other like affections.

Belladonna Plaster.–Soap plaster 3 ounces: melt it by the heat of a water bath: add extract of belladonna 3 ounces and keep constantly stirring the mixture until it acquires a proper consistence.

Cancer Plasters.–1. Wax plaster 1 ounce. extract of hemlock 1 dram, levigated arsenious acid 1/2 dram. 2. Extract of hemlock 1 ounce. extract of henbane 1/2 ounce powdered belladonna 1 dram. acetate of ammonia of sufficient quantity to form a plaster. Should be used with great caution.

Cantharides Plaster.–Melt together yellow wax and suet each 7 1/2 pounds. lard 6 ounces, and resin 3 ounces; while cooling sprinkle in and mix thoroughly 1 pound very finely powdered Spanish flies.

Court Plaster.–This plaster is a kind of varnished silk, and its manufacture is very easy. Bruise a sufficient quantity of isinglass, and let it soak in a little warm water for 24 hours. Expose it to heat over the fire until the greater part of the water is dissipated, and supply its place by proof spirits of wine, which will combine with the isinglass. Strain the whole through a piece of open linen, taking care that the consistence of the mixture shall be such that when cool it may form a trembling jelly. Extend a piece of black or flesh-colored silk on a wooden frame. And fix it in that position by means of tacks or twine. Then apply the isinglass, after it has been rendered liquid by a gentle heal, to the silk with a brush of fine hair (badger's is the best. As soon as this coating is dried, which will not be long, apply a second, and afterward, if the article is to be very superior, a third. When the whole is dry, cover it with two or three coatings of the balsam of peru. This is the genuine court plaster. it is pliable and never breaks, which is far from being the case with spurious articles sold under the same name.

Lead plaster.–Take 1 1/4 pounds of very finely powdered semi vitrified oxide of lead, 1 quart of olive oil and 1/2 pint of water; boil together over a gentle fire, stirring constantly till the oil and litharge unite and form a plaster; if the water nearly all evaporates before the process is completed, add a little boiling water. This is a useful plaster for ulcers. burns, etc.

Linseed Meal Poultice.–To boiling water 1/2 pint. add gradually. constantly stirring, 4 1/2 ounces of linseed or flaxseed meal. or a sufficient quantity to thicken. Used to promote the ripening or suppuration of boils, tumors, etc. A little oil or fresh lard should be added and some smeared over the surface as well to prevent the poultice hardening.

Pitch plaster.–Burgundy pitch 6 parts, yellow resin 8 parts, yellow wax 3 parts, lard 7 parts, turpentine 1 part, palm oil 1 part. linseed oil 1 part; melt together.

Poorman's Plaster.–Melt together. beeswax 1 ounce, tar 3 ounces, resin 3 ounces: spread on paper or muslin.

Spice Plaster.–Take of powdered cloves 1 ounce, ground cinnamon 1 ounce, ground allspice 1 ounce, ground black pepper 2 Ounces, flour 3 or 4 ounces, or enough to mix; mix in a paste with vinegar and spread on muslin. This is a stimulating plaster; if a more powerful one is desired, substitute cayenne for black pepper.

Strengthening Plaster.–Lead plaster 24 parts, white resin 6 parts, yellow wax and olive oil, of each 3 parts, red oxide of iron 8 parts; let the oxide be rubbed with the oil and the other ingredients added, melted; mix the whole well together. This plaster, after being spread over leather. should be cut into strips 2 inches wide and strapped firmly around the joint.

Warming Plaster.–Take of any blistering plaster 1 part, burgundy pitch 14 parts; mix them by means of moderate heat, This plaster Is a stimulant, slightly irritating the skin, and is useful in coughs, colds, whooping cough, sciatica and other local pains.

SYRUPS.

Syrups are saturated solutions of sugar In water, or sugar dissolved in a quantity of water sufficient to make the substance a mass; are used as a vehicle for many medicines, most cough medicines being prepared in this form, also many other preparations. The proper quantity of sugar for making syrups is 2 pounds avoirdupois to every pint of water. Only the very best sugar should be used, and either distilled water or filtered rainwater made the agent for dissolving same. The process should be accomplished over a gentle fire, too much heat producing de-composition; do not keep on fire any longer than is necessary to make a clear, transparent syrup. All ingredients to be added in the preparation of any medicine should be first filtered and made perfectly clear.

Almond.—1. Sweet almonds 1 pound, bitter almonds 1 ounce; blanch, beat them to a smooth paste and make an emulsion with barley water 1 quart, strain; to each pint add of sugar 2 pounds and a tablespoonful of orange flower water, put the mixture In small bottles and keep in a cool place: a little brandy assists in the preservation. 2. Sweet almonds 8 ounces, bitter almonds 2 ounces; blanch, heat in a marble mortar with a wooden pestle to a paste, adding gradually of water 16 fluid ounces, of orange flower water 3 fluid ounces; after straining through a flannel, dissolve 3 pounds of sugar in each pint of the mixture.

Cathartic Syrup.—Best senna leaf 1 ounce, butternut (the Inner bark of the root, dried and bruised) 2 ounces, peppermint leaf 1/2 ounce, fennel seed 1/2 ounce, alcohol 1/2 pint. water 1 1/2 pints, sugar 2 pounds; put all into the spirit and water except the sugar and let stand for 2 weeks, then strain, pressing out from the dregs, adding the sugar and simmering over a gentle fire a few minutes only to dissolve the sugar. For chronic constipation, sick headache, etc.;

a superior remedy. Dose, 1 tablespoonful once a day or less often if the bowels become too loose; if griping is caused, increase the fennel seed and peppermint leaf.

Fuller's Cough Syrup.—Take 6 ounces comfrey root and 12 hands full plantain leaves: cut and beat them together well strain out the juice, then with an equal weight of loafsugar boil to a syrup. Dose, 1 to 2 tablespoons full 3 or 4 times per day.

Gum Syrup.—Dissolve pale and picked gum arabic in an equal weight of water by a gentle heat, add the solution to 4 times its weight of simple syrup, simmer for 2 or 3 minutes, remove the scum and cool. This is a pleasant demulcent; the addition of 1 or 2 fluid ounces of orange flower water to each pint greatly improves it.

Gum Traganth.—Gum traganth 1 ounce, water 32 ounces; macerate for 48 hours, press through a linen cloth and mix the mucilage with 8 pounds of syrup heated to 176 Fahrenheit; strain through a coarse cloth.

Hall's Balsam for the Lungs.—Fluid extract of Ipecac 1/2 ounce. fluid extract of squills 1 ounce, chloroform 1/4 ounce, wine of tar 1 ounce, tincture of opium 1-5 ounce, fluid extract of mullen 1 ounce, syrup enough to make 1 pint.

Hall's Honey of Hoarhound and Tar.—Wine of tar 1 ounce fluid extract of Hoarhound 1 ounce, tincture of opium 1 dram. syrup of orange peel ounce, honey 3 ounces, syrup enough to make 1 pint.

Hive Syrup.—Put 1 ounce each of squills and seneca snake root Into 1 pint of water: boil down to one-half, then strain; then add 1/2 pound of clarified honey containing 12 grains of tartrate of antimony. Dose. for a child, 10 drops to 1 teaspoonful according to age. This is an excellent remedy for croup.

Hoarhound.—1. Dried Hoarhound 1 ounce, Hoarhound water 2 pounds; digest in a water bath for 2 hours, strain and add of white sugar 4 pounds. 2. White hoar bound 1 pound. boiling water 1 gallon; Infuse for 2 hours, press out the liquor, filter and add of sugar a sufficient quantity. This is a fine remedy for coughs and diseases of the lungs. Dose, a tablespoonful at pleasure.

Horseradish.—Scraped horseradish 1 ounce, hot water 8 fluid ounces; mix, let stand until cold, strain and dissolve in the liquor twice its weight of sugar. Dose, 1 dram frequently in hoarseness.

Ipecac.—1. Mix 2 ounces of fluid extract of ipecac in 30 ounces of simple syrup. 2. Fluid extract of ipecac 1 fluid ounce, glycerin 1 fluid ounce. simple syrup 14 fluid ounces; first mix the glycerin with the fluid extract and then add the syrup.

Orange Peel.—1. Tincture of orange peel 1 part. syrup 7 parts; mix. Dose, 1 to 2 drams. 2. Fresh orange peel 18 ounces, sugar 18 pounds, water of sufficient quantity to make syrup.

Piso's Consumption Cure.–Tartar emetic 4 grains, tincture tolu 1/2 ounce, sulphate morphia 4 grams, fluid extract. lobelia 2 drams chloroform 1 dram, fluid extract cannabes; indica 2 drams essence spearmint 10 drops, hot water 8 ounces sugar.4 ounces; dissolve the morphia and tartar emetic in hot water and add the rest.

Rhubarb.–Take 1 1/2 ounces of bruised rhubarb. 1/2 ounce each of bruised cloves and cinnamon, 2 drams bruised nutmeg, 2 pints diluted alcohol, 6 pints pf syrup; macerate the rhubarb and aromatics in the alcohol for 14 days and strain; then by gentle heat evaporate the liquor to 1 pint, and while hot mix with it the syrup previously heated.

Rose.–1. Dried leaves of provence roses 8 ounces, double rose leaves 6 ounces, water 1 pint, sugar 4 pounds; pour the water on the leaves when nearly boiling into a glazed. earthenware vessel; cover it quite close and let it remain In a warm place for 1 day, then strain. The leaves of the damask rose are purgative.2. Dried petals of the damask rose 7 ounces, boiling water 3 pints; macerate for 12 hours; filter and evaporate to 1 quart. and add white sugar 6 pounds, and when cool add rectified spirits 5 1/2 fluid ounces.

Sarsaparilla.-._sarsaparilla 15 ounces, boiling water 1 gallon; macerate for 24 hours; boil to 2 quarts and strain; add of sugar 15 ounces and boil to a syrup.

Senna.–1. Take of Senna ounces, bruised fennel seed 10 drams, boiling water 1 pint; macerate for 6 hours with a gentle heat, then pour out the liquid through a linen cloth and dissolve in it of manna 3 ounces; next add this solution to molasses 3 pounds, which has been boiled almost to the consistency of candy; stir them well together. 2. Senna 4 ounces, boiling water 24 fluid ounces; infuse, strain, add of molasses 48 ounces, and evaporate to a proper consistency. This is an aperient. Dose, 1 to 4 drams.

Squills.–1. Dissolve 24 Troy ounces of sugar in 1 pint of vinegar of squills with gentle heat, and strain while hot. 2. Vinegar of squills 3 pints, white powdered sugar 7 pounds; dissolve by gentle heat.

Tar (Boschee's German Syrup).–Wine of tar 2 ounces, fluid extract squills 1 ounce, tincture opium 2 drams. fluid extract sanguinarie 2 drams, syrup of sugar 8 ounces. Mix.

Wild Cherry.–Moisten 5 ounces of wild cherry bark, coarsely powdered, with water, and let it stand for 24 hours closely covered; then pack it firmly in a glass percolator and gradually pour water on it until 1 pint has passed through, and dissolve in this 28 Troy ounces of crushed sugar.

TINCTURES, ESSENCES AND EL.IXIRS.

Tinctures are alcoholic solutions of the active

medicinal properties of the substances from which they are prepared. They are generally used in liniments and other medicines, and are obtained by percolation and filtration. See Percolation and Filtration.

Essences are somewhat similar, while Elixirs are compounds of various medicinal substances, being mixtures of aromatic wines and tinctures mixed with sugar they are popular, because palatable. Dose. 1 to teaspoonfuls. Among the following formulas will be found many superior remedies, including beef, iron and wine, and many others:

Aconite Tincture.—1. Powdered root 1 part, alcohol to percolate 8 parts; macerate for 48 hours with three-quarters of the alcohol agitating occasionally: pack in a percolator and let it drain, then pour on the remaining spirits. When it ceases to drop press the marc and add alcohol to make up 8 quarts. Dose, 5 to 15 minims. 2 or 3 times a day. 2. Take of aconite root, coarsely powdered, 15 ounces, rectified spirits 1 quart; macerate for 7 days, press and filter.

Aloes Tincture.—Socotrine aloes 1 part, extract of licorice 3 parts, proof spirits (alcohol) 40 parts; macerate 7 days, press and wash the marc with spirits to make 40 parts. Dose, 1 to 2 drams.

Angelica Tincture.—Dried angelica root 1 ounce, proof spirits 6 ounces; digest and filter. Dose, 1 dram.

Aniseed Essence.—Oil of anise 1 part, rectified spirits 4 parts; mix. Use as a stimulant, aromatic and carminative. Dose, 10 to 20 minims. Used also to flavor liquors and to make aniseed water.

Arnica Tincture.—Flowers of arnica montana 1 1/2 ounces, spirits, specific gravity 900, 1 pound; digest for 8 days and strain with expression. Dose, 10 to 30 drops. Used in diarrhea, dysentery, gout, rheumatism, paralysis. etc.

Aromatic Elixir.—Orange peel 4 drams, coriander seed 2 drams, angelica seed 2 1/2 drains, cochineal 1 dram, alcohol 12 ounces, water 10 0unces, glycerin 5 ounces, syrup 6 ounces; reduce the solid ingredients to a moderately line powder and pack firmly in a percolator, mix the other ingredients and percolate 2 pints, adding water enough to make this amount.

Aromatic Tincture.—Cinnamon 4 ounces, cardamon 1 ounce, cloves 1 ounce, galangal root 1 ounce, ginger 1 ounce, all In coarse powder; proof spirits 3 lbs. 2 ozs.; macerate 8 days and strain.

Bark and Protoxide of Iron Elixir.—Elixir of calisaya 15 ounces. crystallized sulphate of iron 128 grains, ammonia and nitric acid, of each sufficient; dissolve the sulphate of iron In boiling water and add to it enough ammonia to precipitate the oxide of iron, wash the precipitate thoroughly with boiling water, collect it on a muslin strainer and press it thoroughly to expel the moisture; then add to it cautiously and by portions enough nitric acid mixed with 3 times its volume of water to re dissolve the precipitate; a slight excess of acid is desired; lastly, filter the solution and mix it up sufficient elixir of calisaya to complete 1 pint.

Beef and Iron Wine.—Sherry wine 14 ounces, simple syrup 2 ounces, extract of beef 4 drams, ammonia-citrate of iron 123 grains, tincture of fresh orange peel 30 minims; mix and filter.

Belladonna Tincture.—1. The dried leaves, in coarse powder, 1 part, proof spirits 20 parts; macerate 48 hours In 15 parts of the spirits, agitating occasionally; pack in a percolator, and when It ceases to drop add the remaining :spirits, let it drain, wash and press the marc, filter and make, up 2 parts. Dose, from 5 to 20 minims. 2. Dried leaves of belladonna 4 ounces, proof spirits 1 quart; macerate for 7 days, press and filter.

Benzoin Tincture.—1. Benzoin 2 ounces,: rectified spirits 10 ounces; digest for 8 days, frequently shaking, then filter. 2. Benzoin 8 parts, prepared storax 6 parts. balsam of tulu 2 parts. socotrine aloes 1 1/2 parts, rectified spirits 80 parts; macerate 7 days, filter, and wash the marc with spirits to make up 80 parts. Dose, 1/2 to 1 dram, triturated with mucilage or yolk of egg. 3. Gum benzoin. coarsely powdered, 3 1/2 ounces, prepared storax 2 1/2 ounces, balsam of tulu 10 drams, socotrine or hepatic aloes, in coarse powder. 5 drams, rectified spirits 1 quart; macerate with frequent agitation for 7 days, and strain.

Bitter Elixir. Extract of buckbean, extract of orange peel, of each 2 parts, peppermint water and alcohol (68 per cent), of each 16 parts, spirits of ether (made of 3 parts alcohol and 1 part ether) 1 part; dissolve and mix.

Buchu Tincture.—Buchu, bruised, 1 part, proof spirits 8. parts; macerate for 48 hours with 3/4 parts of the spirits: pack in a percolator and let it drain, then pour on the rest of the spirits: when it ceases to drop, press and wash the marc, filter and make up in 8 parts. Dose, 1 to 2 drams.

Calisaya Bark Elixir.—Take 8 ounces of calisaya bark, 4 ounces each of orange peel, cinnamon and coriander seed, 1/2 ounce each anise seed, caraway seed, and cardamons; reduce all to a moderate powder. and percolate with 4 pints of alcohol, diluted with 12 pints of water, and add 2 pints of simple syrup.

Camphorated Tincture of Opium.—1. Opium, in coarse powder, 40 grains. benzoic acid 40 grains, camphor 30 grains, oil of anise 1/2 dram, proof spirits 20 ounces: macerate 7 days, strain, wash the marc with spirits and filter 20 ounces. Dose, 15 to 16 minims. 2. Camphor 50 grains, powdered opium and benzoic acid of each 72 grains, oil of aniseed 1 fluid dram, proof spirits 1 quart; macerate for 7 days and filter.

Cantharides Tincture.—Cantharides, in coarse powder, 1 part, proof spirits 80 parts; macerate, agitating occasionally, for 7 days in a closed vessel; strain, press, filter, and add sufficient proof spirits to make up 80 parts, Dose, 5 to 20 minims.

Capsicum Tincture.—1. Capsicum, bruised, 1 part. rectified spirits 27 parts; macerate 48 hours with 3/4 of the spirits, agitating occasionally; pack in a percolator and let it drain, then pour on the remaining spirits; as soon as it ceases to drop, wash the marc with spirits to make up 27 parts. Dose, 10 to 20 minims 2. Capsicum bruised, 10 drams, proof spirits 1 quart; digest 14 days. Dose. 10 to 60 drops in atonic dyspepsia, scarlet fever, ulcerated sore throat, etc., it is also made into a gargle.

Capsienin and Cantharides Tincture.—Cantharides, in fine powder, 10 drams, capsicum 1 dram, diluted alcohol 1 pint: mix and digest for 10 days, and filter. This is a stimulant and rubefacient. Used as a counter irritant in deep-seated, painful affections.

Capsicuin and Veratria Tincture.-_.Dissolve 4 grains of veratria in 1 ounce of concentrated tincture of capsicum.

Cascarilla Essence.—Cascarilla 12 ounces, proof spirits 1 pint; proceed either by digestion or percolation; the product is 8 times the strength of the infusion of cascarilla.

Catechu Wine.—Tincture of catechu 1 part, red wine

12 1/2 parts; mix, and after a few days filter.

Catechu Tincture.–Pale catechu in coarse powder 2 1/2 parts, cinnamon bruised 1 part, proof spirits 20 parts; macerate for 7 days with agitation, strain, press and filter, and add spirits to make 20 parts. Dose, 1/2 to 2 drams.

Celery Elixir (Celery Compound).–For increasing, preserving and producing virility; a cure for sexual debility or loss of manhood. Juniper berries, angelica root, lovage root, of each 1 part, alcohol 12 parts orange flower water and rose water, of each 4 parts, spring water of sufficient quantity; distill 20 parts, and mix the distillate with 12 parts of clarified honey. Dose, 1 to 2 drams.

Celery Essence.–Very fine; used for flavoring. 1. Celery seed, bruised or ground. 4 1/2 ounces, alcohol 1 pint, digest 14 days and strain. 2. Celery seed 7 ounces, alcohol 1 pint: digest as before.

Centaury 'Wine.–Centaury, orange peel, extract of blessed thistle gentian, myrrh and cascarilla, of each 1 dram, sherry wine 2 parts.

Chloroform Tincture.–Mix 2 fluid ounces of chloroform with 8 fluid ounces of alcohol and 10 fluid ounces of compound tincture of cardamons. Dose, 10 to 20 minims.

Cinnamon Tincture.–Cinnamon, bruised, 1 ounce, cardamon seed (bruised without the shells) 1/2 ounce, long pepper and ginger, of each 2% drams, alcohol 1 quart; digest for 7 days. Cordial, aromatic and stomachic.

Clove Essence.—Cloves 3 1/2 ounces, 'proof spirits 3/4 pint, water 1/4 pint: digest 1 week and strain.

Colchicum Tincture.—1. Colchicum seeds, bruised 5 ounces, aromatic spirits of ammonia 1 quart: digest for 7 days, then press and filter. Dose, 20 drops to 1 fluid dram, in gout, etc. 2. Colchicum seeds. bruised, 1 part, proof spirits 8 parts; macerate 48 hours with 6 parts of the spirits, agitating occasionally; pack in a percolator and let it drain, then pour on the remainder of the spirits; when it ceases to drop, wash the marc with spirits to make 8 parts. Dose, 15 to 30 minims.

Colchicum Wine.—An excellent remedy for acute rheumatism, gout and other inflammatory diseases. 1. Coichicura corns, dried and sliced, 4 parts. sherry wine 20 parts; macerate 7 days and strain. Dose, 20 to 30 minims. 2. Dried corns of meadow saffron 8 ounces, sherry wine 1 quart; macerate 7 days and strain. This is a powerful sedative and purgative. Dose, 1/2 to 1 fluid dram.

Cough Elixir—Extracts of blessed thistle and dulcamara. of each 1 dram. cherry laurel water 1 fluid dram. fennel water 1. fluid ounce. Dose, 1 to 2 teaspoons full 3 or 4 times a day; a most useful remedy in nervous coughs.

Cubebs Tincture.—Cubebs, in powder, 1 part, rectified spirits 8 parts; macerate 48 hours with 6 parts of the spirits, agitating occasionally; pack in a percolator and let it drain, pour on the remaining spirits, and when it ceases to drop, wash the marc with spirits to make up 8 parts; Dose. 1 to 2 drams.

Digitalis Tincture.—Digitalis, recently dried and in fine powder, 4 ounces, diluted alcohol a sufficient quantity; moisten the powder with 2 fluid ounces of the alcohol, pack It firmly in a conical percolator and gradually pour diluted alcohol over It until 2 parts of tincture are obtained. It is stimulant, but afterwards sedative, diuretic and narcotic. In overdoses it occasions vomiting, purging, vertigo, delirium and death. Used in inflammatory diseases, phthisis, dropsies, palpitation of the heart. etc.; In mania, epilepsy and asthma. Dose, 10 to 20 drops.

Elecampane Tincture.—Powdered elecampane 4 ounces, proof spirits 1 pint; macerate for 15 days. Tonic, deobstruent and expectorant. Dose, to 2 fluid drams, in dyspepsia, palsy, uterine obstructions, etc.

Ergot Tincture.—Ergot (ground in a coffee mill) 2 1/2 ounces, proof spirits 1 pint; digest for 7 days. strain and filter. Dose, I teaspoonful. Used to excite the action of the uterus in labor.

Iodine Tincture.—Iodine 1/2 dram. Iodide of potassium 1/4 dram, rectified spirits 20 drams: dissolve and filter through filter paper. Dose, 5 to 20 minims. An excellent application for the throat in diphtheria.

Iron Wine.—Ammonia, tartrate of iron 1 1/2 drams. sherry 1 pint; dissolve. Dose, 1 to 5 fluid drams, as a mild chalybeate.

Lavender Tincture.—English oil of lavender 90 minims, English oil of rosemary 10 minims, cinnamon, bruised, 150 grains, nutmeg 150 grains, red sandalwood 300 grains, rectified spirits 40 ounces: macerate the cinnamon, nutmeg and red sandal wood in the spirits for 7 days. then press out and strain: dissolve the oils in the strained tincture and add sufficient spirits to make 40 ounces. Dose, 1/2 to 2 drams.

Lobelia Tincture.—Lobelia, dried and bruised, 1 part, spirits of ether 8 parts; macerate 7 days, press and strain. Dose, 10 to 30 minims, as an antispasmodic.

Myrrh Tincture.—Gum myrrh 2 ounces, alcohol 1 quart; steep 4 days, then filter.

Opium Tincture (Laudanum).—Powdered opium 3 ounces, alcohol 1 quart; macerate 7 days, filter.

Pepsin, Bismuth and Strychnia Elixir.—For dyspepsia, gastralgia, general debility and lack of tone In the general system. Citrate of bismuth and ammonia 256 grains, Hall's solution of strychnia 2 ounces, warm water 1 ounce, elixir of pepsin 13 ounces; dissolve the bismuth in the water by the aid of a few drops of aqua ammonia. Dose, 1 teaspoonful.

Quinine Elixir.—Sulphate of quinine 128 grains, citric acid 20 grains, aqua ammonia of sufficient quantity: simple elixir to make 1 pint. Take 2 portions of elixir; in one dissolve the citric acid, in the other dissolve the quinine by rubbing in the mortar; mix the solutions and add the balance of the elixir; lastly, add aqua ammonia, a few drops at a time, until the mixture is clear:
take care to add no more ammonia than is necessary to clarify the solution, else the ammonia will precipitate the quinine Used in febrile diseases and intermittent and remittent fevers. Dose. 1 to 2 teaspoons full.

Squill Tincture.—Dried squill. bruised, 1 part, proof spirits 8 parts; macerate 48 hours with 6 parts of the spirits, agitating occasionally: pack in a percolator, when It ceases to drop, press. filter and add spirits to make 8 parts. Dose, 15 to 30 minims.

Tolu Tincture.—Balsam of tolu 1 part, rectified spirits 8 parts: dissolve, filter and make up to 8 parts. Dose, 15 to 30 minims. in syrup, for coughs and colds.

Tonic Tincture.—Excellent. Peruvian bark, bruised, 2 ounces. orange peel. bruised, 2 ounces, brandy 2 pints; Infuse 10 days, shake the bottle every day, pour off the liquor and strain. Dose, 1 teaspoonful in a wineglass of water. when languid.

Valerian Tincture.—Valerian. in moderately fine powder, 4 troy ounces diluted alcohol of sufficient quantity; moisten the powder with 1 fluid ounce of the alcohol, macerate for 7 days. strain and filter, using 1 fluid ounce of alcohol to make up quantity needed. This is stimulant and antispasmodic; used in hysteria, etc.

Wild Cherry Bark Tincture.—Wild cherry bark, bruised, 2 ounces, proof spirits 1 pint; digest 14 days, press and filter. Dose, 1 tablespoonful.

POPULAR PATENT MEDICINES.

TONICS, ALTERATIVES, CARMINATIVES, BITTERS, DIURETICS, STOMACHICS, ETC.

In this list will be found the correct formulas for the principal patent medicines now on the market. - The formulas are guaranteed genuine, and the list is a good one. Please read carefully and follow directions closely.

Ayer's Cherry Pectoral.—Take 4 grains of acetate of morphia. 2 fluid drams of tincture of bloodroot, 3 fluid drains each of antimonial wine and wine of ipecacuanha, and 3 fluid ounces syrup of wild cherry mix.

August Flower.—Powdered rhubarb 1 ounce, golden seal 1/4 ounce. aloes 1 dram, peppermint leaves 2 drams, carbonate of potash 2 drams, capsicum 5 grains, sugar 5 ounces, alcohol 3 ounces, water 10 ounces, essence of peppermint, 20 drops: powder the drugs and let stand covered with alcohol and water. equal parts, for 7 days; filter and add through the filter enough diluted alcohol to make 1 pint.

Blood Purifier—B. B. B.—Fluid extract burdock -1 ounce fluid extract of sarsaparilla 1 ounce, fluid extract yellow dock 1 ounce, fluid extract senna 1 oz, syrup 8 ozs., alcohol 2 ozs.; mix.

Castoria.—Pumpkin seed 1 ounce. cenria leaves 1 ounce. rochelle salts 1 ounce, anise seed 1/2 ounce. bicarbonate soda 1 ounce, worm seed 1/2 ounce; mix and thoroughly rub together in an earthen vessel, then put into a bottle and pour over it 4 ounces water and 1 ounce alcohol, and let stand 4 days, then strain off and add syrup made of white sugar, quantity to make 1 pint, then add 1/2 ounce alcohol drops, and 5 drops wintergreen Mix thoroughly, and add to the contents of the bottle, and take as directed.

Canada Catarrh Cure.—Carbolic acid 10 to 20 drops, vaseline 1 to 2 ounces; mix, and use with an atomizer 3 or 4 times per day. Try this, it is excellent.

Cough Drops.—Tincture of aconite 5 drops, tincture of ascelpias 1 dram. glycerin 2 ounces, syrup of wild cherry; mix, and take a teaspoonful every 40 minutes until relieved.

Drops of Life.—Gum opium 1 ounce, gum kino 1 dram, gum camphor 40 grains, nutmeg, powdered, 1/2 ounce, French brandy 1 pint: let stand from 1 to 10 days. Dose, from 30 to 40 drops for an adult; children, half dose.! This is one of the most valuable preparations in the Materia Medica and will in some dangerous hours, when all hope is tied and the system is racked with pain, be the soothing balm which cures the most dangerous diseases to which the human body is liable—flux, dysentery and all summer complaints.

Godfrey's Cordial.—Tincture of opium 6 ounces, molasses 4 pints. alcohol 8 ounces, water 6 pints. carbonate of potash 4 drams, oil of sassafras cut with alcohol 1 dram: dissolve the potash in water. add the molasses, heat over a gentle fire till it simmers. remove the scum, add the other ingredients, the oil dissolved in the alcohol.

Harter's Iron Tonic.—Calisaya bark 2 ounces. citrate of iron 2 ounces. gentian 2 ounces. cardamon seed 2 ounces, syrup 2 ounces. alcohol 2 ounces, water 8 ounces: mix.

Hood's Sarsaparilla.—Fluid extract of sarsaparilla 1 ounce, fluid extract of yellow dock 1 ounce. fluid extract of poke root 1/2 ounce. iodide of potash 1/2 ounce, syrup of orange peel 1 ounce, alcohol 4 ounces, syrup enough to make 1 pint.

Hop Bitters.—Hops 4 ounces. orange peel 2 ounces, cardamon 2 drams, cinnamon 1 dram. Cloves 1/2 dram, alcohol 8 ounces, sherry wine 2 pints. simple syrup 1 pint, water sufficient; grind the drugs.

macerate in the alcohol and wine for 1 week, percolate and add enough syrup and water to make 1
gallon.

Hostetter's Bitters.—Gentian root, ground, 1/2 ounce,
cinnamon bark 1/2 ounce. ciuchona bark, ground,
1/2 ounce, anise seed 1/2 ounce, coriander seed
ground 1/2 ounce, cardamon seed 1/8 ounce, gum
kino 1/4 ounce, alcohol 1 pint, water 4 quarts, sugar
1 pound: mix and let stand for 1 week, pour off the
fluid. boil the drug for a few minutes in 1 quart of
water, strain off and add first the fluid and then the
sugar and water.

Indian Sagwa.—Gentian 1/2 pound, seneca 1/4
pound, cubebs 1/2 pound, rhei 1/4 pound, salts 1/2
pound, aloes 1/3 pound. bicarbonate of soda 2 1/4
pounds. senna 1/3 pound, anise 1/4 pound, coriander 1/4 pound, pareivabrava 5/8 pound, guaiac
5/8 pound, licorice 1 1/4 pounds, alcohol 3 quarts.
water 6 gallons: steep 10 days, percolate and bottle.
The above will fill 65 12-ounce bottles.

Injection Brou.—Water 4 ounces, nitrate of silver 20
grains, tincture of opium 1/2 ounce, sulphate of
bismuth and hydrastis, 2 ounces: mix.

Jayne's Expectorant.—Syrup of squills 2 ounces. tincture of tolu 1 ounce, spirits of camphor 1 dram,
tincture of digitalis 1 dram. tincture of lobelia 1
dram. wine of ipecac 2 drams, tincture of opium 2
drams, antimonia 2 grains; mix.

Jayne's Tonic Vermifuge.—Santonin 20 grains, fluid extract of pink root 3 grams, fluid extract of senna 2 drams, simple elixir 2 ounces, syrup 2 ounces; mix. Dose, 1 tablespoonful night and morning.

S. S. S. Fluid.—Extrart of phytolacca 1 ounce, fluid extract of sarsaparilla 1 ounce, iodide of potash 1 ounce, fluid extract of xanthoxylon 1/2 ounce, fluid extract of Culiver's root 1 ounce, acetate of potash 1 ounce, tincture of cinnamon 1/4 ounce, tincture of cardamon seed 1 ounce, alcohol 4 ounces, sugar 1/2 pound, water 36 ounces; mix.

Smith's Tonic Syrup.—Fowler's solution of arsenic 2 drams, Culiver's root 1 ounce, syrup of orange peel 4 ounces, simple syrup 12 ounces: mix, then add cinchona 40 grains, dissolved in aromatic sulphuric acid; shake to mix well.

Sozodont Fragrant.—Tincture of soap bark 2 ounces, tincture of myrrh 1 dram, glycerine 1/2 ounce, water 1 1/2 ounces, essence of cloves 10 drops, essence of wintergreen 10 drops, tincture of cochineal enough to color; mix. Accompanying the above is a powder composed of prepared chalk, orris root, carbonate magnesia; of equal parts; mix.

Shaker's Extract of Herbs.—Fluid extract of blue flag 20 fluid extract of Culiver's root 20 drops, fluid extract of stalinga 20 drops, fluid extract of poke root 20 drops, fluid extract of butternut 20 drops, fluid extract of dandelion 20 drops, fluid extract of prince pine 10 drops, fluid extract of mandrake 5 drops, fluid extract of gentian 5 drops, fluid extract of calcium 5 drops, fluid extract of black cohose 30 drops, tincture of aloes 30 drops, tincture of capsicum 10 drops, tincture of sassafras 30 drops, borax 1 dram, salt 3/4 drams, syrup 3 ounces, water 8 ounces.

Succus Alterns (McDade's).—Fluid extract of starlinga 1 ounce. fluid extract of sarsaparilla 1 ounce, fluid extract of phytolacca decandra 1/2 ounce, fluid extract of lappa minor 1 ounce, fluid extract of xanthoxylon 1/2 ounce, syrup 14 ounces; mix. Dose, 1 teaspoonful 3 times a day.

Seven Seals of Golden Wonder.—Oil of cajeput 2 drams, oil of sassafras 1/2 ounce, oil of organum 1 dram, oil of hemlock 1 dram. oil of cedar 1 dram, tincture of capsicum 1/4 ounce, alcohol enough to make 1 pint,.

Swain's Vermifuge.—Wormseed 2 ounces. valerian, rhubarb, pink root, white agaric, of each 1 1/4 ounces: boll in sufficient water to yield 3 quarts of decoction and add to It 30 drops of oil of tansy and 45 drops of oil of clover; dissolve in a quart of rectified spirits. Dose, 1 tablespoonful at night.

Warner's Tippecanoe Bitters.—Cardamon seed 2 ounces, nutmeg 1 dram, grains of paradise 1 dram, cloves 1 ounce, cinnamon 2 ounces, ginger 1 ounce, orange peel 1 ounce, lemon peel 1 ounce alcohol 1 gallon, water 1 gallon, sugar 3 pounds; mix and let stand 6 or 7 days and filter. Then add enough water to make 4 gallons.

Warner's Safe Cure.–Take of smart weed 4 pounds, boil for 1 hour with 1 gallon of soft water, adding warm water to supply waste by evaporation; then strain off and add acetate potash 4 ounces, sugar 4 pounds. Boil again till sugar is dissolved, then add alcohol 8 ounces, and flavor with oil of wintergreen cut with alcohol.

Wakefield's Blackberry Balsam.–Blackberries crushed 2 pounds, boiling water 4 ounces, sugar 4 ounces. Jamaica ginger 4 grains, alcohol 2 ounces; mix and add syrup enough to make 16 ounces.

TRIED REMEDIES.

These remedies are not classified, but are efficient for the various troubles for which they are recommended. In this list will be found a little bit of everything, such as corn cures, tapeworm expellers, cough drops, salves, liniments, ointments, pile remedies, pills, etc. Read the list over carefully.

Eye Water.–Table salt and white vitriol, each 1 teaspoonful:
heat them on earthen dish until dry; now add to them soft water 1/2 pint, white sugar 1 teaspoonful, blue vitriol, a piece as large as a common pea. Should this be too strong add a little more water. Apply to the eye 3 or 4 times a day.

To Remove Tapeworms.–Let the patient miss 2 meals. give 2 teaspoonfuls powdered kamala. Should the bowels not move within 24 hours give another teaspoonful of the kamala You may follow this in 2 hours by from 1/2 to 1 ounce of castor oil. This is a positive cure for tapeworm, it, will not make the patient sick. In buying the drug be sure and get kamala, not camellea. Kamala is in appearance like quite red brick dust, and is nearly tasteless, whereas camellea is of a yellowish color.

A Sure Cure for Smallpox.–It is claimed that the following is a sure and never-failing cure for smallpox: One ounce cream of tartar dissolved in a pint of boiling water, to be drank when cold, at intervals. It can be taken at any time, and is a preventative as well as a curative. It is known to have cured in thousands of cases without a failure

Gonorrhea.-_Balsam of copaiba 1 ounce, oil of cubebs 2 drams, laudanum 1 dram, mucilage of gum arabic 2 ounces. sweet spirits nitre 1/2 ounce, compound spirits of lavender 3 drams, camphor water 4 ounces, white sugar 2 drams, oil of partridge berry 5 drops; mix. Dose, 1 tablespoonful 3 or 4 times a day.

Sure Cure for Diphtheria.–Sulpho-calcine and glycerine 1 ounce of each; mix. Apply to throat with a mop every 3 or 4 hours.

Onaulsm.–Fluid extract salix nigra (aments).

Teaspoonful 3 times daily.

Tetter Ointment.—One ounce spirits of turpentine, 1 ounce red percipitate in powder, 1 ounce burgundy pitch in powder. 1 pound hog's lard, melt all these ingredients over a slow fire until the ointment is formed; stir until cold. Spread on a linen rag and apply, to the parts affected.

A Sure Cure for Piles.—Confection of senna 2 ounces, cream of tartar 1 ounce, sulphur 1 ounce, syrup of ginger enough to make a stiff paste; mix. A piece as large as a nut is to be taken as often as necessary to keep the bowels open. One of the best remedies known.

Healing Salve.—Lard 1 pound, resin 1/2 pound, sweet eider bark 1/2 pound; simmer over a slow fire 4 hours, or until it forms. a hard, brown salve. This is for the cure of cuts, bruises, boils old sores and all like ailments; spread on cotton cloth and apply to the parts affected.

Specific Inflammatory Rheumatism.—.Saltpetre. pulverized, 1 ounce. sweet oil 1 pint; bathe the parts affected 3 times a day with this mixture and a speedy cure will be the result.

Another Salve.—Sheep's tallow 1 ounce, beeswax 1 ounce, sweet oil 1/2 ounce, red lead 1/2 ounce, gum camphor 2 ounces; fry all these together in a stone dish, continue to simmer for 4 hours, spread on green basswood leaves or paper and apply to the sore.

Cough Drops.—Tincture of aconite 5 drops, tincture of as celpias 1 dram. glycerine 2 ounces, syrup of wild cherry; mix, and take 1 teaspoonful every 40 minutes until relieved.

Cure for Sore Throat in All Its Different Forms.—Cayenne pepper 2 ounces, common salt 1 ounce, vinegar 1/2 pint; warm over a slow fire and gargle the throat and mouth every hour. Garlic and onion poultice applied to the outside. Castor oil 1 spoonful, to keep the bowels open.

Ointment of Stramonium.—Stramonium leaves 1 pound. lard 3 pounds. yellow wax 1/2 pound; boil the stramonium leaves in the lard until they become pliable, then strain through linen; lastly, add the wax previously melted and stir until they are cold. This is a useful anodyne application in irritable ulcers, painful hemorrhoids and in cutaneous eruptions.

Cathartic Pills.—Extract of colacinth, in powder, 1/2 ounce, jalap. in powder, 3 drams, calomel 3 drams, gamboge, in powder, 2 scruples; mix these together and with water form into mass and roll into 180 pills. Dose, 1 pill as a mild laxative, 2 in vigorous operations. Use in all bilious diseases when purges are necessary.

Lozenges for Heartburn.—Gum arabic 1 ounce, licorice root, pulverized 1 ounce, magnesia 1/4 ounce, add water to make into lozenges; let dissolve

In mouth and swallow. Another Cough Cure.–Good. Take the white of an egg and pulverized sugar; beat to a froth. Take 1 tablespoon full every hour for 3 or 4 hours.

Warts and Corns.–To cure in 10 minutes. Take a small piece of potash and let it stand in the open air until it slacks, then thicken it to a paste with pulverized gum arabic, which prevents it from spreading where it is not wanted.

Tetter Ointment.–Spirits of turpentine 1 ounce; red precipitate, In powder, 1 ounce, burgundy pitch, in powder, 1 ounce, hog's lard 1 pound; melt all these Ingredients over a slow fire until tbe ointment Is formed; stir until cold; spread on a linen rag and apply to the parts affected.

Diphtheria.–Take a clean clay tobacco pipe, put a live coal in it, then put common tar on the fire and smoke it, inhaling and breathing back through the nostrils.

Said to Be Good for Grip.–Peroxide of hydrogen (medicinal) is a marvelous remedy in the treatment of grip or influenza. This medicine should be diluted with water and administered internally, and by sniffing through the nostrils or by spraying the nostrils and throat. The good results from this treatment, which has never been known to fail of producing a speedy cure. Are due to the destruction of the microbe upon which this disease depends. The remedy is simple and within the reach of everybody, and can easily be tested.

Lung Medicine.–Take black cahosh 1/2 ounce, lobelia 1/4 ounce, canker root 3/4 ounce. blackberry root 1/3 ounce, sarsaparilla 1 ounce, pleurisy root 1/2 ounce; steeped in 3 pints of water. Dose. 1 tablespoon full 3 times a day, before eating. Sure cure for spitting blood.

Toothache Drops.–Four ounces pulverized alum, 14 ounces sweet spirits of nitre. Put up In 1 ounce bottles. Retails readily at 25 cents per bottle. This Is the most effective remedy for toothache that was ever discovered, and is a fortune to anyone who will push its sale. It sells at every house.

A Certain Cure for Drunkenness.–Sulphate of iron 5 grains, magnesia 10 grains, peppermint water 11 drams. spirits of nutmeg 1 dram, twice a day. This preparation acts as a tonic and stimulant, and so partially supplies the place of the accustomed liquor and prevents that absolute physical and mental prostration that follows a sudden breaking off from the use of stimulating drinks.

Fever Ague. Ague–Quinine 1 scruple, elixir vitriol 1 dram; dissolve the quinine in the elixir and tincture of black cahosh 14 drops. Dose, 20 drops in a little water once an hour.

Corns, a Sure Cure and Painless Eradication.–Extract of cannabis Indicus 10 grains, salicylic acid 6 grains, colodion 1 ounce; mix and apply with a camel's hair pencil so as to form a thick covering over the corn for

3 or 4 nights. Take a hot foot bath and the corn can easily be removed by the aid of a knife.

Plain Court Plaster that will not stick and remains flexible. Soak isinglass in a little warm water for 24 hours, then evaporate nearly all the water by a gentle heat; dissolve the residue with a little proof spirits of wine, and strain the whole through a piece of open linen. The strained mass should be a stiff jelly when cool. Stitch a piece of silk or sarcenet on a wooden frame with tacks or thread. Melt the jelly and apply it to the silk thinly and evenly with a badger hair brush. A second coating must be applied when the first has dried. When both are dry apply over the whole surface two or three coatings of balsam of peru. This plaster remains quite pliable, and never breaks.

A Cure for Cancer.—The following has been used by a New York physician with great success: Take red oak bark and boil it to the thickness of molasses then mix with sheep's tallow of equal proportion spread it on leaves of linnwood, green, and keep the plaster over the ulcer. Change once In 8 hours.

To Strengthen and Invigorate the System.—Two drams essential salt of the round leaf cornel 1 scruple extract rhubarb, 1 scruple ginger powder. Make into pills, and take for a dose 2 or 3 times a day.

Chilblains.—We glean these two prescriptions from the British Medical Journal. They are now being used in this country, and with good results, 1. Belladonna liniment drams. aconite liniment 1 dram. carbolic acid 5 minims flexible colodion 1 ounce. Mix and apply every night with a camel's hair pencil. 2. Flexible colodion 4 drams, castor oil 4 drams. spirits of turpentine 4 drams. Use 3 times daily with camel's hair brush.

How to Remove Pain and Soreness from Wounds.– The value of the smoke from burned wool to remove the pain and soreness from wounds of all kinds, or from sores is great, and it will give immediate relief from the intense pain caused by a gathering. The easiest way to prepare this is to cut all-wool flannel if you haven't the wool–into narrow strips: take some hot ashes with a few small live coals on a shovel. sprinkle some of the flannel, strips on it. and hold the injured member in the smoke for five or ten minutes. using plenty of flannel to make a thick smoke. Repeat as often as seems necessary, though one smoking is usually enough.

Dropsy, Cure for.–Take of bruised juniper berries, mustard seed. and ginger, 1/2 ounce each, bruised horseradish and parsley root, 1 ounce each sound old cider, 1 quart; infuse Dose, a wineglass full 3 times a day.

Catarrh, A Simple Remedy for–Catarrh is an inflammation of the mucous membrane. especially of the air passages of the head and throat, with an exudation on its free surface. Treatment; Simple but effective. Take 1 ounce each of fine salt, pulverized borax and baking soda. mix thoroughly together and dissolve in

1/2 pint of water. To use take 1 tablespoon full of the solution to 2 or 3 of warm water, and snuff 'up the head at bedtime. The salt stimulates, the borax cleanses and heals, and the soda soothes; use softwater.

Influenza or "Grippe," Treatment for.—It is reported as having been quite fatal in France in 1311 and 1403. In 1570 it also prevailed, and In 1557 spread over Europe, and extended to America. It occurred again in 1729, 1743, 1775, 1782, 1833, 1837, with notable violence. In the United States, one of the most remarkable epidemics for extent, was that of 1843, Another was that of 1872, following nearly the course of the epizootic among horses of the latter part of that year. The last epidemic (1890) has been a remarkable one for its extent, invading all Europe and the United States. Mild cases require housing and little more. The following prescriptions will be found excellent: Take of antipyrine 18 grains, Dover's powder 12 grains, powdered extract valerian 3 grains; mix, and divide into 6 capsules. Take one every 2 hours. If there be a tight cough, take the following: Take of muriate of ammonia 30 grains, deodorized tincture of opium 1 dram, syrup of senega snakeroot 1/2 ounce distilled water 1 ounce, syrup of balsam tolu enough to maloa 3 fluid ounces; mix, and take a teaspoon full every 2 hours. Great prostration, especially in old people, may call for support by quinine and stimulants, as hot whisky punches.

Conclusion

It is our sincerest hope that you have found in this book, some help. As we were writing this book, we found that there were so many of our friends that we have helped through the years that said, "It's about time" so we knew that we were doing the right thing. As I said at the beginning of this book, I am trying not to let 40 years of research go to waste. Some of these treatments seem almost unbelievable to you, but understand that they are meant to change your body's chemistry in order to allow your body to help itself. So in other words, just because these treatments sound strange, they initiate a chemical change in your system that allows it to fight back, and fight back until the problem is resolved.

These are the alternatives that I want you to know about. You can always go to a regular doctor and take their prescribed medications, sometimes with terrible side effects that might just be worse then the original health problem. Or try our methods that have proven to help, without the serious side effects caused by prescription drugs. Understand, that I have no intention to replace your physician, as they are far more advanced in the practice of medicine then I am. I am just trying to give you some healthy alternatives and some new information that might just save your life.

I would like to thank all of the people and publications that have helped in the process of publishing this book. Their knowledge and wisdom has helped me to bring you this offering. Please read

the bibliography for a list of the authors that I would
like to thank and to suggest, for your reading library.

Bibliography

Forty Something Forever
By: Harold and Arlene Breacher Co-Authors

Left For Dead
By: Dick Quinn

Alpha Lipolic Acid Breakthrough
By: Burt Berkson M.D., Ph.D.

Grow Young With HGH
By: Ronald Klatz

Natural Progesterone Cream
By: Norman Shealy, M.D., Ph.D.

How To Stay Out Of The Doctors Office
By: Dr. Edward Wagner with Sylvia Goldfarb

The Cure Is In The Cupboard
By: Dr. Cass Ingram

Aqua Vitae
By: Roy Jacobsen

Olive Leaf Extract
By: Martin Walker

The Prostate Cancer Protection

By: Dr. Bob Arnot

Physicians Desk Reference
By: Medical Economics, Inc.

Dr. Whitakers Guide to Natural Healing
By: Julian Whitaker M.D.

The Healing Foods
By: Patricia Hausman and Judith Hurley

Index

A

F

G

H

K

L

M

Printed in the United States
By Bookmasters